Street by Street

BOLTON

HORWICH, WALKDEN, WESTHOUGHTON

Adlington, Aspull, Atherton, Blackrod, Edgworth, Farnworth, Kearsley, Little Lever, Swinton, Tottington, Tyldesley

CW00555848

lst edition May 2002

© Automobile Association Developments Limited 2002

 **Ordnance Survey®** This product includes map data licensed from Ordnance Survey® with the permission of the Controller of Her Majesty's Stationery Office. © Crown copyright 2002. All rights reserved. Licence No: 399221.

Published by AA Publishing (a trading name of Automobile Association Developments Limited, whose registered office is Millstream, Maidenhead Road, Windsor, Berkshire SL4 5GD. Registered number 1878835).

The Post Office is a registered trademark of Post Office Ltd. in the UK and other countries.

Mapping produced by the Cartographic Department of The Automobile Association. A00965

A CIP Catalogue record for this book is available from the British Library.

Printed by GRAFIASA S.A., Porto Portugal.

The contents of this atlas are believed to be correct at the time of the latest revision. However, the publishers cannot be held responsible for loss occasioned to any person acting or refraining from action as a result of any material in this atlas, nor for any errors, omissions or changes in such material. The publishers would welcome information to correct any errors or omissions and to keep this atlas up to date. Please write to Publishing, The Automobile Association, Fanum House (FH17), Basing View, Basingstoke, Hampshire, RG21 4EA.

Ref: ML203

Key to map pages — ii-iii

Key to map symbols — iv-1

Enlarged scale pages — 2-3

Street by Street — 4-55

Index – towns & villages — 56

Index – streets — 57-75

Index – featured places — 76-78

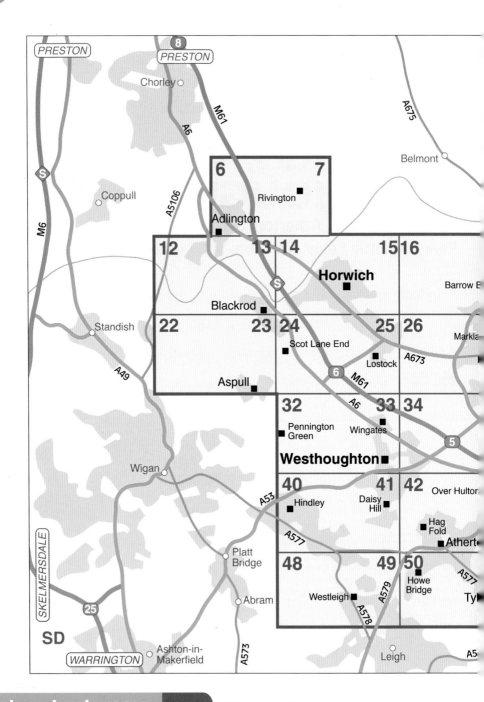

ii

PRESTON

PRESTON

8

Chorley

M61

A6

A675

Belmont

Coppull

A5106

6 **7**

Rivington

Adlington

12 **13** **14** **15** **16**

Horwich

Barrow E

M6

S

A49

Blackrod

22 **23** **24** **25** **26**

Standish

Markl

Scot Lane End

Lostock

A673

6

M61

Aspull

32 **33** **34**

A6

Pennington
Green

Wingates

5

Westhoughton

Wigan

40 **41** **42**

Over Hulton

A53

Hindley

Daisy
Hill

Hag
Fold

A577

Athert

SKELMERSDALE

Platt
Bridge

48 **49** **50**

Howe
Bridge

A577

25

Abram

Westleigh

A579

A578

Ty

SD

WARRINGTON

Ashton-in-
Makerfield

A573

Leigh

A5

husband in pub — Paul Stubbs
38 years.

↓

Jane. ?

to family home.

refused to leave
assaulted
and ...
Step mother
+ father.

husband threw her
out,

Step mother
taken her home.

Pauline Eckersley
01942 8796 11

0767976

Annette Eckersley.
Kaye.
14 Dumbarton Green
Beech Hill
Wigan.

IAN HUGHES
12 CALVERLEIGH CLOSE
BOLTON
01204 660508
He has the photo

8630
01042 708412

2552

D Relief Collar Numbers and Names

11568 - Andy Livesey
15273 - Aaron Tomlison

14009 - Rachel Dempsey
14057 - ~~Barry~~ Horner
KARL

2647 - Pete Hayes
19685 - Andy Prior

19507 - Gary Alty
15365 - Rob Knight

17094 - Martin Sibbit
13143 - Gill Hardman

11222 - Ian Roby
18560 - Steve Malone

13401 - Paul Griffiths

1. BOOKED ON

2. AVAILABLE AT OFFICE

3. ON PATROL

4. REFS

5. ON ROUTE TO INCIDENT

6. AT SCENCE

7. ENQS - BUT AVAILABLE

8. PASSENGERS

9. ESCORT

10. COURT

11. GONE

5505 - Dave Hartwell
19249 - Phil Sharpe

15300 - Brian Newbold
16250 - Dave Shott

Ins 12519 Wood
Sgt 6811 Kuysner   KUSNYER
Sgt 4524 Baybutt

6655 ANDY SMITH

6220 DAVE PERCIVAL.

9 a

V

blue Peugot 206

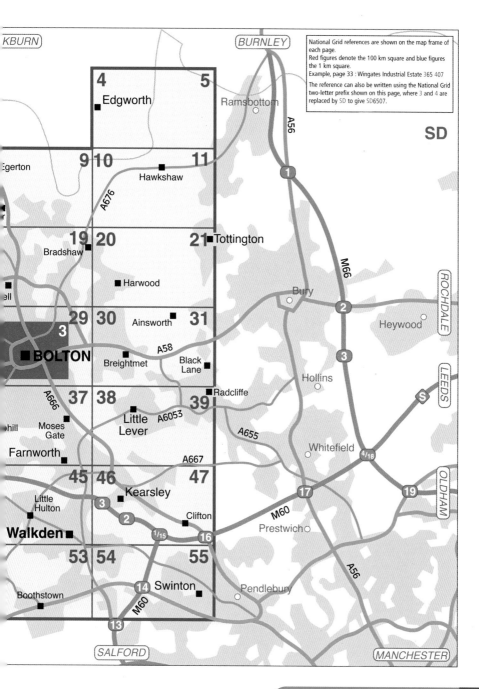

KBURN

BURNLEY

Ramsbottom

National Grid references are shown on the map frame of each page.
Red figures denote the 100 km square and blue figures the 1 km square.
Example, page 33 : Wingates Industrial Estate 365 407

The reference can also be written using the National Grid two-letter prefix shown on this page, where 3 and 4 are replaced by SD to give SD6507.

SD

4 Edgworth **5**

Egerton **9 10** Hawkshaw **11**

A676

A56

19 20 Bradshaw Harwood **21** Tottington

Bury

M66

ROCHDALE

Heywood

29 30 Ainsworth **31**
3
■BOLTON Breightmet Black Lane
A58

Hollins

LEEDS

S

37 38 Little Lever A6053 **39** Radcliffe
A666 Moses Gate
A655
Whitefield
4/18

hill Farnworth

A667

45 46 Kearsley **47**
Little Hulton **3**
2 Clifton
Walkden■ **1/15** **16**

17

M60

Prestwich

19

OLDHAM

A56

53 54 **55**
Boothstown **14** Swinton Pendlebury
M60
13

SALFORD

MANCHESTER

4.2 inches to 1 mile

Scale of main map pages 1:15,000

0   1/4   miles   1/2   3/4   1
0   1/4   1/2   kilometres   3/4   1   1 1/4   1 1/2

Junction 9	Motorway & junction	⊖	Underground station
Services	Motorway service area	⊖	Light Railway & station
	Primary road single/dual carriageway	+++++++++	Preserved private railway
Services	Primary road service area	LC	Level crossing
	A road single/dual carriageway	•—•—•—•	Tramway
	B road single/dual carriageway	- - - - - - -	Ferry route
	Other road single/dual carriageway	....	Airport runway
	Minor/private road, access may be restricted	- · - · - · -	Boundaries - borough/district
← ←	One-way street	⋁⋁⋁⋁⋁⋁⋁	Mounds
	Pedestrian area	**93**	Page continuation 1:15,000
:- - - - - - - :	Track or footpath	**7**	Page continuation to enlarged scale 1:10,000
	Road under construction		River/canal, lake, pier
⊢ - - - - ⊣	Road tunnel		Aqueduct, lock, weir
AA	AA Service Centre	465 ▲ Winter Hill	Peak (with height in metres)
P	Parking		Beach
P+🚌	Park & Ride		Coniferous woodland
🚌	Bus/Coach station		Broadleaved woodland
	Railway & main railway station		Mixed woodland
	Railway & minor railway station		Park

Cemetery	Theme Park
Built-up area	Abbey, cathedral or priory
Featured building	Castle
City wall	Historic house or building
24-hour Accident & Emergency hospital	National Trust property (Wakehurst Place NT)
Post Office	Museum or art gallery
Public library	Roman antiquity
Tourist Information Centre	Ancient site, battlefield or monument
Petrol station (Major suppliers only)	Industrial interest
Church/chapel	Garden
Toilet	Arboretum
Toilet with disabled facilities	Farm or animal centre
Public house (AA recommended)	Zoological or wildlife collection
Restaurant (AA inspected)	Bird collection
Theatre or performing arts centre	Nature reserve
Cinema	Visitor or heritage centre
Golf course	Country park
Camping (AA inspected)	Cave
Caravan Site (AA inspected)	Windmill
Camping & Caravan Site (AA inspected)	Distillery, brewery or vineyard

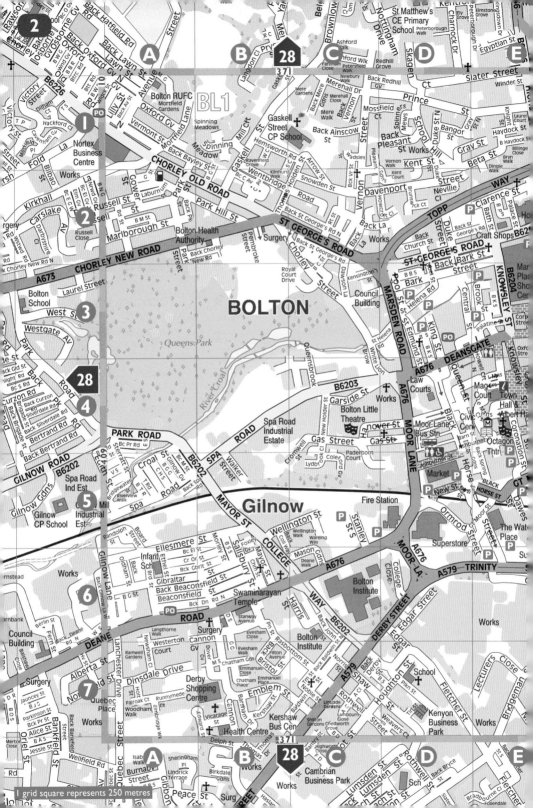

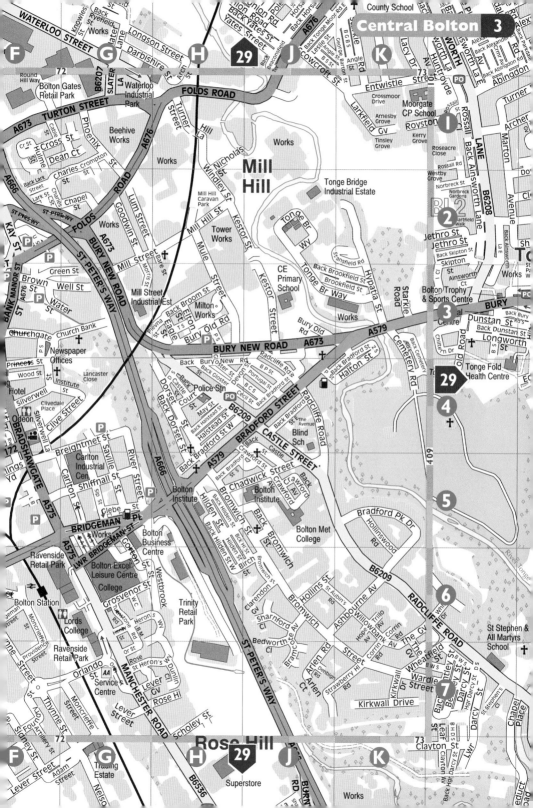

B6214

E   F   G   H

77   78   18

Lancashire County
Bury

1

2

17

Holcombe CE
Primary School

3

Moor Road

B6214

RAMSBOTTOM

Holcombe Hey
Fold Farm

Peel
Tower

Peel Walk

Cross Lane

Hol

Moorbottom Road

Moorbottom Road

4

Road

Moorbottom Road

416

Old Holcombe Road

CARR ROAD

Carnwood Hey

Carr Av

Lumb

Holcombe Lee

Vines St

5

Hazelhurst

LUMB CARR ROAD

Works

Spenleach Lane

**Holcombe
Brook**

Redisher Lane

Redisher
Cft

Park Rd

Woodhey Rd

High Sc

A676

E   F   **II**   G   H

77   78

wkshaw

Yarrow
Reservoir

Dean
Head
Lane

Wilcock's
Farm

E

F

G

H

63

64

Moses
Cocker's

I

15

2

Rivington

House

Sheep

Hall

Lane

Lane

Lane

Rivington
Primary
School

Rivington Lane

3

41

Belmont Road

Rivington
Country
Park

Lever Park

4

Tan Pits
Farm

Rivington
Lane

5

Rivington
Reservoirs

413

Cross

The
Castle

63

ime ford
lage

E

F

I4

G

H

64

Rivington & Blackrod
High School

Old Will's Lane

A673

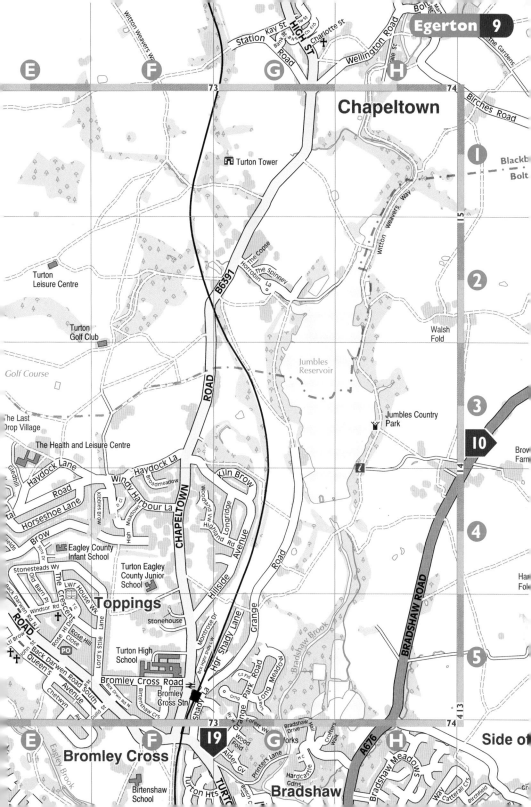

Chapeltown

E F G H

73 74 Birches Road

I Blackb
Bolt

Turton Tower

B6391 The Copse
The Spinney
Horrobin La
Witton Weavers Way

Turton
Leisure Centre

2 Walsh
Fold

Turton
Golf Club

Golf Course

Jumbles
Reservoir

3
10

The Last
Drop Village

The Health and Leisure Centre

Jumbles Country
Park

Haydock Lane
Windy Harbour La
Broadmeadow
Haydock La
Kiln Brow
Woodrow
Woodland Vw
Highland Rd
Longridge

4

Road
Horseshoe Lane
Brow
High
Meadows
Kibbles Brow
CHAPELTOWN
ROAD
Avenue
Grange
Road

BRADSHAW ROAD

Eagley County
Infant School
Stonesteads Wy
Turton Eagley
County Junior
School

Bradshaw Brook

Back Darwen Rd
Old Barn Pl
The Crescent
Lwr House Wk
Windsor Rd
Toppings
Rose Hill
Stonehouse
Hillside
Montrose Dr

5

ROAD
John St
Rose Close
Lord's Stile Lane
Bck High Shady La
Hgr Shady Lane
Bradshaw
Drive
413

PO
Turton High
School
Grange Park Road
Long Meadow

Queen's
Bromley Cross Road
Bromley
Cross Stn
CS Fld
Grma

Chetwyn
Avenue
Guild St
Back Dewn Rd N
Birtenshaw Crs
Shady La
73 Turton Hts
74

E F 19 G H

Bromley Cross **Side of**

Eagley Brook
Birtenshaw
School
TURTON
Grange Park Road
Wood
Fold
Alder Gv
Printers Lane
Forest Ww
Bradshaw
Hall
Works
Crater's Walk
Hardcastle
Gdns
A676
Bradshaw Meadows
Way Catterall Crs
Birchfield

Bradshaw

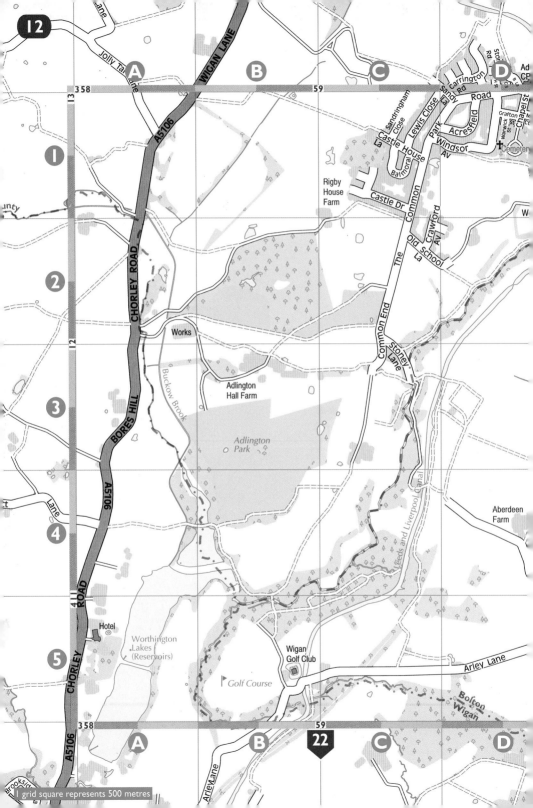

ADLINGTON

Grimef
Village

Grove
Avenue

RAILWAY ROAD

Mayfield Av

Belmont

Abbey Gv

A673

BOLTON ROAD

Shawes

M61

Cole

Grimeford Lane

Rivington

62

13

Headless Cross

E Adlington
Station

Meadow
Street

Railway
View

F

6
61

G

H

Grimeford
Industrial Estate

I

A673

Adlington Cricket
Club

Huyton
Road

Road

Works

CHORLEY

ROAD

A6

Grimeford Lane

Greenland

Lane

2

M61

62

12

3

Hotel

Bolton W

Dark

BLACKROD
BROW

CHORLEY ROAD

Blackrod

Lancashire County
Bolton

Factory
Brow

Anderson Lane

14

4

Crowshaw
Farm

Lane

Harrison Crs

Ainse
Road

Clifton Dr

Hill

Lane

Nightingale Rd

Thirlmere Rd

BLACK
HORSE ST

St Catherines Dr

Coniston
Road

Folds

Lthm Rd

Whitehall Lane

Fryent Close

Carlton Close

5

Surgery

Council
Building

Vicarage Rd W

CHURCH STREET

Ridgway

Bramh St

Brown st

Scotland

Little

Scotland

Blundell

Lane

Blackrod
Church
School

Vicarage Lane

Vicarage

Half Acre Lane

NEW STREET

PO
Road

Vauze House

Castlecroft Av

Cemetery

Grn W

MANCHESTER ROAD

62

Hillside
Avenue

E

Bolton
Wigan

F

Feras Lane

Tuckers

61

23

Sibberings
Farm

G

Wynridge Drive

Chig

Green
Barn

Thursford Crove

Shawbury

STATION RD

H

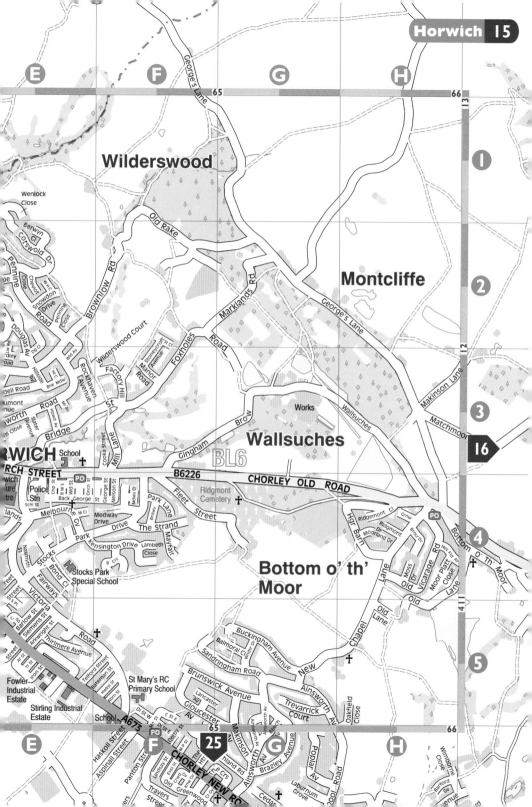

Wilderswood

Wenlock
Close

Old Rake

Montcliffe

Brownlow Rd

Marklands Rd

George's Lane

Wilderswood Court

Foxholes Road

Manor Road

Factory Hill

Stoneycroft Avenue

Works

Wallsuches

Wallsuches

Makinson Lane

Matchmoor

RWICH

School

RCH STREET

Police
Stn

Cooke Street

George St

Nelson St

Mill Lane

Gingham Brow

BL6

B6226

CHORLEY OLD ROAD

Ridgmont Cemetery

Ridgemont Cl

Ridgmont Dr

Moorland Dr

Melbourne Cl

Medway Drive

Park Lane

Fleet Street

Park Kensington Drive

The Strand

Mayfair

Lambeth Close

High Barn

Vicarage Rd

Moss

Old Lane

Moor Platt
Close

Bottom o' th'
Moor

Stocks Park
Special School

Chapel Lane

Old Lane

New Road

Buckingham Avenue

Balmoral Cl

Sandringham Road

Ainsworth Av

Trevarrick
Court

Oakfield
Close

Fowler
Industrial
Estate

Stirling Industrial
Estate

A673

St Mary's RC
Primary School

Brunswick Avenue

Lancaster
Av

Gloucester
AV

Makinson

Poplar
Av

Brazley Avenue

Laburnum
grove

Cedar

Windborne
Close

CHORLEY NEW RO

16

Coal Pit Road

Ⓐ Holdens Farm Ⓑ Gilligant's Ⓒ Ⓓ

3 66   13   67

1

Burnt Edge Lane

Col

2

Walker Fold

12

Makinson Lane

Edge Lane

Walker Fold Road

3

Matchmoor Lane

Old Harts Farm

◀**15**

PO

4

Moss Dr

Vicarage R

Egmont

Moor Platt Close

Bottom O' Th' Moor Lane

Shepherd's Drive

B6226 CHORLEY OLD ROAD MONTSERRAT BROW

Old

Old

411

B6402

OLD KILN LANE

5

3 66   67   B

Ⓐ Wimborne Close Ⓑ ▼**26** Ⓒ Ⓓ

Barford

High Rid Reservoir

1 grid square represents 500 metres

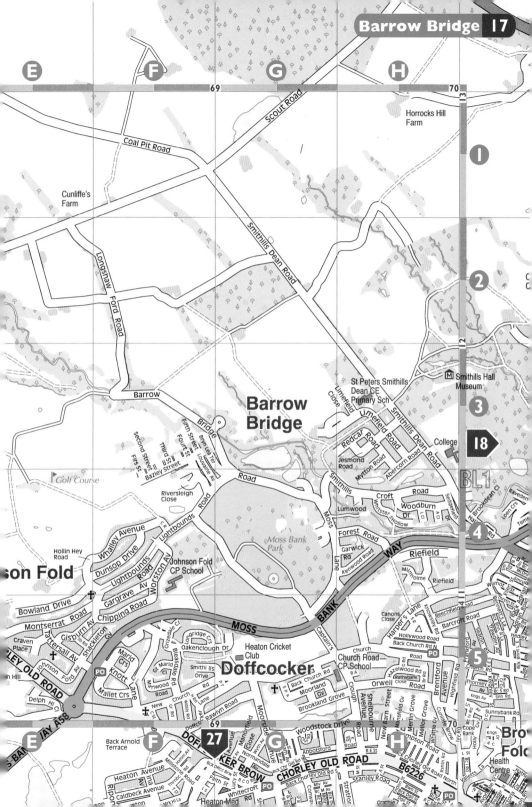

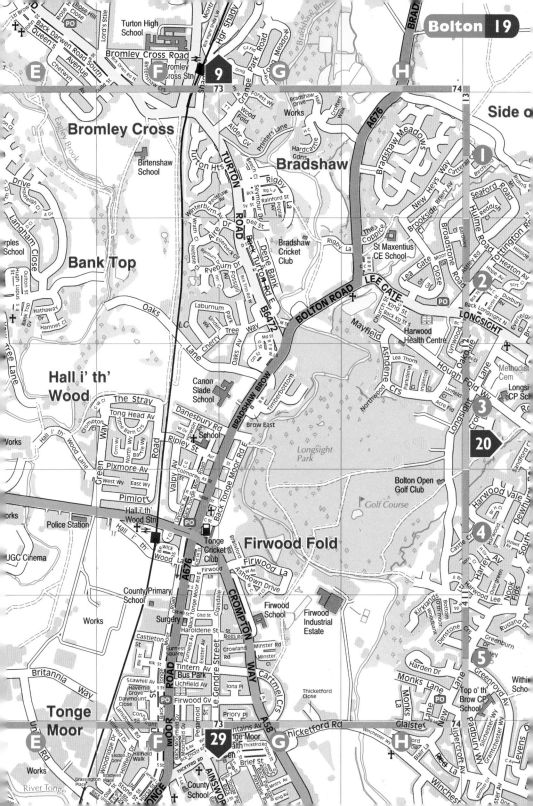

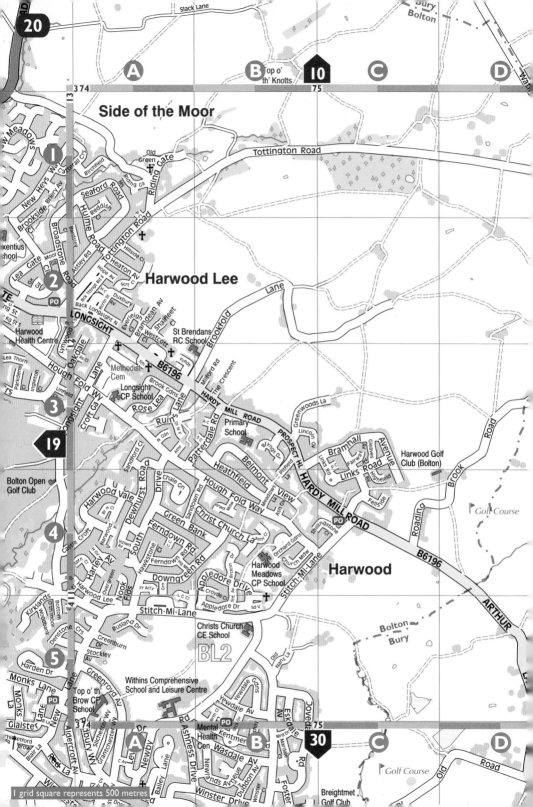

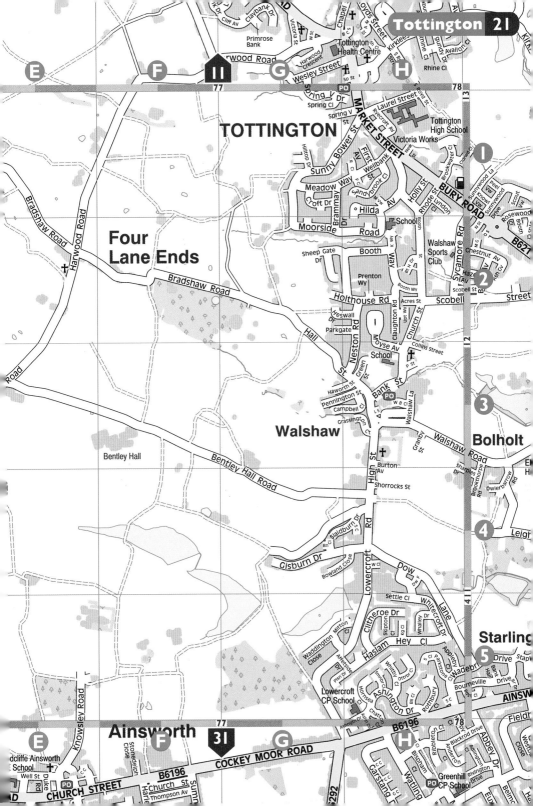

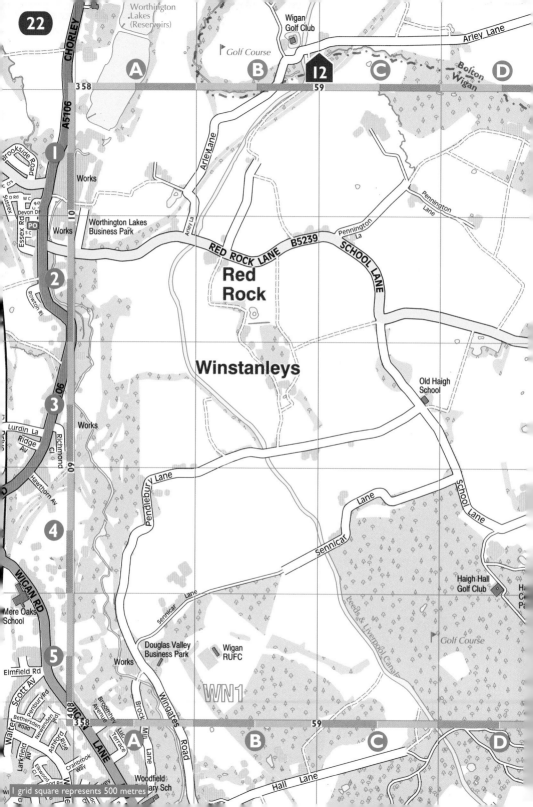

A B I2 C D

358 59

Worthington Lakes (Reservoirs)

Wigan Golf Club

Wigan Golf Club

Arley Lane

Golf Course

Bolton Wigan

CHORLEY

A5106

Arley Lane

Works

Brookside Road

C Crs

Sussex Rd

D Rd W C

Devon Dr

Essex Rd

PO

Worthington Lakes Business Park

Works

Arley La

RED ROCK LANE B5239

Pennington La

SCHOOL LANE

Pennington Lane

Red Rock

Rowton Rl

2

10

60

Winstanleys

Old Haigh School

3

Lurdin La

Ridge Av

Richmond Cl

Hawthorn Av

Works

60

Pendlebury Lane

Lane

4

Sennicar

School Lane

WIGAN RD

Mere Oaks School

Sennicar

Lane

Haigh Hall Golf Club

Ha
C
Pa

5

Elmfield Rd

Scott Av

Denbury Rd

Bethersden Rd

Newlands Rd

Ashford Rd

Douglas Valley Business Park

Works

Wigan RUFC

WN1

Golf Course

Leeds & Liverpool Canal

408

358

LANE

Walter

Larkfield Av

Elkwood Rd

Cranbrook Way

Broomthey Avenue

Lilac Terrace

Mill Lane

Brock

Wingates Road

A B C D

Woodfield mary Sch

Hall Lane

grid square represents 500 metres

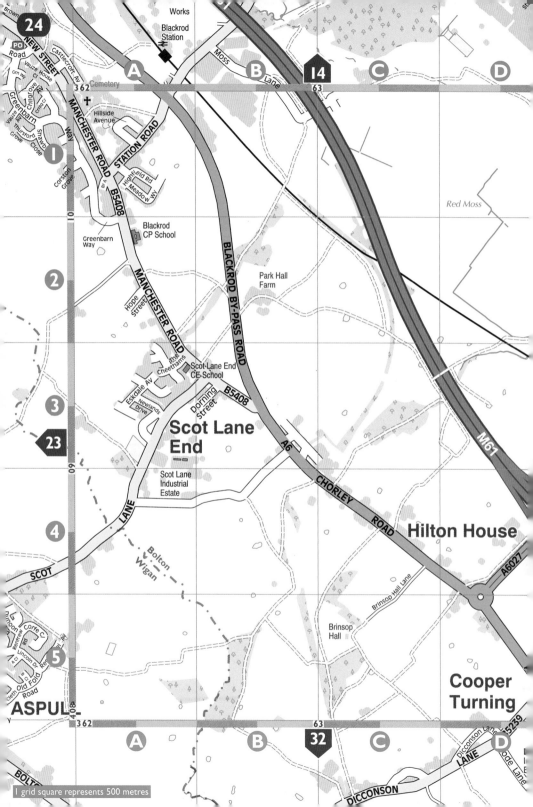

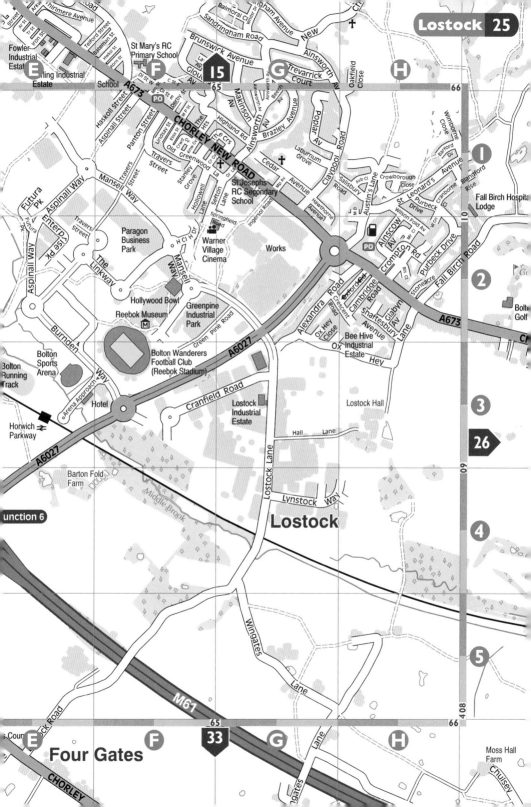

Arkw
Thirlmere Avenue
Telford Street
Blakeman St
Hawks St
Abn St

Balmoral Avenue
Sandringham Road
Brunswick Avenue
Ainsworth Av
New
Ch

Fowler Industrial Estate
St Mary's RC Primary School

ling Industrial Estate

E
School
A673
PO

Haskoll Street
Aspinall Street
Panton Street
Travers Street
Stanley Grove
Old Greenwood La

F
DISLW
C St E
DISLWF
Derby St
M P E
Esso St
M G W
15
65

Brunswick Avenue
Makinson Av
Highland Rd
Gloucester Av
The Hts
Lindsay St
The Crs
Sefton Lane
Hollowell Lane
Springfield Road
Ingersol Road

Trevarrick court
Ainsworth Av
Brazley Av
Poplar Av
G
Cedar
Avenue

Laburnum Grove
Claypool Road

Oakfield Close

H
66

Futura Pk
Futura

Aspinall Way
Mansel Way
Travers Way
Travers Street

St Josephs RC Secondary School

St
Hawthorne Avenue

Salisbury Road
Austin's Lane
Crowborough Close
St Leonard's
Purbeck Drive
Wilson Fold Av

Wimborne Close
Barford Gv
Cranmore Av
Blandford Rise

Fall Birch Hospital Lodge

I

Enterp (rise) Pk
Enterp
Aspinall Way

The Linkway
Mansel Way

Paragon Business Park

H Cl H Dr
Warner Village Cinema

Works

Ainscow
Crompton Rd
Purbeck Drive
Stoneacre

St Leonard's Av

Fall Birch Road

A673
Cr
2

Bolton Golf

Aspinall Way
Burnden Way

Hollywood Bowl
Reebok Museum
M

Greenpine Industrial Park
Green Pine Road

PO
Alexandra Road
Oxford Rd
Cambridge Road
Crescent
Ox Hey Close
Bee Hive Industrial Estate
Ox Hey

Shaftesbury Avenue
Gladyn Av
Hey

Bolt

A6027

3

Bolton Sports Arena
Bolton Running Track

Bolton Wanderers Football Club (Reebok Stadium)

A6027

Hotel
Cranfield Road
Lostock Industrial Estate
Hall Lane

Lostock Hall

26

Horwich Parkway
A6027

Barton Fold Farm

Middle Brook
Lostock Lane

Lynstock Way

Lostock

4

unction 6

60

Wingates Lane

5

M61
65

E
F
33
65
G
Gates Lane
Wingates Lane
H

Four Gates

Moss Hall Farm

CHORLEY

408
66

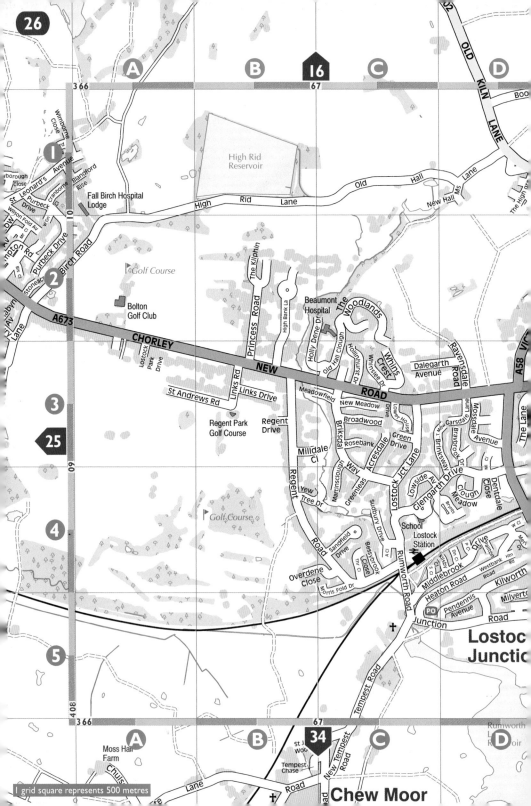

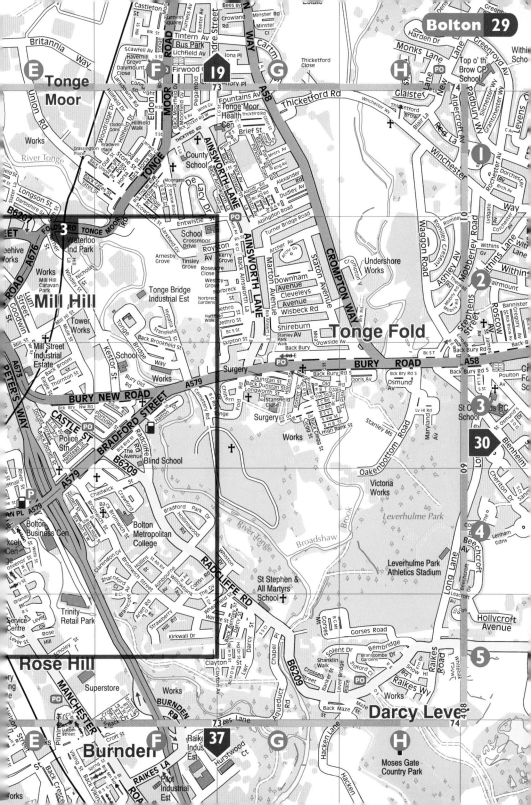

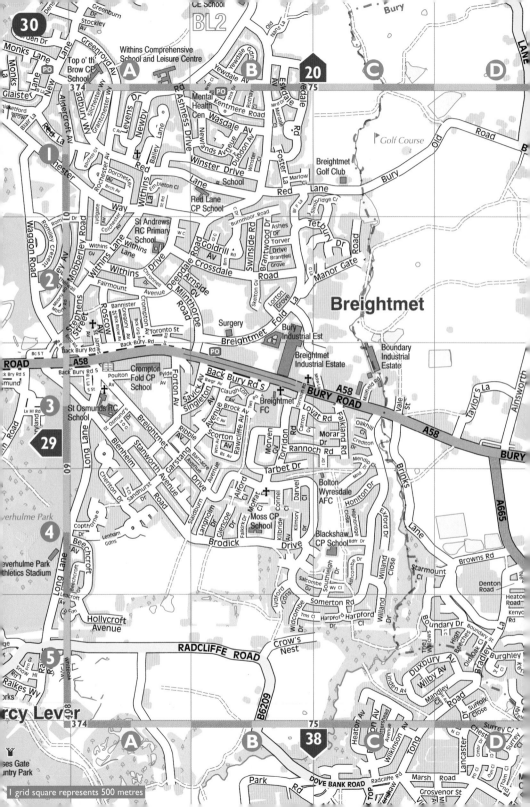

Greenburn Dr
CE School
Bury
LANE

Stockley AV
Greenroyd Av

Withins Comprehensive
School and Leisure Centre

Monks Lane
Top o' th'
Brow CP
School

A
B
C
D

Mental
Health
Cen

Old Road

Golf Course

Breightmet
Golf Club

Red Lane

I

Winster Drive

Red Lane
CP School

Bury

St Andrews
RC Primary
School

Withins Lane

Goldrill
Drive

Crossdale
Road

2

Manor Gate

Tetbury
Dr

Breightmet

Waggon Road

Mobberley Road

Surgery
Breightmet

Bury
Industrial Est

Breightmet
Industrial Estate

Boundary
Industrial
Estate

ROAD
A58

Crompton
Fold CP
School

Back Bury Rd S

BURY ROAD
A58

BURY

St Osmunds RC
School

Breightmet
FC

3

29

Breightmet

Bolton
Wyresdale
AFC

Brinks Lane

A665

Moss CP
School

Blackshaw
CP School

4

rhulme Park

Brodick
Drive

Starmount
Cl

Denton
Road

Browns Rd

Hollycroft
Avenue

Somerton Rd

Duxbury
Wilby Av

Burghley

5

RADCLIFFE ROAD
Crow's
Nest

rcy Lever
374

A
B
38
C
D

ses Gate
untry Park

Park
DOVE BANK ROAD
Radcliffe Rd

Grosvenor St

1 grid square represents 500 metres

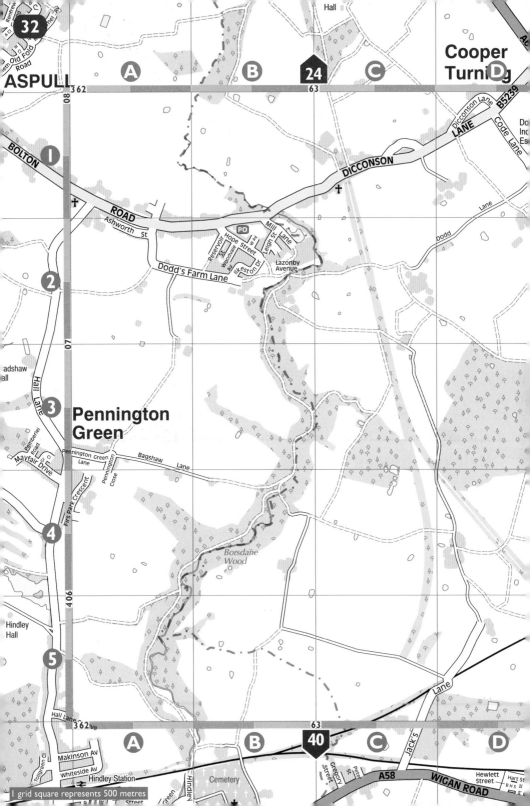

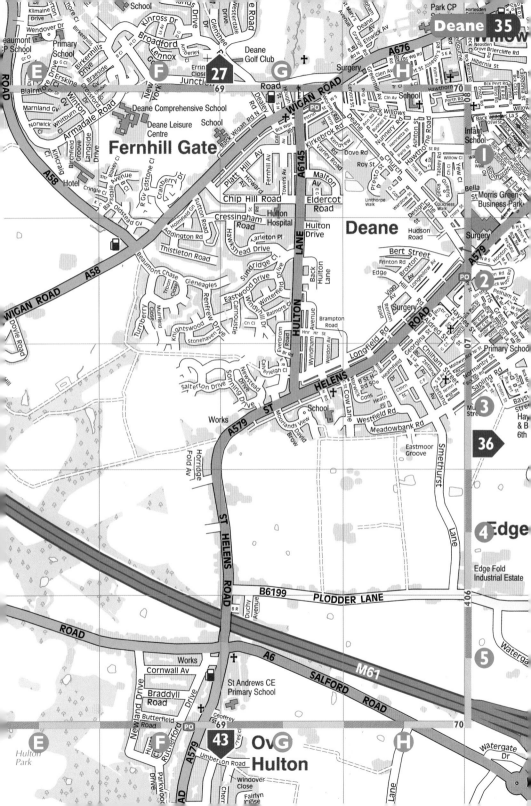

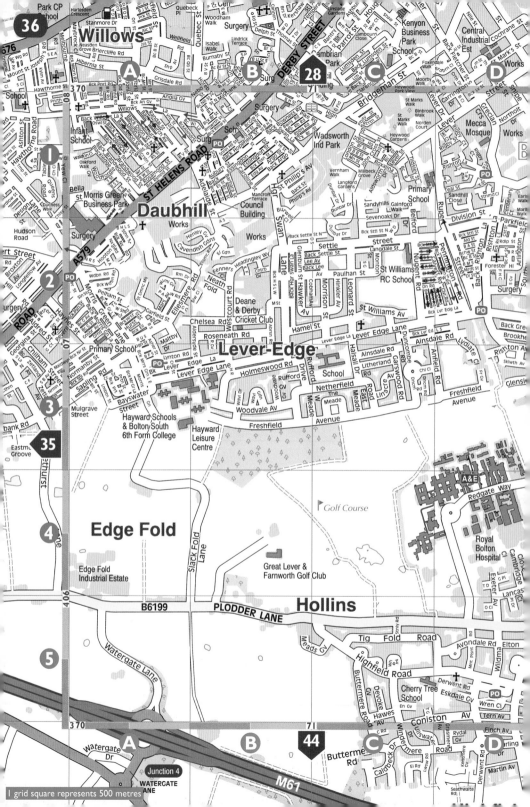

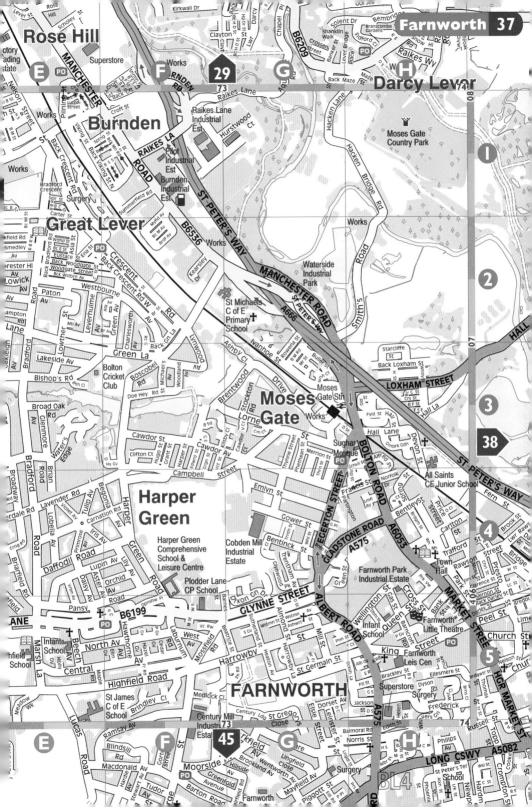

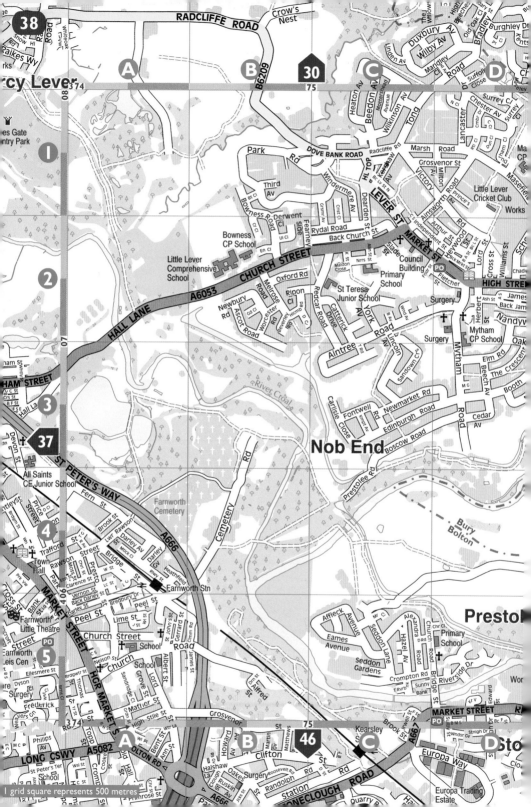

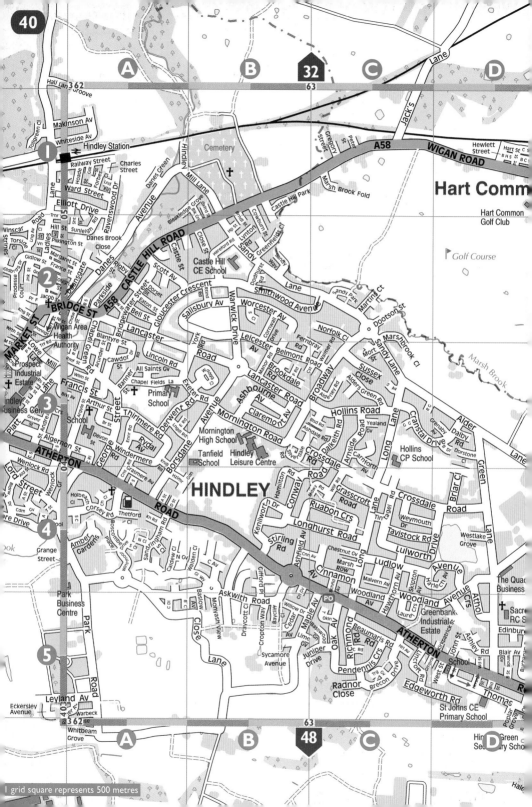

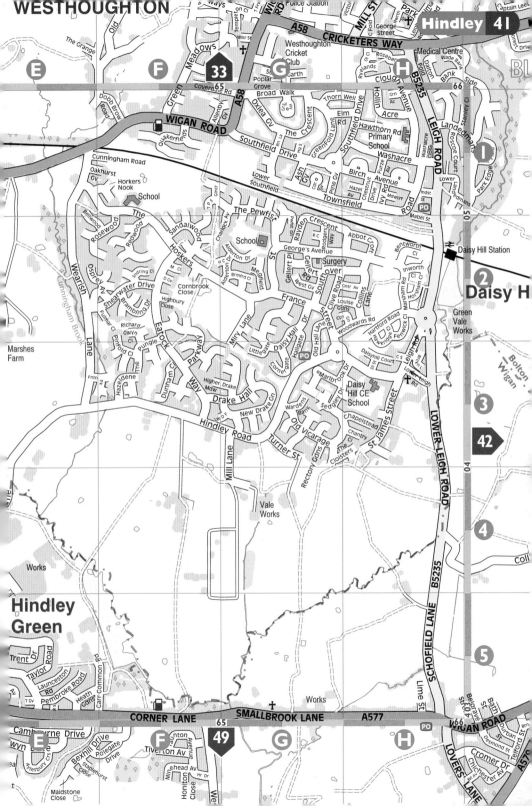

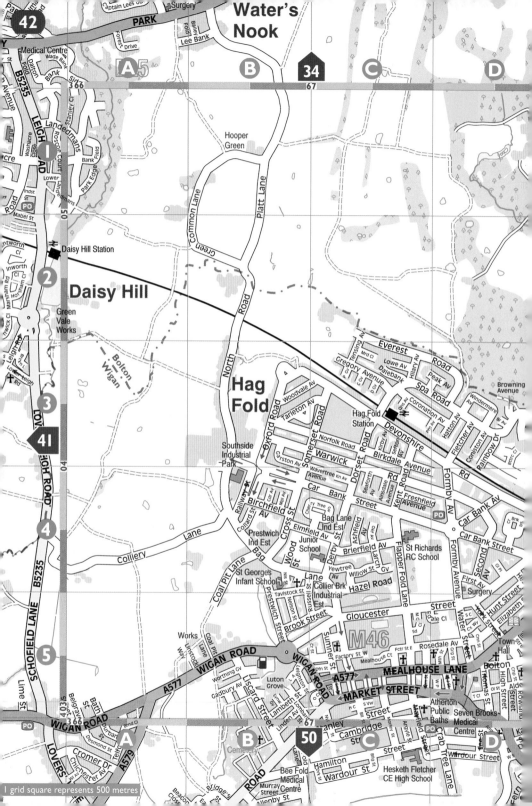

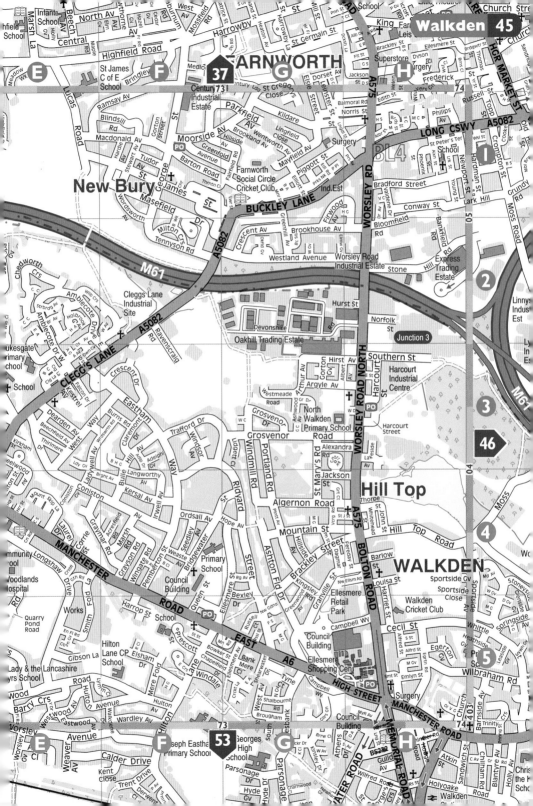

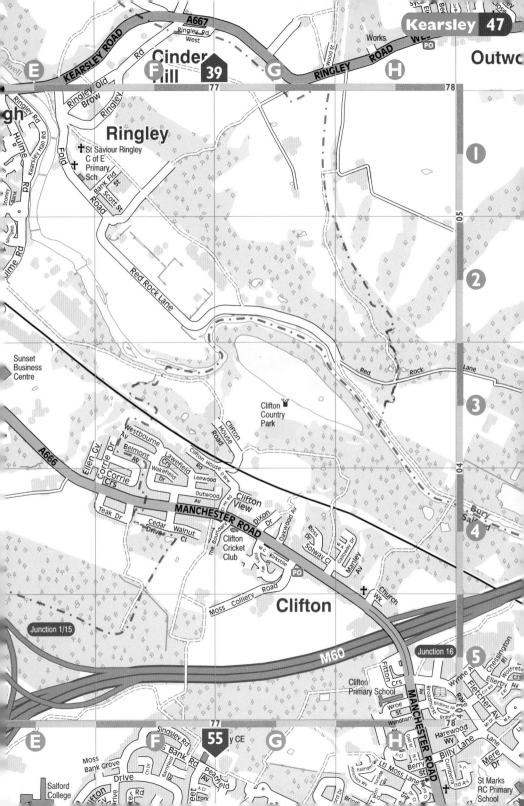

A667
Ringley Rd West
Kearsley Road
Cinder Hill `39`
Ringley Old Brow
Ringley Rd
Ringley Road
Ringley
Works
Outwo
PO

Ringley
77
78

St Saviour Ringley C of E Primary Sch
Ringley Rd
Kearsley Hall Rd
Hulme Rd
Storey Bank
Bank Fld St
Scott St
Fold
Road
Springs

Hulme Rd

Red Rock Lane

05

Sunset Business Centre

Red Rock Lane

04

Clifton Country Park

A666
Westbourne Av
Clifton House Road
Ellen Gv
Corrie Dr
Belmont Av
Lawefield Rd
Clifton House Drw
Corrie Crs
Wakefield Dr
Leewood
Outwood Av
Clifton View
Teak Dr
Cedar Drive
Walnut Cl
The Boundary
MANCHESTER ROAD
Dixon Dr
Oakwood Av
Ross Dr
W U
Galloway Dr
Manley Av

Clifton Cricket Club
W G Pl
Kirkstile Pl
Ford St
Solway Cl
PO

Moss Colliery Road
Clifton
Church Wk
Bury Salford
04

Junction 1/15

M60

Junction 16

5

Clifton Primary School
Wroe St
Wyndham
Fifton Crs
Broadhurst
Brdhrst St
Wynne Av
Rake
Chesshagton Rd
Ellerby Av
Wolfreton
Fletcher Av
MANCHESTER ROAD
Harewood Wy
Mere Dr

77
78

E
Sindsley Rd
F
s Bank Rd
Peafield Av
y CE `55`
G
H
Berry St
Billy Lane
Lane

Moss Bank Grove
Barfield
Drive
Rd
York
Ealinger Wy
Hinchley Wy
Ltl Moss Lane
Torside
Cumberla
Brindl
Salford College
St Marks RC Primary School

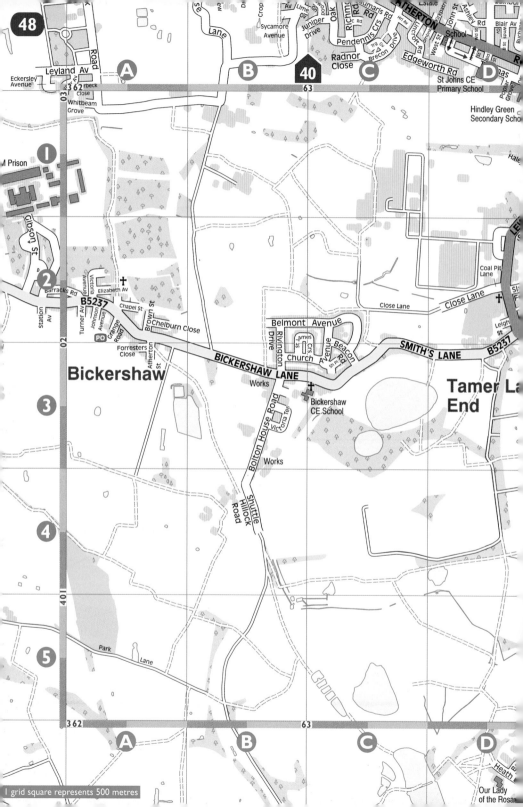

48

Leyland Av

Eckersley Avenue

A

03 3 **62** rbeck Close

Whitbeam Grove

sycamore Avenue

crop

Lime

Oak

Juniper Drive

Pendennis Rd

Radnor Close

B

40

Richmond Rd

Beaumaris Rd

Lincoln Drive

Brecon Drive

C

63

ATHERTON

School

West St

John St

Ashley Rd

Blair Av

Edgeworth Rd

St Johns CE Primary School

D

Hindley Green Secondary Scho

I

M Prison

Glasson St

Hale

Coal Pit Lane

2

Barracks Rd

B5237

Victoria Avenue

Johnson Avenue

Turner Av

Chapel St

Elizabeth Av

Brown St

Grange Road

station Av

02

PO

Chelburn Close

Forresters Close

Atherton St

Bickershaw

Close Lane

Close Lane

Belmont Avenue

Rivington Drive

James St

Crs

Church

Avenue

Beacon Rd

Leigh St

Leigh St

SMITH'S LANE

B5237

3

BICKERSHAW LANE

Works

Victoria Ter

Bickershaw CE School

Tamer La End

Bolton House Road

4

Shuttle Hillock Road

401

Works

5

Park Lane

362

A

63

B

C

Heath

D

Our Lady of the Rosa

1 grid square represents 500 metres

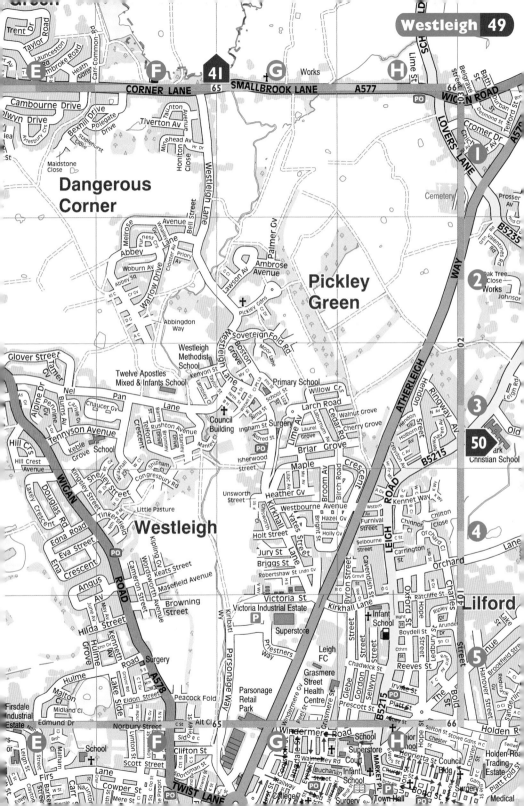

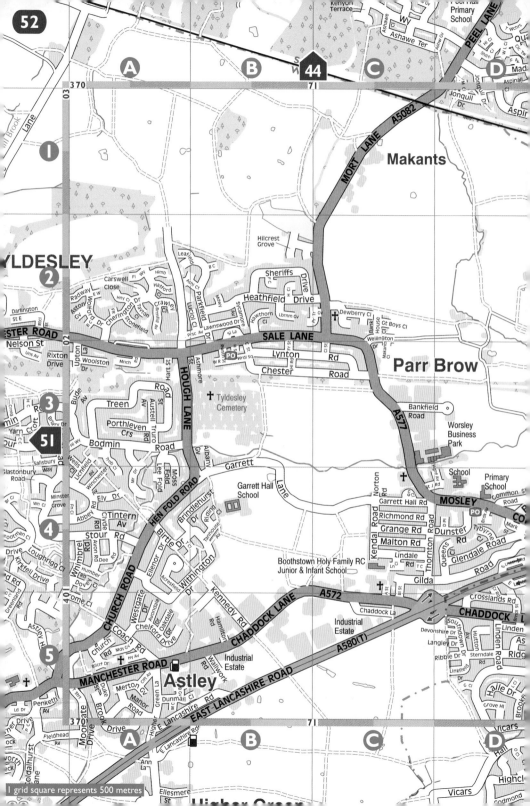

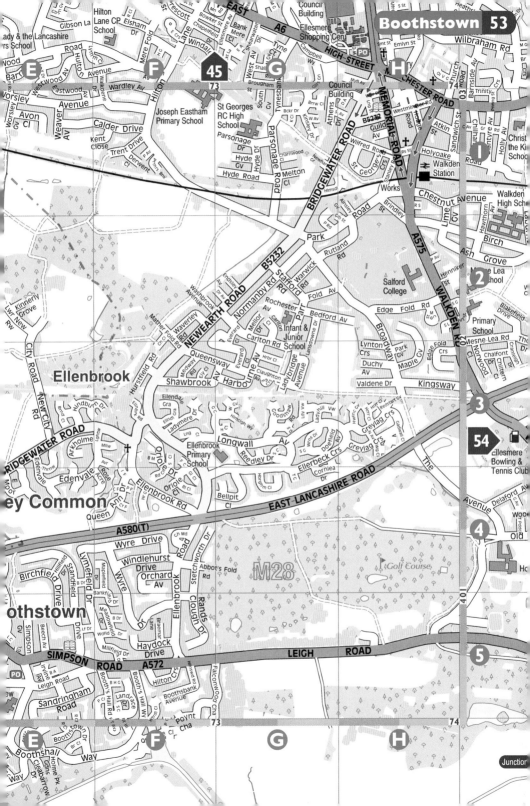

Adlington	6 B5	Doffcocker	17 G5	Hilton House	24 C4	Prestolee	
Affetside	10 D4	Dunscar	8 B3	Hindley	40 B4	Ramsbottom	
Ainsworth	31 F1	Eagley	8 D5	Hindley Green	41 E5	Red Rock	
Anderton	6 B4	Edge Fold	36 A4	Hindsford	50 D1	Ringley	
Aspull	23 H5	Edgworth	4 A3	Holcombe Brook	11 H1	Rivington	
Astley	52 A5	Egerton	8 C2	Hollins	36 B5	Roe Green	
Astley Bridge	18 C3	Ellenbrook	53 E3	Horrocks Fold	8 A5	Rose Hill	
Atherton	43 E5	Farnworth	37 G5	Horwich	14 D3	Scot Lane End	
Bank Top	19 E2	Fernhill Gate	35 F1	Howe Bridge	50 B2	Shakerley	
Barrow Bridge	17 G3	Firwood Fold	19 G4	Hunger Hill	34 D2	Sharples	
Bickershaw	48 A3	Four Gates	33 E1	Johnson Fold	16 D4	Side of the Moor	
Black Lane	31 H4	Four Lane Ends	21 F2	Kearsley	46 D2	Stoneclough	
Blackrod	13 G4	Gilnow	2 B5	Lever-Edge	36 B3	Swinton	
Boothstown	53 E5	Gin Pit	51 F4	Lilford	50 A5	Tamer Lane End	
Bottom o' th' Moor	15 G4	Great Lever	37 E2	Linnyshaw	46 A5	Tonge Fold	
Bradley Fold	31 E3	Greenheys	44 B3	Little Hulton	44 D4	Tonge Moor	
Bradshaw	19 G1	Greenmount	11 G2	Little Lever	38 D1	Toppings	
Breightmet	30 C2	Grimeford Village	14 A1	Little Scotland	13 E5	Tottington	
Bromley Cross	19 E1	Hag Fold	42 B3	Lostock	25 G4	Turton Bottoms	
Brownlow Fold	28 A1	Haigh	23 F3	Lostock Junction	26 D5	Tyldesley	
Burnden	37 E1	Halfway Houses	31 E3	Makants	52 C1	Walkden	
Chapeltown	9 H1	Hall i' th' Wood	19 E3	Markland Hill	27 E2	Wallsuches	
Chequerbent	34 C4	Halliwell	18 C4	Mill Hill	3 H2	Walshaw	
Chew Moor	34 C1	Harper Green	37 F4	Montcliffe	15 H2	Wardley	
Cinder Hill	39 F5	Hart Common	40 D1	Moorside	55 F4	Water's Nook	
Clifton	47 G5	Harwood	20 C4	Moses Gate	37 G3	Westhoughton	
Cooper Turning	24 D5	Harwood Lee	20 A2	Mosley Common	52 D4	Westleigh	
Cox Green	8 D3	Hawkshaw	11 E1	New Bury	45 E1	Wilderswood	
Daisy Hill	42 A2	Hazelhurst	5 H5	Newtown	55 G2	Willows	
Dales Brow	55 F5	Hazelhurst	54 D5	Nob End	38 C3	Wingates	
Dangerous Corner	49 E1	Heaton	27 G2	Over Hulton	43 G1	Winstanleys	
Darcy Lever	29 H5	Higher Folds	51 E5	Parr Brow	52 C3	Worsley	
Daubhill	36 A1	Highfield	44 D1	Pennington Green	32 A3		
Deane	35 H2	Hill Top	45 H4	Pickley Green	49 G2		

USING THE STREET INDEX

Street names are listed alphabetically. Each street name is followed by its postal town or area locality, the Postcode District, the page number, and the reference to the square in which the name is found.

Standard index entries are shown as follows:

Abbey Cl *RAD* M26 ....**31** G5

Street names and selected addresses not shown on the map due to scale restrictions are shown in the index with an asterisk or with the name of an adjoining road in brackets:

Acresfield Cl *HOR/BR* * BL6.................**13** G4

Albert Colliery Est
   WGNE/HIN
   (off Bolton House Rd) WN2 ....**48** B3

GENERAL ABBREVIATIONS

ACC	ACCESS	CTS	COURTS	HGR	HIGHER	MTN	MOU
ALY	ALLEY	CTYD	COURTYARD	HL	HILL	MTS	MOUN
AP	APPROACH	CUTT	CUTTINGS	HLS	HILLS	MUS	MU
AR	ARCADE	CV	COVE	HO	HOUSE	MWY	MOTO
ASS	ASSOCIATION	CYN	CANYON	HOL	HOLLOW	N	N
AV	AVENUE	DEPT	DEPARTMENT	HOSP	HOSPITAL	NE	NORTH
BCH	BEACH	DL	DALE	HRB	HARBOUR	NW	NORTH
BLDS	BUILDINGS	DM	DAM	HTH	HEATH	O/P	OVE
BND	BEND	DR	DRIVE	HTS	HEIGHTS	OFF	O
BNK	BANK	DRO	DROVE	HVN	HAVEN	ORCH	ORC
BR	BRIDGE	DRY	DRIVEWAY	HWY	HIGHWAY	OV	OV
BRK	BROOK	DWGS	DWELLINGS	IMP	IMPERIAL	PAL	P
BTM	BOTTOM	E	EAST	IN	INLET	PAS	PA
BUS	BUSINESS	EMB	EMBANKMENT	IND EST	INDUSTRIAL ESTATE	PAV	PAV
BVD	BOULEVARD	EMBY	EMBASSY	INF	INFIRMARY	PDE	PUBLIC H
BY	BYPASS	ESP	ESPLANADE	INFO	INFORMATION	PH	PUBLIC H
CATH	CATHEDRAL	EST	ESTATE	INT	INTERCHANGE	PK	P
CEM	CEMETERY	EX	EXCHANGE	IS	ISLAND	PKWY	PAR
CEN	CENTRE	EXPY	EXPRESSWAY	JCT	JUNCTION	PL	P
CFT	CROFT	EXT	EXTENSION	JTY	JETTY	PLN	P
CH	CHURCH	F/O	FLYOVER	KG	KING	PLNS	P
CHA	CHASE	FC	FOOTBALL CLUB	KNL	KNOLL	PLZ	P
CHYD	CHURCHYARD	FK	FORK	L	LAKE	POL	POLICE ST
CIR	CIRCLE	FLD	FIELD	LA	LANE	PR	P
CIRC	CIRCUS	FLDS	FIELDS	LDG	LODGE	PREC	PRE
CL	CLOSE	FLS	FALLS	LGT	LIGHT	PREP	PREPARA
CLFS	CLIFFS	FLS	FLATS	LK	LOCK	PRIM	PR
CMP	CAMP	FM	FARM	LKS	LAKES	PROM	PROME
CNR	CORNER	FT	FORT	LNDG	LANDING	PRS	PRI
CO	COUNTY	FWY	FREEWAY	LTL	LITTLE	PRT	P
COLL	COLLEGE	FY	FERRY	LWR	LOWER	PT	P
COM	COMMON	GA	GATE	MAG	MAGISTRATE	PTH	P
COMM	COMMISSION	GAL	GALLERY	MAN	MANSIONS	PZ	P
CON	CONVENT	GDN	GARDEN	MD	MEAD	QD	QUAD
COT	COTTAGE	GDNS	GARDENS	MDW	MEADOWS	QU	Q
COTS	COTTAGES	GLD	GLADE	MEM	MEMORIAL	QY	Q
CP	CAPE	GLN	GLEN	MKT	MARKET	R	R
CPS	COPSE	GN	GREEN	MKTS	MARKETS	RBT	ROUNDA
CR	CREEK	GND	GROUND	ML	MALL	RD	R
CREM	CREMATORIUM	GRA	GRANGE	ML	MILL	RDG	R
CRS	CRESCENT	GRG	GARAGE	MNR	MANOR	REP	REP
CSWY	CAUSEWAY	GT	GREAT	MS	MEWS	RES	RESE
CT	COURT	GTWY	GATEWAY	MSN	MISSION	RFC	RUGBY FOOTBALL
CTRL	CENTRAL	GV	GROVE	MT	MOUNT	RI	RI

......RAMP	SPR	.....SPRING	TPK	....TURNPIKE	VLG	......VILLAGE
......ROW	SQ	....SQUARE	TR	....TRACK	VLS	.....VILLAS
......SOUTH	ST	....STREET	TRL	....TRAIL	VW	.....VIEW
......SCHOOL	STN	....STATION	TWR	....TOWER	W	.....WEST
......SOUTH EAST	STR	....STREAM	U/P	...UNDERPASS	WD	....WOOD
......SERVICE AREA	STRD	....STRAND	UNI	..UNIVERSITY	WHF	...WHARF
......SHORE	SW	...SOUTH WEST	UPR	....UPPER	WK	...WALK
......SHOPPING	TDG	....TRADING	V	....VALE	WKS	...WALKS
......SKYWAY	TER	....TERRACE	VA	....VALLEY	WLS	...WELLS
......SUMMIT	THWY	..THROUGHWAY	VIAD	...VIADUCT	WY	...WAY
......SOCIETY	TNL	....TUNNEL	VIL	...VILLA	YD	...YARD
......SPUR	TOLL	....TOLLWAY	VIS	...VISTA	YHA	...YOUTH HOSTEL

STCODE TOWNS AND AREA ABBREVIATIONS

......Atherton	CHLYE	....Chorley east/	LEIGH	....Leigh	TYLD	....Tyldesley
......Bolton		Adlington/Whittle-le-Woods	LHULT	....Little Hulton	WALK	....Walkden
......Bolton east	EDGW/EG	....Edgworth/Egerton	RAD	....Radcliffe	WGN	....Wigan
LL.....Bolton south/Little Lever	FWTH	....Farnworth	SWIN	....Swinton	WGNE/HIN	..Wigan east/Hindley
EC.....Chorley/Eccleston	HOR/BR	..Horwich/Blackrod	TOT/BURYW	..Tottington/Bury west	WHTF	....Whitefield
					WHTN	....Westhoughton

ndex - streets　　　　　　　　　**Abb - Ast**

A

CI RAD M26	31	G5
Ct RAD M26	39	G1
Dr SWIN M27	55	G3
Gv CHLYE PR6	6	A5
La LEIGH WN7	49	F2
Rd TYLD M29	52	A4
Sq LEIGH WN7	49	F2
St LEIGH WN7	49	H5
gdon Wy LEIGH WN7	49	F2
's Fold Rd WALK M28	53	F4
sford Rd BOL BL1	27	G1
t St BOLS/LL BL3	28	C5
/BR BL6	14	D3
orn Rd BOL BL1	17	H4
ethy St HOR/BR BL6	15	F5
don Rd BOLE BL2	29	G2
am St HOR/BR BL6	14	D3
Av SWIN M27	55	G5
Gv LHULT M38	45	F3
hi Dr LHULT M38	45	F3
hi St RAD M26	31	H5
am Dr BOL BL1	2	A5
ton St BOLS/LL BL3	36	B2
Rd BOL BL1	18	A5
de Dr TOT/BURYW BL8	21	G5
k Av RAD M26	38	C5
w Av HOR/BR BL6	25	H2
ale Av ATH M46	42	C4
le Rd BOLS/LL BL3	36	C2
Rd HOR/BR BL6	13	F4
Gv WALK M28	53	H1
t BOL BL1	27	G1
orth Av HOR/BR BL6	25	G1
orth Hall Rd BOLE BL2	30	D3
orth La BOLE BL2	29	F1
orth Rd BOLS/LL BL3	38	C2
M26	31	H5
orth St BOL BL1	18	A5
e Rd BOLS/LL BL3	38	C3
BOLE BL2	19	F2
orth St WHTN BL5	33	G2
t BOL BL1	18	A4
y CI RAD M26	52	B3
arle Rd SWIN M27	55	C4
a St BOLS/LL BL3	28	A5
Av WALK M28	45	G3
Colliery East		
E/HIN		
Bolton House Rd) WN2	48	B3
Gv FWTH BL4	37	H5
on CI WGNE/HIN WN2	23	G4
Rd BOL BL1	27	G2
H BL4	37	G4
Rd SWIN M27	27	F2
St BOLS/LL * BL3	38	D2
W/EG BL7	8	B1
H BL4	45	H1
S BL4	14	D3
St BOLS/LL BL3	28	C5
H BL4	46	C2
BL5	33	G2

Aldbury Ter BOL * BL1	28	B1
Alderbank HOR/BR BL6	14	B4
Alderbank CI FWTH BL4	46	B2
Aldercroft Av BOLE BL2	29	H1
Alder Dr SWIN M27	55	E2
Alderfold St ATH M46	42	D5
Alder Gv BOLE BL2	19	C1
Alder La WGNE/HIN WN2	40	D3
Alderley Av BOL BL1	18	C2
Alderley Rd WGNE/HIN WN2	40	C3
Alderminster Av LHULT M38	45	E3
Alders Green Rd		
WGNE/HIN WN2	40	C3
Alder St ATH M46	42	D5
BOLS/LL BL3	36	D2
Aldersyde St BOLS/LL BL3	36	B2
Alderton Dr WHTN BL5	41	C2
Aldford Dr ATH M46	43	E4
Aldford Gv BOLS/LL BL3	30	D5
Aldred St BOLS/LL BL3	35	H2
LEIGH WN7	49	C3
Aldsworth Dr BOLS/LL BL3	36	C1
Alexander Briant Ct		
FWTH (off Parkfield Av) BL4	45	C1
Alexander Rd BOLE BL2	29	C1
Alexander St TYLD M29	51	C3
Alexandra Rd FWTH BL4	46	C2
HOR/BR BL6	25	C2
RAD M26	38	C5
WALK M28	45	C3
Alexandra St BOLS/LL * BL3	36	B1
FWTH BL4	45	H1
Alexandria Dr WHTN BL5	34	B5
Alford CI BOLE BL2	30	B4
Alfred Av WALK M28	54	C4
Alfred St BOLS/LL BL3	29	F5
EDGW/EG BL7	8	B1
FWTH BL4	37	H3
TYLD M29	51	F2
WALK M28	45	H5
Algernon Rd WALK M28	45	C4
Algernon St SWIN M27	55	F3
Alice St BOLS/LL BL3	28	A5
Allan St TYLD M29	51	F3
Allenby Gv WHTN BL5	41	F1
Allenby Rd SWIN M27	55	E5
Allenby St ATH M46	50	B1
Allendale Gdns BOL BL1	18	C5
Allen St BOLS/LL BL3	38	C2
RAD M26	39	C2
Allerton CI WHTN BL5	34	A4
Allesley CI WHTN BL5	34	A4
All Saints Gv WGNE/HIN WN2	40	A3
All Saints' St BOL BL1	2	E2
Allsopp St BOL BL1	2	E6
Alma Rd WHTN BL5	33	H5
Alma St ATH M46	42	C5
BOLS/LL BL3	36	A1
FWTH* BL4	46	D3
LEIGH WN7	49	C3
RAD M26	31	H5
TYLD M29	51	F3
Almond Gv BOL * BL1	18	D4
Almond St BOL BL1	18	D4
FWTH BL4	37	G5
Alnwick CI WGNE/HIN WN2	23	H5
Alpine Dr LEIGH WN7	49	E3
Alston Lea ATH M46	43	E4
Alston St BOLS/LL * BL3	36	C2
Amber Gdns WGNE/HIN WN2	40	A4
Amber Gv WHTN BL5	33	H3
Amberley CI BOLS/LL BL3	27	F5
Amblecote Dr East LHULT M38	45	E2
Amblecote Dr West LHULT M38	45	E2
Ambleside CI BOLE BL2	20	B3
Ambrose Av LEIGH WN7	49	G2
Anchor La FWTH BL4	37	G3
Anderton CI TOT/BURYW BL8	31	H1

Anderton Ct		
HOR/BR (off Bolton Rd) BL6	14	C2
Anderton La CHLYE PR6	14	A4
Anderton St CHLYE PR6	6	A5
Andrew Ct TOT/BURYW BL8	11	H3
Andrew La BOL BL1	18	D1
Anfield Rd BOLS/LL BL3	36	C3
Angelo St BOL BL1	18	B4
Angle St BOLE BL2	29	F1
Anglezarke Rd CHLYE PR6	6	A5
Anglia Gv BOLS/LL BL3	36	A1
Angus Av LEIGH WN7	49	E4
Annis Rd BOLS/LL BL3	35	H1
Ann St FWTH BL4	46	A1
LEIGH WN7	49	C3
Ansdell Rd HOR/BR BL6	15	E3
Anson Av SWIN M27	55	G5
Anson Rd SWIN M27	55	G5
Anson St BOL BL1	18	D4
Anyon Vls		
HOR/BR		
(off Catherine St East)	14	C3
Appleby CI TOT/BURYW BL8	21	H5
Appleby Gdns BOLE * BL2	29	E1
Appledore Dr BOLE BL2	20	B5
Aqueduct Rd BOLS/LL BL3	37	C1
Arbor Gv LHULT M38	44	C4
Archer Av BOLE BL2	29	C2
Archer Gv BOLE BL2	29	C2
Archer St WALK M28	52	C5
Arch St BOL BL1	3	H1
Ardens CI SWIN M27	55	F1
Ardley Rd HOR/BR BL6	15	E3
Argo St BOLS/LL BL3	36	B1
Argyle CI WALK M28	45	G3
Argyle St ATH M46	50	C1
SWIN M27	55	C4
WGNE/HIN WN2	40	A3
Arkholme WALK M28	53	E3
Arkwright CI BOL BL1	28	A1
Arkwright St HOR/BR BL6	15	E5
Arlen Ct BOLE BL2	3	J7
Arlen Rd BOLE BL2	3	J7
Arley La CHLY/EC PR7	12	D5
WGN WN1	22	B1
WGNE/HIN WN2	22	B2
Arley Wy ATH M46	51	E1
Arlington Av SWIN M27	55	F5
Arlington St BOLS/LL BL3	36	D2
Armadale Rd BOLS/LL BL3	35	E1
Armitage Av LHULT M38	44	D4
Armitage Gv LHULT M38	44	D4
Armstrong St HOR/BR BL6	15	E5
Arncot Rd BOL BL1	18	D2
Arnesby Gv BOLE BL2	3	K1
Arnfield Dr WALK M28	53	F5
Arnold Rd EDGW/EG BL7	8	D4
Arnold St BOL BL1	18	A5
Arnside Gv BOLE BL2	30	A2
Arnside Rd WGNE/HIN WN2	40	C3
Arran CI BOLS/LL BL3	27	E4
Arran Gv RAD M26	31	C5
Arrowhill Rd RAD M26	31	H2
Arrow St BOL BL1	2	C1
Arthur Av WALK M28	45	C3
Arthur La BOLE BL2	20	C4
Arthur St BOLS/LL BL3	38	C2
FWTH BL4	37	H5
SWIN M27	55	F4
WALK M28	53	H2
WGNE/HIN WN2	40	A3
Artillery St BOLS/LL BL3	3	F7
Arundale WHTN BL5	33	H3
Arundel Dr LEIGH WN7	49	H5
Arundel Rd BOL BL1	18	C2
SWIN M27	55	E2
WGNE/HIN WN2	40	A3
Ascot Dr ATH M46	43	E4
Ascot Rd BOLS/LL BL3	38	B2

Ashawe CI LHULT M38	44	C5
Ashawe Gv LHULT M38	44	D5
Ashawe Ter LHULT M38	44	C5
Ashbank Av BOLS/LL BL3	27	E4
Ashbee St BOL BL1	18	C4
Ashbourne Av BOLE BL2	3	K6
WGNE/HIN WN2	40	B3
Ashbourne CI LEIGH WN7	49	F2
Ashbourne Gv WALK M28	54	A3
Ashburner St BOL BL1	2	D4
Ashbury CI BOLS/LL BL3	2	C7
Ashby CI BOLS/LL BL3	37	F2
Ashby Gv LEIGH WN7	49	E3
Ashcombe Dr BOLE BL2	30	C4
RAD M26	31	F5
Ashcott CI HOR/BR BL6	26	D5
Ashcroft St WGNE/HIN WN2	40	A4
Ashdale Av BOLS/LL BL3	27	E4
Ashdale Rd WGNE/HIN WN2	40	B3
Ashdene Crs BOLE BL2	19	H3
Ashdown Dr BOLE BL2	19	C4
WALK M28	52	C4
Ash Dr SWIN M27	55	E1
Asher St BOLS/LL BL3	36	A2
Ashes Dr BOLE BL2	30	B2
Ashfield Av ATH M46	42	C4
WGNE/HIN WN2	40	B4
Ashfield Dr WGNE/HIN WN2	23	C5
Ashfield Gv BOL BL1	19	E1
Ashfield Rd CHLYE PR6	6	B4
Ashford Av SWIN M27	55	E5
WALK M28	52	B5
Ashford CI BOLE BL2	20	A3
Ashford Wk BOL BL1	28	C1
Ash Gv BOL BL1	27	H2
BOLE BL2	20	B4
TOT/BURYW BL8	11	H1
WALK M28	54	A2
WHTN BL5	41	H4
Ashington CI BOL BL1	17	H4
Ashington Dr TOT/BURYW BL8	21	H5
Ashlands Av SWIN M27	55	E5
WALK M28	53	E4
Ash Lawns BOL BL1	27	H3
Ash Leigh Dr BOL BL1	27	E2
Ashley Av BOLE BL2	29	H2
SWIN M27	55	F5
Ashley Crs SWIN M27	55	F4
Ashley Dr LEIGH WN7	49	E3
SWIN M27	55	F5
Ashley Rd WGNE/HIN WN2	40	B5
Ashling Ct TYLD M29	52	A2
Ashmore St TYLD M29	52	B3
Ashness CI HOR/BR BL6	14	B4
Ashness Dr BOLE BL2	30	A1
Ashover CI EDGW/EG BL7	18	D1
Ashridge CI HOR/BR BL6	26	C4
Ash Rd FWTH BL4	46	B3
Ash St BOLE BL2	3	C5
TYLD M29	51	C2
Ashton Field Dr LHULT M38	45	C4
Ashton St BOLS/LL BL3	38	D2
BOLS/LL BL3	38	D2
Ashurst CI BOLE BL2	20	B4
Ashwell St BOLE BL2	19	F4
Ashwood RAD M26	46	D1
Ashwood Av WALK M28	45	D1
Ashworth CI BOLS/LL BL3	39	E2
Ashworth La BOL BL1	18	D2
Ashworth St FWTH BL4	37	C5
WGNE/HIN WN2	32	A5
Asia St BOLS/LL BL3	37	E2
Askwith Rd WGNE/HIN WN2	40	B5
Aspen CI WHTN BL5	33	H3
Aspinall Av WALK M28	44	D5
Aspinall Crs WALK M28	52	D1
Aspinall St HOR/BR BL6	25	F1
Aspinall Wy HOR/BR BL6	25	E1
Aster Av FWTH BL4	37	E4

Astley Hall Dr *TYLD* M29 .....51 H5
Astley La *BOL* BL1.....18 C4
Astley Rd *BOLE* BL2 .....20 A2
Astley St *BOL* BL1.....18 C5
  TYLD M29.....51 G3
Aston Dr *WALK* M28.....52 A2
Athens Dr *WALK* M28.....53 C1
Atherfield *BOLE* BL2.....20 A3
Atherleigh Gv *LEIGH* WN7.....49 H4
Atherleigh Wy *LEIGH* WN7.....49 H3
Atherton Rd *WGNE/HIN* WN2.....40 C5
Atherton St *CHLY/EC* PR7.....13 E1
  WGNE/HIN WN2.....48 A3
Athlone Av *BOL* BL1.....18 A2
Athol Crs *WGNE/HIN* WN2.....40 D4
Atholl Cl *BOLS/LL* BL3.....27 F4
Atkinson Av *BOLS/LL* BL3.....37 F2
Atkin St *WALK* M28.....53 H1
Auberson Rd *BOLS/LL* BL3.....36 B2
Auburn St *BOLS/LL* BL3.....36 B1
Augustus St *BOLS/LL* BL3.....37 E1
Austin's La *HOR/BR* BL6.....25 H1
Avallon Cl *TOT/BURYW* BL8.....11 H5
Avebury Cl *HOR/BR* BL6.....25 H1
Avenue St *BOL* BL1.....2 A1
The Avenue *BOLE* BL2.....3 J4
  CHLYE PR6.....6 A4
  LEIGH WN7.....49 H5
  WALK M28.....53 H3
  WHTN BL5.....33 H4
Averhill *WALK* M28.....53 F3
Aviary Rd *WALK* M28.....54 A5
Avocet Cl *LEIGH* WN7.....50 A5
Avoncliff Cl *BOL* BL1.....18 B4
Avon Cl *WALK* M28.....53 E1
Avondale Dr *TOT/BURYW* BL8.....11 H2
  TYLD M29.....52 A5
Avondale Rd *FWTH* BL4.....36 D5
Avondale St *BOL* BL1.....28 A1
Avonhead Cl *HOR/BR* BL6.....14 B4
Avon Rd *FWTH* BL4.....46 D3
  TYLD M29.....52 A4
Avon St *BOL* BL1.....27 H1
Aylesbury Crs *WGNE/HIN* WN2.....49 E1
Aylesford Wk *BOL* * BL1.....28 C1
Ayr St *BOLE* BL2.....19 F3
Ayrton Gv *LHULT* M38.....45 E3

B

Babylon La *CHLYE* PR6.....6 C3
Back Abingdon Rd *BOLE* BL2.....29 G1
Back Adrian Rd *BOL* BL1.....18 A5
Back Adrian Rd East *BOL* * BL1.....18 A5
Back Ainscow St *BOL* BL1.....2 C1
Back Ainsworth La *BOLE* BL2.....29 F1
Back Ainsworth La East
  BOLE BL2.....29 G1
Back Ainsworth St *BOL* * BL1.....18 A4
Back Alder St *BOLS/LL* BL3.....36 D2
Back Alexander Rd *BOLE* BL2.....29 G1
Back Alexandra St *BOLS/LL* BL3.....36 A1
Back Alfred St *BOLS/LL* * BL3.....37 E1
Back Alice St *BOLS/LL* BL3.....28 A5
  BOLS/LL BL3.....38 D2
Back Alicia St *BOLS/LL* * BL3.....37 H1
Back Alston St *BOLS/LL* BL3.....36 C2
Back Anglia Gv *BOLS/LL* BL3.....36 A1
Back Annis Rd *BOLS/LL* BL3.....35 H1
Back Anson St *BOL* * BL1.....18 D4
Back Apple Ter *BOL* * BL1.....18 B5
Back Argo St *BOLS/LL* BL3.....36 D2
Back Arlington St *BOLS/LL* BL3.....36 D2
Back Arnold St *BOL* BL1.....18 A5
Back Arnold Ter *BOL* BL1.....27 F1
Back Ashbee St *BOL* BL1.....18 C4
Back Ash St *BOLE* BL2.....3 G5
Back Ashton St *BOLS/LL* * BL3.....35 H1
Back Ashworth La *BOL* BL1.....18 D2
Back Astley St *BOL* BL1.....18 C5
Back Augustus St *BOLS/LL* * BL3.....37 E1
Back Augustus St West
  BOLS/LL * BL3.....37 E1
Back Avenue St *BOL* BL1.....2 A1
Back Avondale St *BOL* BL1.....28 A1
Back Baldwin St *BOLS/LL* * BL3.....2 C7
Back Baldwin St North
  BOLS/LL BL3.....2 C7
Back Banbury St *BOLE* BL2.....29 G2
Back Bankfield St *BOLS/LL* BL3.....28 A5
Back Bantry St *BOLS/LL* * BL3.....37 E2
Back Barbara St *BOLS/LL* BL3.....36 B1
Back Bark St *BOL* BL1.....2 D5
Back Bashall St *BOL* BL1.....18 A3
Back Battenberg Rd *BOL* * BL1.....28 A2
Back Baxendale St *BOL* BL1.....18 C3
Back Bayley St *BOL* BL1.....2 A1
Back Baythorpe St *BOL* * BL1.....18 D5
Back Baytorpe St North
  BOL * BL1.....18 D4
Back Beaconsfield St
  BOLS/LL BL3.....2 A6
Back Beaconsfield Ter
  BOLE * BL2.....29 F1
Back Bedford St *BOL* BL1.....28 A2

Back Beech St *BOL* BL1.....18 D5
Back Beechwood St
  BOLS/LL BL3.....36 D2
Back Belmont Rd *BOL* BL1.....18 C2
Back Belmont Rd East *BOL* BL1.....18 C2
Back Bennett's La *BOL* BL1.....18 A5
Back Bennett's La East
  BOL BL1.....18 A5
Back Bentinck St *BOL* BL1.....27 H1
Back Bentley St *BOLE* BL2.....29 G5
Back Bertrand Rd *BOL* BL1.....28 A3
Back Beverley Rd *BOL* BL1.....28 A2
Back Birley St *BOL* BL1.....18 C3
Back Blackbank St *BOL* BL1.....18 C3
Back Blackburn Rd *BOL* BL1.....18 D5
Back Blackburn Rd East
  EDGW/EG BL7.....8 B1
Back Blackburn Rd West
  BOL BL1.....18 C3
  EDGW/EG* BL7.....8 C4
Back Blackwood St *BOL* BL1.....18 D4
Back Blackwood St
  BOLS/LL BL3.....37 E1
Back Bolton St *BOL* BL1.....18 D5
Back Boundary St *BOL* BL1.....18 B5
Back Bowen St *BOL* BL1.....27 H1
Back Bowness Rd *BOLS/LL* BL3.....36 B1
Back Bradford St *BOLS/LL* BL3.....37 E1
Back Bradford Rd West
  BOLS/LL BL3.....37 E2
Back Bradford St *BOLE* BL2.....3 J4
Back Bradford St East *BOLE* BL2.....3 J4
Back Bradford St South
  BOLE BL2.....3 H5
Back Bradford St West *BOLE* BL2.....3 H5
Back Bradshaw *BOLE* BL2.....19 G3
Back Bradshaw Brow West
  BOLE * BL2.....19 G3
Back Bradshawgate *BOL* * BL3.....3 F5
Back Bradshaw Rd East
  BOLE BL2.....19 H2
Back Brandon St *BOLS/LL* BL3.....36 B1
Back Brandon St North
  BOLS/LL BL3.....36 B1
Back Brandwood St
  BOLS/LL BL3.....36 A1
Back Bridgeman St *BOLS/LL* BL3.....36 B1
Back Bridge St *BOL* * BL1.....2 E2
Back Brigade St *BOL* BL1.....28 A3
Back Brindley St *BOL* BL1.....18 D5
Back Brink's Pl *BOL* * BL1.....2 C3
Back Bristol Av *BOLE* BL2.....29 G1
Back Bristol St *BOLS/LL* BL3.....2 B6
Back Bromwich St *BOLE* BL2.....3 J5
Back Brookfield St *BOLE* BL2.....3 J3
Back Broom St *BOLE* BL2.....3 H3
Back Bryce St *BOLS/LL* BL3.....28 C5
Back Burnaby St *BOLS/LL* BL3.....28 B5
Back Burnham Av *BOLS/LL* BL3.....27 G1
Back Bury New Rd *BOL* BL1.....28 A1
Back Bury New Rd East
  BOL * BL3.....3 J3
Back Bury Old Rd *BOLE* * BL2.....3 H3
Back Bury Rd *BOLE* BL2.....29 H3
Back Bury Rd East *BOLE* BL2.....29 G3
Back Bury Rd South *BOLE* BL2.....29 G3
Back Bushell St *BOLS/LL* * BL3.....35 H1
Back Calder Rd *BOLS/LL* BL3.....36 C2
Back Caledonia St *BOLS/LL* BL3.....28 A5
Back Calvert Rd *BOLS/LL* BL3.....36 D2
Back Canada St *BOL* * BL1.....18 A5
  HOR/BR BL6.....14 D4
Back Carter St *BOLS/LL* BL3.....37 E1
Back Castle St *BOLE* BL2.....3 H4
Back Cecilia St *BOLS/LL* BL3.....37 E1
Back Cecil St *BOLE* BL2.....3 J4
Back Cemetery Rd East
  BOLE BL2.....3 K3
Back Cestrian St *BOLS/LL* BL3.....36 D2
Back Chalfont St *BOL* BL1.....18 D5
Back Chapel St *HOR/BR* * BL6.....15 E4
  TOT/BURYW BL8.....11 H5
Back Chapman St *BOL* BL1.....27 H1
Back Charles Holden St
  BOL BL1.....2 A5
Back Chaucer St *BOL* BL1.....28 B1
Back Cheapside *BOL* BL1.....2 E4
Back Chorley New Rd *BOL* BL1.....2 A2
Back Chorley New Rd North
  BOL BL1.....27 H3
Back Chorley Old Rd *BOL* BL1.....27 G1
Back Chorley Old Rd North
  BOL BL1.....27 G1
Back Chorley Old Rd South
  BOL BL1.....27 G1
Back Chorley St *BOL* BL1.....2 C3
Back Chorley St East *BOL* * BL1.....2 C2
Back Church Av *BOLS/LL* BL3.....36 A1
Back Church Rd *BOL* BL1.....17 G5
Back Church Rd North *BOL* BL1.....17 H5
Back Church St *BOLE* BL2.....3 D2
  BOLS/LL BL3.....38 C2
Back Clarendon Rd *BOLE* BL2.....29 G5
Back Clarke St *BOL* * BL1.....28 A2
Back Clay St East
  EDGW/EG* BL7.....9 E5
Back Clay St West
  EDGW/EG* BL7.....9 E5

Back Clegg's Bldgs *BOL* * BL1.....2 C2
Back Clegg St *BOLE* BL2.....29 G3
Back Cloister St *BOL* * BL1.....18 A5
Back Clyde St *BOL* BL1.....18 C5
Back Cobden St *BOL* BL1.....18 B4
Back Colenso Rd *BOLE* * BL2.....29 H3
Back College Wy *BOLS/LL* BL3.....2 B5
Back Columbia Rd *BOL* * BL1.....28 A2
Back Common St *WHTN* BL5.....40 D1
Back Coniston St *BOL* * BL1.....18 D4
Back Coop St *BOL* BL1.....18 C3
Back Corson St *FWTH* BL4.....37 H3
Back Cotton St *BOL* BL1.....18 B5
Back Cox Green Rd North
  EDGW/EG BL7.....8 D4
Back Crawford Av *BOL* * BL1.....3 J5
Back Crawford St *BOLE* * BL2.....3 J5
Back Crescent Av *BOL* BL1.....2 B2
Back Crescent Rd *BOLS/LL* BL3.....37 E1
Back Crescent Rd West
  BOLS/LL BL3.....37 E2
Back Croft La *BOLS/LL* BL3.....37 F1
Back Cromer Av *BOLE* BL2.....29 G1
Back Croston St *BOLS/LL* BL3.....36 A1
Back Crown St *HOR/BR* BL6.....14 C3
Back Crumpsall St North
  BOL BL1.....18 C4
Back Cundey St *BOL* BL1.....28 A1
Back Curzon Rd *BOL* BL1.....28 A3
Back Cyril St *BOLS/LL* * BL3.....29 E5
Back Daisy St *BOLS/LL* BL3.....36 A1
Back Darley St *FWTH* BL4.....38 A5
Back Darwen Rd North
  EDGW/EG BL7.....8 C3
Back Darwen Rd South
  EDGW/EG BL7.....9 E5
Back Darwin St *BOL* * BL1.....18 B5
Back Deal St *BOLS/LL* BL3.....36 D2
Back Deane Church La
  BOLS/LL * BL3.....35 H1
Back Deane Church La West
  BOLS/LL * BL3.....35 H1
Back Deane Rd *BOLS/LL* BL3.....28 A5
Back Deane Rd North
  BOLS/LL BL3.....2 A6
Back Derby St *BOLS/LL* BL3.....2 C7
Back Design St *BOLS/LL* BL3.....35 H1
Back Devonshire Rd *BOL* BL1.....27 G1
Back Dijon St *BOLS/LL* BL3.....36 A1
Back Dijon St North
  BOLS/LL BL3.....36 A1
Back Dobie St *BOLS/LL* * BL3.....37 E1
Back Doffcocker Brow *BOL* BL1.....27 F1
Back Dorset St *BOLE* BL2.....3 H4
Back Dougill St *BOL* BL1.....27 H1
Back Dougill St South *BOL* * BL1.....27 H1
Back Drummond St *BOL* * BL1.....18 C3
Back Ducie Av *BOL* BL1.....28 A3
Back Duncan St *HOR/BR* * BL6.....15 E4
Back Dunstan St *BOLE* BL2.....29 G3
Back Duxbury St *BOL* * BL1.....18 B5
Back Earnshaw St
  BOLS/LL BL3.....36 A2
Back Eastbank St *BOL* BL1.....18 D4
Back Eckersley Rd *BOL* BL1.....18 C4
Back Edditch Gv *BOLE* BL2.....29 G3
Back Eden St *BOL* BL1.....18 C3
Back Edgmont Av
  BOLS/LL * BL3.....36 B1
Back Elgin St *BOL* BL1.....18 B5
Back Ellesmere Rd *BOLS/LL* BL3.....36 A1
Back Ellesmere St *BOLS/LL* BL3.....2 A6
Back Elmwood Gv *BOL* * BL1.....28 A2
Back Elmwood Gv West
  BOL * BL1.....28 A2
Back Emmett St *HOR/BR* BL6.....14 D4
Back Empire Rd *BOLE* BL2.....29 H2
Back Empress St *BOL* BL1.....27 H1
Back Ena St *BOLS/LL* BL3.....37 E2
Back Ernest St *BOL* BL1.....28 A4
Back Eskrick St *BOL* * BL1.....18 B5
Back Eskrick St East *BOL* * BL1.....18 B5
Back Eskrick St South *BOL* BL1.....18 B5
Back Eskrick St West *BOL* * BL1.....18 B5
Back Essingdon St *BOLS/LL* BL3.....36 B1
Back Essingdon St South
  BOLS/LL BL3.....36 B1
Back Eustace St *BOLS/LL* BL3.....37 E2
Back Euxton St *BOLS/LL* BL3.....36 B1
Back Everton St North
  BOL * BL1.....18 D5
Back Ewart St *BOL* BL1.....18 C5
Back Fairhaven Rd *BOL* BL1.....18 D4
Back Fair St *BOLS/LL* BL3.....36 A3
Back Fern St East *BOLS/LL* BL3.....28 A4
Back Fletcher St *RAD* M26.....46 D1
Back Fletcher St
  BOLS/LL BL3.....28 C5
Back Flora St *BOLS/LL* * BL3.....36 C1
Back Florence Av *BOL* BL1.....18 D3
Back Fortune St *BOLS/LL* BL3.....29 F5
Back Frances St *BOLS/LL* BL3.....28 B5
Back Frank St *BOL* * BL1.....28 B5
Back Fylde St *FWTH* BL4.....37 H3
Back Gainsborough Av
  BOLS/LL BL3.....36 A2
Back Garside Gv *BOL* * BL1.....18 A5
Back Gaskell St *BOL* BL1.....2 B2
Back Gaskell St East *BOL* * BL1.....2 B2
Back Gaythorne St *BOL* * BL1.....18 D4

Back George Barton St
  BOLE BL2.....2
Back George St *BOLS/LL* BL3.....3
  HOR/BR BL6.....3
Back Gibraltar St *BOLS/LL* BL3.....
Back Gibraltar St South
  BOLS/LL BL3.....
Back Gilnow Gv *BOL* BL1.....
Back Gilnow La *BOLS/LL* * BL3.....
Back Gilnow La West
  BOLS/LL BL3.....
Back Gilnow Rd *BOL* BL1.....
Back Glen Av *BOLS/LL* * BL3.....
Back Glen Bott St *BOL* * BL1.....
Back Gloster St *BOL* * BL1.....
Back Goldsmith St *BOLS/LL* BL3.....3
Back Gordon Av *BOLS/LL* BL3.....
Back Gorses Mt *BOLE* BL2.....
Back Grafton St *BOL* * BL1.....
Back Grantham Cl *BOL* * BL1.....
Back Grasmere St *BOL* * BL1.....
Back Greenhalgh St
  BOLS/LL * BL3.....
Back Greenland Rd
  BOLS/LL BL3.....
Back Green La South *BOLS/LL* BL3.....
Back Gregory Av *BOLE* BL2.....
Back Grendon St *BOLS/LL* BL3.....
Back Gresham St *BOL* * BL1.....
Back Grove St *BOL* BL1.....
Back Hadwin St *BOL* * BL1.....
Back Halliwell Rd *BOL* * BL1.....
Back Halliwell Rd South
  BOL * BL1.....
Back Halstead St *BOL* * BL1.....
Back Hargreaves St *BOL* BL1.....
Back Harper's La South
  BOL * BL1.....
Back Hartington St *BOL* * BL1.....3
Back Hart St *WHTN* BL5.....
Back Hatfield Rd *BOL* BL1.....
Back Hawthorne Rd
  BOL * BL1.....3
Back Hawthorne Rd East
  BOL * BL1.....3
Back Hawthorn Rd West
  BOL * BL1.....
Back Haydn St *BOL* BL1.....
Back Haydock St *BOL* BL1.....
Back Hengist St *BOLE* BL2.....
Back Hennon St *BOL* BL1.....
Back Henrietta St
  BOLS/LL * BL3.....
Back Henry Lee St *BOLS/LL* BL3.....3
Back High Bank St *BOLE* BL2.....
Back Higher Darcy St
  BOLS/LL BL3.....2
Back Higher Shady La West
  EDGW/EG BL7.....
Back Higher Swan La
  BOLS/LL BL3.....
Back Higher Swan La
  West *BOLS/LL* BL3.....
Back High St *BOLS/LL* BL3.....
Back High St South
  BOLS/LL BL3.....
Back High St West
  BOLS/LL * BL3.....
Back Hilden St *BOLE* BL2.....
Back Hilden St West *BOLE* BL2.....
Back Holland St *BOLE* BL2.....
Back Holland St East *BOL* * BL1.....
Back Holly Pl *BOL* BL1.....
Back Holly St *BOL* BL1.....
Back Hopefield St *BOLS/LL* BL3.....
Back Horeb St East
  BOLS/LL * BL3.....
Back Horsa St *BOLE* BL2.....
Back Horsa St North *BOLE* * BL2.....
Back Hotel St *BOL* * BL1.....
Back Hough La East
  EDGW/EG BL7.....
Back Howarden St *BOL* * BL1.....
Back Howcroft St
  BOLS/LL * BL3.....
Back Hughes St *BOL* BL1.....
Back Hulton La *BOLS/LL* BL3.....
Back Hulton La South
  BOLS/LL * BL3.....
Back Hulton La West
  BOLS/LL * BL3.....
Back Hurst St *BOLS/LL* BL3.....
Back Huxley St *BOL* BL1.....
Back Irlam St *BOL* BL1.....
Back Irlam St North *BOL* * BL1.....
Back Ivy Bank Rd *BOL* BL1.....
Back Ivy Rd *BOL* BL1.....
Back Ivy Rd West *BOL* * BL1.....
Back James St *BOLS/LL* BL3.....
Back Jauncey St *BOLS/LL* BL3.....
Back John Brown St *BOL* * BL1.....
Back John Cross St
  BOLS/LL * BL3.....
Back Johnson St *BOL* * BL1.....
Back John St *BOLS/LL* BL3.....
Back Keighley St *BOL* BL1.....
Back Kendal Rd *BOL* BL1.....

Kingholm Gdns BOL * BL1 ....28 B1
Kingsley St BOL BL1 ....18 B5
King St BOL BL1 ....2 D3
King St North
  W/EG BL7 ....8 D4
King St South BOLE BL2 ....19 H2
Knowsley Rd BOL * BL1 ....17 H5
Knowsley St BOL BL1 ....2 E3
Kylemore Av
  S/LL * BL3 ....27 H5
La BOL BL1 ....2 C2
N BL1 ....43 H2
Lark St BOL BL1 ....3 F2
Latham St BOL BL1 ....18 D5
Lawn St BOL BL1 ....28 A1
Leachfield St BOL BL1 ....18 B4
Leach St BOLS/LL BL3 ....28 C5
Lee Av BOLS/LL BL3 ....36 A2
Lena St BOL BL1 ....18 D5
Lenora St BOLS/LL * BL3 ......27 H5
Lever Edge La
  S/LL BL3 ....36 A3
Lever Edge La South
  S/LL BL3 ....36 C2
Lever St BOLS/LL BL3 ....36 C1
Lever St North
  S/LL BL3 ....38 C1
Lever St South
  S/LL * BL3 ....5 G3
Lightburne Av BOL BL1 ....27 H3
Lilly St BOL * BL1 ....2 A1
Lincoln Rd BOL * BL1 ....28 A2
Lindley St BOLS/LL * BL3 ......38 D2
Longden St BOL BL1 ....28 A2
Longfield Rd
  S/LL 35 H2
Long La BOLE BL2 ....30 A3
Longsight North BOLE BL2 ....20 A2
Longsight South BOLE BL2 ....19 H2
Longworth St
  W/EG BL7 ....8 B1
Lord St BOLS/LL BL3 ....38 D2
Loxham St BOLS/LL BL3 ....37 H3
Lumsden St BOLS/LL BL3 ......28 C5
Luton St BOLS/LL BL3 ....37 E1
Lytton St BOL BL1 ....28 B1
Mackenzie St BOL BL1 ....18 B5
Malvern Av BOL BL1 ....27 C1
Manchester Rd BOLE BL2 ......3 C6
S/LL BL3 ....37 G3
Manchester Rd East
  E * BL2 ....3 G7
Manchester Rd South
  S/LL BL3 ....29 E5
Manchester Rd West
  S/LL BL3 ....37 F1
Maple St BOLS/LL * BL3 ....2 B7
Marion St South
  S/LL * BL3 ....37 G3
Market St BOLS/LL BL3 ....38 D2
  M26 ....46 D1
Markland Hill La BOL BL1 ......27 F1
Markland Hill La East
  * BL1 ....27 F1
Markland Hill La West
  * BL1 ....27 F1
Marlborough St BOL BL1 ....2 A2
Marsh Fold La BOL * BL1 ......28 A2
Mary St BOLS/LL * BL3 ....2 B7
Mawdsley St BOL BL1 ....2 E4
Maxwell St BOL * BL1 ....18 C3
Maybank St BOL BL1 ....28 B5
Mayfield As BOLS/LL BL3 ......37 F2
Mayor St BOL BL1 ....2 E2
Mayor St North BOL * BL1 ......2 A5
Maze St BOLS/LL BL3 ....29 G5
Mcdonna St BOL BL1 ....18 A4
Mckean St BOLS/LL BL3 ....37 E1
Mckean St North
  S/LL * BL3 ....37 E1
Melbourne Rd
  S/LL BL3 ....28 A5
Mellor Gv BOL BL1 ....27 H1
Mellor Gv West BOL * BL1 ......27 H1
Melrose Av BOL BL1 ....27 G1
Melville St BOLS/LL BL3 ....37 E2
Mercia St BOLS/LL BL3 ....28 A5
Meredith St BOLS/LL BL3 ......36 D2
Mere Gdns BOL BL1 ....2 C1
Merlin Gv BOL * BL1 ....27 H1
Methwold St
  S/LL * BL3 ....36 A1
Milford Rd BOLS/LL BL3 ....36 C1
Miller St BOL * BL1 ....18 C3
Mill St North
  W/EG BL7 ....8 D4
Mill St South
  W/EG BL7 ....8 D4
Minorca St BOLS/LL * BL3 ......36 C1
Moorfield Gv BOLE BL2 ....29 F1
Morningten Rd East
  BL1 ....28 A2
Morris Green La
  S/LL BL3 ....36 A2
Morris Green La East
  S/LL BL3 ....36 A2
Moss Ter BOL BL1 ....2 E2
Mowbray St BOL * BL1 ....27 H1
Murton Ter BOL BL1 ....18 D3
Musgrave Rd BOL BL1 ....28 A2

Back Musgrave Rd North
  BOL BL1 ....28 A2
Back Nelson St BOLS/LL BL3 ....36 B1
Back Nelson St HOR/BR * BL6 ....15 F4
Back Nevada St BOL BL1 ....28 C1
Back Newhall La BOL BL1 ......2 A5
Back Newport Rd BOLS/LL * BL3 ....37 E1
Back Newport St BOL * BL1 ....2 E5
Back Newton St BOL BL1 ......18 C5
Back Nixon Rd BOLS/LL BL3 ....36 A2
Back Normanby St BOLS/LL BL3 ....36 A3
Back Norris St BOLS/LL * BL3 ....38 C2
Back Northern Gv BOL BL1 ....28 A1
Back Nunnery Rd BOLS/LL BL3 ....35 H1
Back Nut St BOL * BL1 ....18 B5
Back Olaf St BOLE BL2 ....29 F1
Back Oldham St BOLS/LL BL3 ....2 A6
Back Olga St BOL BL1 ....18 B5
Back Olga St North BOL * BL1 ....18 B5
Back Oriel St BOLS/LL BL3 ....28 A5
Back Osborne Gv BOL BL1 ....28 A1
Back Oxford Gv North BOL BL1 ....28 A1
Back Packer St BOL * BL1 ......18 A5
Back Palace St BOL * BL1 ......2 E2
Back Palm St BOL BL1 ....18 C4
Back Parkdale Rd BOLE BL2 ....29 C1
Back Parkfield Rd BOLS/LL BL3 ....37 E2
Back Parkinson St
  BOLS/LL * BL3 ....28 A5
Back Park Rd BOL BL1 ....2 A4
Back Park St BOL BL1 ....2 A5
Back Park Vw EDGW/EG BL7 ....18 D1
Back Park View Rd
  BOLS/LL * BL3 ....36 A1
Back Partington St BOLS/LL BL3 ....36 A3
Back Patterson St
  BOLS/LL * BL3 ....35 G1
Back Peabody St BOLS/LL BL3 ....36 C1
Back Peace St BOLS/LL BL3 ....28 B5
Back Pedder St BOL BL1 ....28 A1
Back Penarth Rd BOLS/LL BL3 ....28 A5
Back Pennington Rd
  BOLS/LL * BL3 ....36 C2
Back Peveril St BOLS/LL * BL3 ....35 H2
Back Pikes La West BOLS/LL BL3 ....36 B2
Back Pine St BOL BL1 ....18 D5
Back Pleasant St BOL BL1 ......2 D1
Back Poplar Av BOL BL1 ....18 D3
Back Portugal St BOLE BL2 ....3 J4
Back Preston St BOLS/LL BL3 ....37 F1
Back Primrose St BOL * BL1 ....18 A5
Back Primula St BOL BL1 ......18 A5
Back Progress St BOL * BL1 ....28 D1
Back Quebec St BOLS/LL BL3 ....38 A5
Back Queensgate BOL BL1 ....28 A2
Back Queen St BOL * BL1 ......2 A2
Back Radcliffe Rd East
  BOLE * BL2 ....3 J4
Back Railway Vw CHLY/EC PR7 ....13 H1
Back Raimond St BOL BL1 ......18 A4
Back Rainshaw St BOL BL1 ....18 D3
Back Randal St BOLS/LL * BL3 ....36 B1
Back Range St BOL BL1 ....36 B1
Back Raphael St BOL BL1 ......28 A1
Back Rawlinson St
  HOR/BR * BL6 ....14 D3
Back Rawson Rd BOL BL1 ......14 D3
Back Rawson Rd North BOL BL1 ....28 A1
Back Redhill Gv BOL BL1 ....2 C1
Back Ribblesdale Rd
  BOLS/LL * BL3 ....36 B1
Back Richelieu St BOLS/LL BL3 ....37 E1
Back Rigby La North BOLE * BL2 ....19 G1
Back Rigby La South BOLE BL2 ....19 G1
Back Rishton La BOLS/LL BL3 ....36 D1
Back Rishton La East
  BOLS/LL BL3 ....36 D2
Back Rock Av BOL BL1 ....18 A4
Back Roland Rd BOLS/LL BL3 ....28 A5
Back Romer St BOLE BL2 ......29 G3
Back Rosamond St BOLS/LL BL3 ....36 A1
Back Roscow Av BOLE BL2 ....30 A2
Back Roseberry St
  BOLS/LL * BL3 ....36 A1
Back Rossini St BOL BL1 ....18 B4
Back Rowena St BOLS/LL * BL3 ....37 G3
Back Rowland St BOLS/LL * BL3 ....35 H2
Back Roxalina St BOLS/LL BL3 ....36 C1
Back Rudolph St BOLS/LL BL3 ....36 D2
Back Rumworth St BOLS/LL BL3 ....36 B1
Back Rushton Rd BOL * BL1 ....27 H1
Back Russell Cl BOL * BL1 ......28 A1
Back Russell St BOL * BL1 ......28 A1
Back Rutland Gv BOL BL1 ......28 A1
Back Ryefield St BOL BL1 ......29 E1
Back St Ann St BOL BL1 ....28 A2
Back St Augustine St BOL BL1 ....18 B5
Back St George's Rd BOL BL1 ....2 C1
Back St George's Rd North
  BOL BL1 ....2 B2
Back St Helens Rd
  BOLS/LL * BL3 ....36 B1
Back St Helens Rd South
  BOLS/LL BL3 ....35 H3
Back St Philip's Av
  BOLS/LL BL3 ....36 B1
Back St Thomas St East
  BOL * BL1 ....18 B5
Back Salisbury St BOLS/LL BL3 ....2 B5
Back Salisbury Ter BOLE BL2 ....29 H3

Back Sandon St West
  BOLS/LL * BL3 ....36 B1
Back Sapling Rd BOLS/LL BL3 ....35 H3
Back Sapling Rd South
  BOLS/LL * BL3 ....35 H3
Back Scowcroft St BOLE BL2 ....29 F1
Back Settle St BOLS/LL BL3 ....36 B2
Back Settle St North
  BOLS/LL BL3 ....36 B2
Back Seymour St BOL BL1 ......18 D4
Back Shakerley Rd ATH * M46 ....51 F2
Back Sharman St BOLS/LL BL3 ....29 F5
Back Sherwood St BOL * BL1 ....27 H1
Back Shipton St BOL BL1 ......18 A5
Back Short St ATH M46 ....51 E2
Back Shuttle St BOLS/LL * BL3 ....2 C6
Back Silverdale Rd BOL BL1 ....28 A3
Back Skipton St BOLE BL2 ....29 G2
Back Smethurst La BOLS/LL BL3 ....35 H3
Back Smethurst La West
  BOLS/LL * BL3 ....35 H3
Back Sofa St BOL BL1 ....27 H1
Back Soho St BOL BL1 ....28 A5
Back Somerset Rd BOL BL1 ....27 H5
Back Somerville St BOL * BL1 ....18 A4
Back Southfield st BOLS/LL BL3 ....37 F1
Back South St BOLS/LL BL3 ....36 C2
Back South View St BOLE BL2 ....29 G3
Back Spa Rd BOLS/LL BL3 ......2 A5
Back Spa Rd North BOL * BL1 ....2 A5
Back Spa Rd West BOL * BL1 ....2 A5
Back Springfield St BOLS/LL BL3 ....37 E1
Back Spring Gdns BOL BL1 ......2 E4
Back Stainsbury St BOLS/LL BL3 ....36 A1
Back Stewart St BOL BL1 ......28 C1
Back Stone St BOLE BL2 ....29 F1
Back Sunlight Rd BOL BL1 ......28 A3
Back Sunning Hill St
  BOLS/LL * BL3 ....36 B1
Back Sunnyside Rd BOL BL1 ....18 A5
Back Swan La BOLS/LL BL3 ....36 B1
Back Talbot St BOL BL1 ....18 D3
Back Tavistock Rd BOL BL1 ....2 A5
Back Thicketford La BOLE * BL2 ....29 G1
Back Thicketford Rd West
  BOLE BL2 ....29 F1
Back Thomasson Cl BOL BL1 ....28 C1
Back Thorns Rd BOL BL1 ......18 C4
Back Thorn St BOL BL1 ....18 C5
Back Thorpe St BOL BL1 ....18 B5
Back Thurnham St
  BOLS/LL * BL3 ....36 A2
Back Tonge Moor Rd BOLE BL2 ....19 F4
Back Tonge Moor Rd East
  BOLE BL2 ....19 F4
Back Tonge Old Rd BOLE BL2 ....29 G3
Back Tottington Rd East
  BOLE BL2 ....20 A2
Back Tudor St BOLS/LL BL3 ....36 A1
Back Turton Rd BOLE BL2 ......19 G2
Back Turton Rd West BOLE BL2 ....19 G2
Back Uganda St BOLS/LL BL3 ....36 A2
Back Ulleswater St BOL BL1 ....18 D5
Back Union Rd BOLE BL2 ....29 E1
Back Unsworth St South
  BOLS/LL BL3 ....28 B5
Back Uttley St BOL BL1 ....18 B5
Back Venice St BOLS/LL BL3 ....36 A1
Back Vernon St BOL BL1 ....2 C2
Back Vernon St South BOL * BL1 ....2 C2
Back Vickerman St BOL BL1 ....18 B5
Back Victoria Gv BOL BL1 ......28 A1
Back Victoria Gv North BOL BL1 ....28 A1
Back Victory Seat BOL BL1 ......28 A2
Back View St BOLS/LL BL3 ....28 B5
Back Viking St North
  BOLS/LL BL3 ....37 E1
Back Vincent St BOL * BL1 ......2 A5
Back Vine St BOLS/LL * BL3 ....28 A4
Back Viola St BOL BL1 ....18 C4
Back Waldeck St BOL BL1 ......28 A2
Back Walnut St BOL BL1 ....18 D4
Back Wapping St BOL BL1 ......18 B5
Back Wardle St EDGW/EG BL7 ....3 K7
Back Waverley Rd BOL BL1 ....18 C4
Back Webster St BOLS/LL BL3 ....37 F1
Back Westbourne Av
  BOLS/LL * BL3 ....37 E2
Back Weston St North
  BOLS/LL * BL3 ....37 E2
Back Weston St South
  BOLS/LL BL3 ....36 D1
Back Westwood Rd BOL * BL1 ....28 A2
Back Whittle Gv BOL * BL1 ....27 H1
  BOLS/LL BL3 ....35 G1
Back Wigan Rd BOLS/LL BL3 ....27 H5
Back Wigan Rd North
  BOLS/LL BL3 ....27 H5
  BOLS/LL BL3 ....35 G1
Back Wigan Rd South
  BOLS/LL * BL3 ....35 H1
Back Willows BOLS/LL BL3 ....35 H1
Back Willows La North
  BOLS/LL * BL3 ....36 A1
Back Willows La South
  BOLS/LL * BL3 ....35 H1
Back Wilmot St BOL * BL1 ......18 A4
Back Wilton St BOL BL1 ....18 D4

Back Windermere St BOL BL1 ....18 D4
Back Windsor Gv BOL BL1 ......28 A1
Back Wolfenden St BOL * BL1 ....18 C5
Back Woodbine Rd BOLS/LL BL3 ....36 A2
Back Woodfield St
  BOLS/LL * BL3 ....37 E2
Back Woodgate St BOLS/LL BL3 ....37 E2
Back Wood St HOR/BR BL6 ....15 E4
Back Worcester St BOL BL1 ....28 C1
Back Wordsworth St BOL BL1 ....18 B5
Back Worsel St BOLS/LL BL3 ....36 A1
Back Worsel St North
  BOLS/LL * BL3 ....36 A1
Back Wright St HOR/BR BL6 ....14 D3
Back Wynne St BOL BL1 ....18 D3
Back Yates St BOLE BL2 ....29 E1
Badder St BOL * BL1 ....2 E2
Bag La ATH M46 ....42 B4
Bagot St SWIN M27 ....55 E2
Bagshaw La WGNE/HIN WN2 ....32 A3
Bailey Fold WHTN BL5 ....34 B5
Bailey La BOLE BL2 ....30 A1
Baines St BOL BL1 ....14 D3
Bain St SWIN M27 ....55 H4
Baker St FWTH BL4 ....46 D2
Balcary Gv BOL BL1 ....27 H2
Baldrine Dr WGNE/HIN WN2 ....40 D3
Baldwin St BOLS/LL BL3 ....2 C1
  WGNE/HIN WN2 ....40 D5
Balliol St SWIN M27 ....55 G3
Balmoral CHLY/EC PR7 ....12 C1
Balmoral Rd BOLS/LL BL3 ......38 C2
Balmoral Cl HOR/BR BL6 ......15 G5
Balmoral Dr LEIGH WN7 ....50 D5
Balmoral Rd FWTH BL4 ....45 G1
Balmore Cl BOLS/LL BL3 ....35 G2
Balshaw Cl BOLS/LL BL3 ....28 A5
Bamber Cft WHTN BL5 ....33 G2
Bamber Wk BOLS/LL * BL3 ....28 B5
Bamburgh Cl RAD M26 ....31 E5
Bampton Cl WHTN BL5 ....33 G4
Banbury Ms SWIN M27 ....55 F2
Banbury St BOLE BL2 ....29 G1
Bancroft Rd SWIN M27 ....55 G2
Bangor St BOL BL1 ....2 D1
Banker St BOLS/LL BL3 ....29 G5
Bank Fld WHTN BL5 ....42 A1
Bankfield Cl BOLE BL2 ....31 E1
Bankfield Dr WALK M28 ....53 E5
Bankfield Rd FWTH BL4 ....45 H1
  TYLD M29 ....52 C3
Bankfield St BOLS/LL BL3 ......28 A5
Bank Field St RAD M26 ....47 F1
Bank Gv LHULT M38 ....44 D2
Bankhall Cl WGNE/HIN WN2 ....48 D2
Bank Hey
  WHTN (off Bolton Rd) BL5 ....33 H5
Bank House Cl TYLD M29 ......52 C2
Bank La LHULT M38 ....44 D2
Bank Meadow Fold BOLE BL6 ....15 E3
Bank Mere Cl WALK M28 ......45 G5
Bank Side WHTN BL5 ....33 H5
Bank Stanway Av BOLS/LL * BL3 ....2 B6
Bank St BOL BL1 ....3 F5
  FWTH BL4 ....37 H5
  TOT/BURYW BL8 ....21 H3
Bank Top Gv BOL BL1 ....19 E2
Bank Wd BOL BL1 ....27 F3
Banner St WGNE/HIN WN2 ....40 A3
Bannister St BOLE BL2 ....30 A2
Bantry St BOLS/LL BL3 ....28 C5
Barbara Rd BOLS/LL BL3 ......35 G3
Barbara St BOLS/LL BL3 ....28 A5
Barberry Bank EDGW/EG BL7 ....8 B2
Barbury Cl LEIGH WN7 ....49 H4
Barchester Av BOLE BL2 ....30 A1
Barcroft Rd BOL BL1 ....17 H5
Bardon Cl BOL * BL1 ....28 B1
Bardsley Cl BOLE BL2 ....19 H2
Bare St BOL BL1 ....3 H2
Barford Gv HOR/BR BL6 ....25 H1
Bark St BOL BL1 ....2 D3
  BOLS/LL * BL3 ....46 D3
Bark St East BOL BL1 ....2 E2
Bar La BOL BL1 ....18 C2
Barley Brook Meadow BOL BL1 ....18 D1
Barlow Ct
  WALK (off Barnside Av) M28 ....46 A5
Barlow Park Av BOL BL1 ....18 B2
Barlow St HOR/BR BL6 ....15 E5
  WALK M28 ....45 H4
Barnabys Rd WHTN BL5 ....33 F2
Barn Acre HOR/BR BL6 ....24 A1
Barnacre Av BOLE BL2 ....30 B3
Barn Ct
  BOLE (off Thicketford Rd) BL2 ....19 G5
Barncroft Dr HOR/BR BL6 ......15 H4
Barncroft Rd FWTH BL4 ....37 H5
Barnes Cl FWTH BL4 ....37 F4
Barnes St FWTH BL4 ....46 C4
Barnes Ter FWTH BL4 ....46 C4
Barnet Rd BOL * BL1 ....17 H5
Barnfield Cl EDGW/EG BL7 ....8 C2
  RAD M26 ....39 G2
  TYLD M29 ....52 C3
Barnfield Dr WALK M28 ....53 F5
  WHTN BL5 ....33 G3
Barnfield Rd SWIN M27 ....55 F1
Barn Hl WHTN BL5 ....33 G4
Barn Hill Ter WHTN BL5 ....33 G4

Barnsdale CI *BOLE* BL2 ....31 E1
Barnside Av *WALK* M28 ....54 A1
Barnston CI *BOL* BL1 ....18 D3
Barn St *BOL* BL1 ....2 D4
Barnwood CI *BOL* * BL1 ....28 C1
Barnwood Dr *BOL* BL1 ....28 C1
Barnwood Ter *BOL* BL1 ....28 C1
Baron Fold Crs *LHULT* M38 ....44 D3
Baron Fold Gv *LHULT* M38 ....44 D3
Baron Fold Rd *LHULT* * M38 ....44 D3
Baron Wk *BOLS/LL* BL3 ....39 E2
Barrett Av *FWTH* BL4 ....46 B1
Barrie St *LEIGH* WN7 ....49 F3
Barrie Wy *BOL* BL1 ....19 F3
Barrisdale CI *BOLS/LL* BL3 ....27 F5
Barron Meadow *LEIGH* WN7 ....49 F4
Barrow Bridge Rd *BOL* BL1 ....17 F3
Barrows Ct *BOL* * BL1 ....2 E5
Barrowshaw CI *WALK* M28 ....53 G1
Barrs Fold CI *WHTN* BL5 ....33 F2
Barrs Fold Rd *WHTN* BL5 ....33 F3
Barry Crs *WALK* M28 ....45 E5
Barsham Dr *BOLS/LL* BL3 ....2 B7
Barton Rd *FWTH* BL4 ....45 F1
Barton St *FWTH* BL4 ....46 A1
Barwell Sq *FWTH* BL4 ....37 F3
Bashall St *BOL* BL1 ....18 D4
Basil St *BOLS/LL* BL3 ....2 C7
Baslow Av *WGNE/HIN* WN2 ....40 B4
Basswood Gn *WGNE/HIN* WN2 ....40 C5
Bateman St *HOR/BR* BL6 ....15 F5
Batheaston Gv *LEIGH* WN7 ....49 F4
Bath St *ATH* M46 ....42 A5
  BOL BL1 ....2 E2
Battenberg Rd *BOL* * BL1 ....28 A2
Baxendale St *BOL* BL1 ....18 C3
Baxter's Rw *WGNE/HIN* WN2 ......48 D1
Baycliff CI *WGNE/HIN* WN2 ....40 B5
Bayley Ct *BOL* * BL1 ....2 A1
Baysdale Av *BOLS/LL* BL3 ....35 F1
Bayswater St *BOLS/LL* BL3 ....36 A3
Baythorpe St *BOL* BL1 ....18 D4
Bazley St *BOL* BL1 ....17 F4
Beacon Av *ATH* M46 ....50 A1
Beacon Rd *WGNE/HIN* WN2 ......48 C3
Beaconsfield St *BOLS/LL* BL3 ......2 B6
Beatrice Rd *BOL* * BL1 ....28 A2
  WALK M28 ....54 D4
Beatrice St *FWTH* BL4 ....37 F5
  SWIN M27 ....55 F2
Beatty Dr *WHTN* BL5 ....33 G4
Beaufort Av *SWIN* M27 ....55 F4
Beaumaris Rd *WGNE/HIN* WN2 ..40 C5
Beaumont Av *HOR/BR* BL6 ....15 E3
Beaumont Cha *BOLS/LL* BL3 ......35 F2
Beaumont Dr *BOLS/LL* BL3 ....27 E5
Beaumont Rd *HOR/BR* BL6 ....14 D3
  HOR/BR BL6 ....27 E4
Beck Gv *WALK* M28 ....54 A2
Beckside *TYLD* M29 ....51 E3
Bede St *BOL* BL1 ....18 A5
Bedford Av *SWIN* M27 ....55 G4
  WALK M28 ....53 G2
Bedford Dr *ATH* M46 ....50 A2
Bedford St *BOL* BL1 ....2 A2
  EDGW/EG BL7 ....8 B2
Bedworth Bl *BOLE* BL2 ....3 J7
Beech Av *ATH* M46 ....43 E5
  BOLS/LL BL3 ....38 D3
  CHLYE PR6 ....6 B4
  FWTH BL4 ....37 E5
  FWTH BL4 ....46 D3
  HOR/BR BL6 ....25 G1
  RAD M26 ....39 H5
  WALK M28 ....53 E5
Beech CI *BOLE* BL2 ....19 G1
Beechcroft Av *BOLE* BL2 ....30 A4
Beechcroft Gv *BOLE* BL2 ....30 A4
The Beeches
  ATH (off George St) M46 ....42 D5
  BOL BL1 ....18 B1
Beechfield Av *LHULT* M38 ....45 E3
  WGNE/HIN WN2 ....40 C4
Beechfield Rd *BOL* BL1 ....17 H5
Beech Gv *LHULT* M38 ....44 C3
Beech St *ATH* M46 ....43 E5
  BOL BL1 ....18 D5
  SWIN M27 ....55 F3
Beechwood Crs *TYLD* M29 ....51 G5
Beechwood Dr *WALK* M28 ....54 D5
Beechwood St *BOLS/LL* BL3 ......36 C3
Beedon Av *BOLS/LL* BL3 ....38 C1
Bee Fold La *ATH* M46 ....50 B1
Beehive Gn *WHTN* BL5 ....34 B4
Beeston St *EDGW/EG* BL7 ....19 E1
Beeston Gv *LEIGH* WN7 ....50 D4
Begonia Av *FWTH* BL4 ....37 E4
Belcroft Dr *LHULT* M38 ....44 C2
Belcroft Gv *LHULT* * M38 ....44 C3
Belford Dr *BOLS/LL* BL3 ....36 C1
Belgrave Crs *HOR/BR* BL6 ....15 F4
Belgrave Gdns *BOL* BL1 ....18 C5
Belgrave St *ATH* M46 ....42 A5
  BOL BL1 ....18 C5
Belgrave St South *BOL* BL1 ......28 C1
Bellairs St *BOLS/LL* BL3 ....36 A2
Bella St *BOLS/LL* BL3 ....36 A1
Bellingham CI *TOT/BURYW* BL8 ..21 H5
Bellpit CI *WALK* M28 ....53 G4
Bell St *LEIGH* WN7 ....49 F2

  WGNE/HIN WN2 ....40 A2
Bellwood *WHTN* BL5 ....41 E1
Belmont Av *ATH* M46 ....43 F4
  FWTH BL4 ....47 F3
  WGNE/HIN WN2 ....48 B2
Belmont Dr *WGNE/HIN* WN2 ......23 G5
Belmont Rd *BOL* BL1 ....18 B1
  CHLYE PR6 ....6 B5
  WGNE/HIN WN2 ....40 B3
Belmont Vw *BOLE* BL2 ....20 B3
Belvedere Av *ATH* M46 ....43 F4
Belvedere CI *LEIGH* WN7 ....50 D4
Belvedere Rd *CHLYE* PR6 ....6 B4
Belvoir St *BOLE* BL2 ....29 G3
Bembridge Dr *BOLS/LL* BL3 ......29 H5
Bennet St *RAD* M26 ....39 F1
Bennett's La *BOL* BL1 ....18 A5
Benson St *EDGW/EG* * BL7 ....4 A4
Bentham CI *TOT/BURYW* BL8 ....21 G4
Bent Hill St *BOLS/LL* * BL3 ....35 G1
Bentinck St *BOL* BL1 ....27 H1
Bentley Ct *FWTH* BL4 ....37 G4
Bentley Fold Cottages
  TOT/BURYW (off High St) BL8 ....21 H3
Bentley Hall Rd
  TOT/BURYW BL8 ....21 F3
Bentley St *FWTH* BL4 ....37 H4
Bent Spur Rd *FWTH* BL4 ....46 C3
Bent St *FWTH* BL4 ....46 A1
Bentworth CI *WHTN* BL5 ....41 H2
Beresford Av *BOLS/LL* BL3 ....28 A5
Berkeley Crs *RAD* M26 ....31 E5
Berkeley Rd *BOL* BL1 ....18 C3
Berlin St *BOLS/LL* BL3 ....28 A4
Bernard Gv *BOL* BL1 ....18 A5
Berne Av *HOR/BR* BL6 ....14 C4
Bernice St *BOL* BL1 ....18 A5
Berryfold Wy *TYLD* M29 ....51 G3
Berry St *CHLYE* PR6 ....6 A4
  SWIN M27 ....55 H1
Bertha St *BOL* BL1 ....18 B5
Bertrand Rd *BOL* BL1 ....28 A3
Berwick CI *WALK* M28 ....52 D4
Berwyn CI *HOR/BR* BL6 ....15 E2
Beryl Av *TOT/BURYW* BL8 ....11 H5
Beryl St *BOL* BL1 ....18 D4
Bessybrook CI *HOR/BR* BL6 ......26 C4
Beta St *BOL* BL1 ....2 D1
Beverley Rd *BOL* BL1 ....28 A2
  BOLS/LL BL3 ....38 B2
Bewick St *BOLE* BL2 ....19 F4
Bewley Gv *LEIGH* WN7 ....46 D1
Bexhill CI *BOLS/LL* BL3 ....39 E2
Bexhill Dr *WGNE/HIN* WN2 ....45 G5
Bexley Dr *LHULT* M38 ....45 G5
Bexley St *WGNE/HIN* WN2 ....40 A2
Bickershaw Dr *WALK* M28 ....53 G1
Bickershaw La *WGNE/HIN* WN2 ..52 A5
Bickley Gv *TYLD* M29 ....52 A5
Bideford Dr *BOLE* BL2 ....30 C4
Bidston CI *TOT/BURYW* BL8 ......21 H5
Big Fold *HOR/BR* * BL6 ....13 H5
Bilbao St *BOL* BL1 ....2 E1
Billinge CI *BOL* BL1 ....2 E1
Billy La *SWIN* M27 ....55 H1
Binbrook Wk *BOLS/LL* BL3 ....54 H1
Bingham St *SWIN* M27 ....55 H3
Birch Av *WHTN* BL5 ....41 H1
Birches Rd *EDGW/EG* BL7 ....10 A1
Birchfield *BOLE* BL2 ....20 A1
Birchfield Av *ATH* M46 ....42 B4
Birchfield Dr *WALK* M28 ....53 E4
Birchfield Gv *BOLS/LL* BL3 ....35 E1
Birchfold CI *LHULT* M38 ....45 E3
Birchgate Wk *BOL* BL1 ....28 C5
Birch Rd *ATH* M46 ....42 C5
  FWTH BL4 ....46 B2
  LEIGH WN7 ....49 H4
  WALK M28 ....54 A2
Birch St *BOLE* BL2 ....3 H6
  TYLD M29 ....51 G2
Birkdale Av *ATH* M46 ....42 C3
Birkdale Gdns *BOLS/LL* BL3 ......28 B5
Birkenhills Dr *BOLS/LL* BL3 ......27 E5
Birkett CI *BOL* BL1 ....18 B1
Birkett Dr *BOL* BL1 ....18 B1
Birley St *LEIGH* WN7 ....50 A5
Birtenshaw Crs *EDGW/EG* BL7 ....9 F5
Birtle Dr *TYLD* M29 ....52 A4
Bishopbridge CI *BOLS/LL* BL3 ..36 D1
Bishop's CI *BOLS/LL* BL3 ....37 E3
Bishop's Rd *BOLS/LL* BL3 ....37 E3
Bispham Av *BOLE* BL2 ....30 B3
Bispham CI *TOT/BURYW* BL8 ....31 H1
Bispham St *BOLE* * BL2 ....29 G2
Blackbank St *BOL* BL1 ....18 D5
Blackburn Rd *BOL* BL1 ....18 C4
  EDGW/EG BL7 ....8 B1
Blackcap CI *WALK* M28 ....53 F4
Blackcroft CI *SWIN* M27 ....55 G3
Blackhorse Av *HOR/BR* * BL6 ....13 G5
Blackhorse CI *HOR/BR* BL6 ......13 G4
Black Horse St *BOL* BL1 ....2 D3
  FWTH BL4 ....46 A1
Blackledge Gv *RAD* * M26 ....13 G4
Blackledge St *BOLS/LL* BL3 ......36 A1
Black Moss CI *RAD* * M26 ....39 F2

Blackrod Brow *HOR/BR* BL6 ......13 F3
Blackrod By-Pass Rd
  HOR/BR BL6 ....24 B2
Blackrod Dr *TOT/BURYW* BL8 ....31 H1
Blackshaw La *BOLS/LL* BL3 ......28 A4
Blackthorne CI *BOL* BL1 ....27 G1
Blackwood St *BOLS/LL* BL3 ......37 E1
Blair Av *LHULT* M38 ....45 F4
  WGNE/HIN WN2 ....40 D5
Blair La *BOLE* BL2 ....20 D1
Blairmore Dr *BOLS/LL* BL3 ....35 E1
Blair St *EDGW/EG* BL7 ....8 D4
  FWTH BL4 ....46 C2
Blakefield Dr *WALK* M28 ....54 A2
Blake Gdns *BOL* BL1 ....18 B5
Blake St *BOL* BL1 ....18 B5
  EDGW/EG BL7 ....9 E5
Blakey CI *BOLS/LL* BL3 ....35 F1
Blandford Av *WALK* M28 ....54 B3
Blandford CI *ATYLD* M29 ....51 G2
Blandford Ri *HOR/BR* BL6 ....26 A1
Blantyre Av *WALK* M28 ....54 A1
Blantyre St *SWIN* M27 ....55 F3
  WGNE/HIN WN2 ....40 A2
Blaydon CI *WGNE/HIN* WN2 ......23 H5
Bleakledge Gn *WGNE/HIN* WN2 ..40 A2
Bleakledge Gv *WGNE/HIN* WN2 ..40 A4
Bleak St *BOLE* BL2 ....19 F5
Bleasdale CI *HOR/BR* BL6 ....25 H2
Bleasdale Rd *BOL* BL1 ....17 F5
Bleasedale Rd *WGNE/HIN* WN2 ..40 B3
Blenheim Dr *LEIGH* WN7 ....51 E4
Blenheim Rd *BOLE* BL2 ....30 A3
Blenheim St *BOLS/LL* BL3 ....35 H3
Blethyn St *BOLS/LL* BL3 ....35 H3
Blewberry CI *LEIGH* WN7 ....49 H4
Bligh Rd *WHTN* BL5 ....33 G4
Blindsill Rd *FWTH* BL4 ....45 F1
Bloomfield Dr *WALK* M28 ....53 E4
Bloomfield Rd *FWTH* BL4 ....45 H2
Bloomfield St *BOL* BL1 ....18 C4
Blossom St *TYLD* M29 ....51 G2
Blundell La *HOR/BR* BL6 ....13 E5
Blundell St *BOL* BL1 ....2 E5
Boardman CI *BOL* BL1 ....18 C5
Boardman St *BOL* BL1 ....18 C5
  HOR/BR BL6 ....13 H5
Board St *BOLS/LL* BL3 ....2 A5
Bodiam Rd *TOT/BURYW* BL8 ....11 H3
Bodmin Rd *TYLD* M29 ....51 H3
Bold St *BOL* BL1 ....2 E5
  LEIGH WN7 ....49 H5
  SWIN M27 ....55 H1
Bollin CI *FWTH* BL4 ....46 C2
Bollings Yd *BOL* BL1 ....3 F5
Bolton House Rd
  WGNE/HIN WN2 ....48 B4
Bolton Old Rd *ATH* M46 ....42 D5
Bolton Rd *ATH* M46 ....43 F4
  BOLE BL2 ....19 G2
  BOLS/LL BL3 ....34 D3
  CHLYE PR6 ....4 A4
  EDGW/EG BL7 ....4 A4
  FWTH BL4 ....37 H3
  RAD M26 ....39 F1
  TOT/BURYW BL8 ....11 E2
  WALK M28 ....45 H4
  WGNE/HIN WN2 ....23 G5
  WHTN BL5 ....33 H5
Bolton St *RAD* M26 ....39 H2
Bond CI *HOR/BR* BL6 ....15 E4
Bond St *ATH* M46 ....51 F2
Boonfields *EDGW/EG* BL7 ....9 F4
Boothby Rd *SWIN* M27 ....55 G2
Booth Hall Dr *TOT/BURYW* BL8 ..21 H2
Booth Rd *BOLS/LL* BL3 ....38 D3
Boothsbank Av *WALK* M28 ....53 F5
Booth's Hall *WALK* M28 ....53 F5
Booth's Hall Gv *WALK* M28 ......53 F5
Booth's Hall Rd *WALK* M28 ......53 F5
Booth's Hall Wy *WALK* M28 ......53 F5
Booth St *BOL* BL1 ....18 A4
  TOT/BURYW BL8 ....21 H2
Booth Wy *TOT/BURYW* BL8 ......21 H2
Boot La *BOL* BL1 ....26 D1
Border Brook La *WALK* M28 ......53 E4
Bores Hl *WGN* WN1 ....12 A3
Borrowdale Av *BOL* BL1 ....27 G2
Borsdane Av *WGNE/HIN* WN2 ....40 A4
Borsden St *SWIN* M27 ....55 F2
Boscobel Rd *BOLS/LL* BL3 ....37 F5
Boscombe Pl *WGNE/HIN* WN2 ..40 A4
Boscow Rd *BOLS/LL* BL3 ....38 C3
Boston Gv *LEIGH* WN7 ....49 G2
Boston St *BOL* * BL1 ....18 C5
Bosworth St *HOR/BR* BL6 ....14 D3
Bottom o'th' Knotts Brow
  EDGW/EG BL7 ....10 B1
Bottom o'th' Moor *BOLE* BL2 ....19 H5
  HOR/BR BL6 ....14 H4
Boundary Dr *BOLS/LL* BL3 ....30 C5
Boundary Gdns *BOL* * BL1 ....18 B5
Boundary Rd *SWIN* M27 ....55 H1
Boundary St *BOL* BL1 ....18 B5
  BOLS/LL BL3 ....30 D5
  TYLD M29 ....51 G2
The Boundary *SWIN* M27 ....47 F4
Bournbrook Av *LHULT* M38 ....45 E2
Bourne Av *SWIN* M27 ....55 H4
Bourneville Dr *TOT/BURYW* BL8 ..21 H5

Bourton Ct *TYLD* M29 ....51 G5
Bowden St *BOLS/LL* * BL3 ....15 ..
Bowen St *BOL* BL1 ....18 ..
Bowgreave Av *BOLE* BL2 ....31 ..
Bowkers Rw *BOL* * BL1 ....2 ..
Bowker St *WALK* M28 ....53 ..
Bowland CI *TOT/BURYW* BL8 ....21 ..
Bowland St *BOL* BL1 ....18 ..
Bowness Rd *BOLS/LL* BL3 ....36 ..
  BOLS/LL BL3 ....36 ..
Bowstone Hill Rd *BOLE* BL2 ......20 ..
Bow St *BOL* BL1 ....2 ..
Boydell St *LEIGH* WN7 ....49 ..
Boyle St *BOL* BL1 ....18 ..
Brabham Ms *SWIN* M27 ....47 ..
Bracken Av *WALK* M28 ....53 ..
Bracken CI *BOL* BL1 ....18 ..
Bracken Lea *WHTN* BL5 ....41 ..
Bracken Rd *ATH* M46 ....50 ..
Brackley Av *TYLD* M29 ....51 ..
Brackley Rd *WHTN* BL5 ....33 ..
Brackley St *FWTH* BL4 ....37 ..
  WALK M28 ....54 ..
Bracondale Av *BOL* BL1 ....17 ..
Bradbourne CI *BOLS/LL* BL3 ......29 ..
Braddyll Rd *WHTN* BL5 ....41 ..
Bradford Crs *BOLS/LL* BL3 ....36 ..
Bradford Lea *WHTN* BL5 ....41 ..
Bradford Park Dr *BOLE* BL2 ......29 ..
Bradford Rd *WGNE/HIN* WN2 ....40 ..
Bradford St *BOLE* BL2 ....29 ..
  FWTH BL4 ....37 ..
Bradley Fold Rd *BOLS/LL* BL3 ....38 ..
Bradley La *BOLS/LL* BL3 ....38 ..
Bradshaw Brow *BOLE* BL2 ....20 ..
Bradshawgate *BOL* * BL1 ....3 ..
Bradshaw Hall Dr *BOLE* BL2 ......20 ..
Bradshaw Hall Fold
  BOLE (off Bradshaw Rd) BL2 ....20 ..
Bradshaw Mdw *BOLE* BL2 ....20 ..
Bradshaw Rd *BOLE* BL2 ....20 ..
  TOT/BURYW BL8 ....21 ..
Bradshaw St *ATH* M46 ....43 ..
  FWTH BL4 ....37 ..
  RAD M26 ....39 ..
Bradwell Pl *BOLE* BL2 ....30 ..
Brady St *HOR/BR* BL6 ....13 ..
Braemar La *WALK* M28 ....53 ..
Braeside Gv *BOLS/LL* BL3 ....2 ..
Brailsford Rd *BOLE* BL2 ....20 ..
Brakesmere Gv *LHULT* M38 ......44 ..
Brambling Gv *WHTN* BL5 ....41 ..
Bramcote Av *BOL* BL1 ....27 ..
Bramdean Av *BOLE* BL2 ....30 ..
Bramford CI *WHTN* BL5 ....41 ..
Bramhall Av *BOLE* BL2 ....30 ..
Bramhall St *BOLS/LL* BL3 ....36 ..
Bramley CI *SWIN* M27 ....47 ..
Bramley Rd *EDGW/EG* BL7 ....9 ..
Brammay Dr *TOT/BURYW* BL8 ..21 ..
Brampton Rd *BOLS/LL* BL3 ....36 ..
Brampton St *ATH* * M46 ....43 ..
Brancker St *WHTN* BL5 ....41 ..
Brandon St *BOLS/LL* BL3 ....35 ..
Brandwood CI *WALK* M28 ....53 ..
Brandwood St *BOLS/LL* BL3 ......36 ..
Branscombe Gdns *BOLS/LL* BL3 ..35 ..
Bransdale CI *BOLS/LL* BL3 ....35 ..
Brantfell Gv *BOLE* BL2 ....30 ..
Brantwood Dr *BOLE* BL2 ....30 ..
Brathay CI *BOLE* BL2 ....30 ..
Braybrook Dr *BOL* BL1 ....17 ..
Brayford Dr *WGNE/HIN* WN2 ....40 ..
Brazley Av *BOLS/LL* BL3 ....35 ..
  HOR/BR BL6 ....26 ..
Breaktemper *WHTN* BL5 ....41 ..
Breckland Dr *BOL* BL1 ....17 ..
Breckles Pl *BOLS/LL* * BL3 ....3 ..
Brecon Dr *WGNE/HIN* WN2 ......40 ..
Bredbury Dr *FWTH* BL4 ....46 ..
Breeze Hl *ATH* M46 ....43 ..
Breeze Hill Rd *ATH* M46 ....43 ..
Breightmet Dr *BOLE* BL2 ....30 ..
Breightmet Fold La *BOLE* BL2 ....20 ..
Breightmet St *BOLE* BL2 ....3 ..
Brentford Av *BOL* BL1 ....17 ..
Brentford St *BOLS/LL* BL3 ....36 ..
Brentwood Av *WALK* M28 ....52 ..
Brentwood Dr *FWTH* BL4 ....45 ..
Brentwood Rd *CHLYE* PR6 ....6 ..
  SWIN M27 ....55 ..
Brereton Dr *WALK* M28 ....53 ..
Brett Rd *WALK* M28 ....53 ..
Brian Rd *FWTH* BL4 ....36 ..
Briar CI *WGNE/HIN* WN2 ....40 ..
Briarcroft Dr *ATH* M46 ....43 ..
Briarfield *EDGW/EG* BL7 ....9 ..
Briarfield Rd *FWTH* BL4 ....45 ..
  WALK M28 ....54 ..
Briar Gv *LEIGH* WN7 ....49 ..
Briar Hill Av *LHULT* M38 ....44 ..
Briar Hill CI *LHULT* M38 ....44 ..
Briar Hill Gv *LHULT* M38 ....44 ..
Briar St *BOLE* * BL2 ....3 ..
Briary Dr *TYLD* M29 ....51 ..
Bride St *BOL* BL1 ....2 ..
Bridgecroft St *WGNE/HIN* WN2 ..40 ..
Bridgeman Pl *BOLE* BL2 ....3 ..
Bridgeman St *BOLS/LL* BL3 ......35 ..
  FWTH BL4 ....37 ..

...mere Cl *RAD* M26 ....31 H5
...s Ct *BOL* * BL1 ....2 E5
...'s St *ATH* M46 ....50 B1
...st *BOL* BL1 ....2 E2
... BL4 ....38 A4
.../BR BL6 ....15 E3
... M28 ....38 D5
...water Rd *WALK* M28 ....55 E4
...water St *BOL* BL1 ....2 E5
...Ct M38 ....37 H5
...T M38 ....45 F4
...E/HIN WN2 ....40 A2
...n La *BOLE* BL2 ....29 H1
...t *BOLE* BL2 ....29 C1
...iffe Rd *BOLS/LL* BL3 ....28 A5
...eld Av *ATH* M46 ....42 C4
...olme Av *EDGW/EG* BL7 ....8 C3
...y Rd West *SWIN* M27 ....55 G2
...Av *BOLE* BL2 ....19 H1
...e St *BOL* BL1 ....28 C5
...Fold Cl *EDGW/EG* BL7 ....8 C2
...Fold Rd *EDGW/EG* BL7 ....8 C2
...st *LEIGH* WN7 ....49 G4
...on Av *BOL* BL1 ....27 G1
...st *LEIGH* WN7 ....49 G4
...al Wy *HOR/BR* BL6 ....26 C3
...eld Av *TYLD* M29 ....52 A2
...ehurst Dr *TYLD* M29 ....52 A4
...st *TYLD* M29 ....51 H5
...E/HIN WN2 ....40 B1
...ey Av *WALK* M28 ....53 E5
...y Cl *ATH* M46 ....50 A1
... BL4 ....37 F5
..." BL4
...y St *HOR/BR* * BL6 ....15 E5
... M27 ....55 H1
... M28 ....52 D5
...La *BOL* BL2 ....30 C3
...RW
.../BR (off Wildersmoor) BL6....15 F2
...way *HOR/BR* BL6 ....15 F2
...o Hall La *WHTN* BL5 ....24 C5
...Hall Wy *WHTN* BL5 ....33 H3
...Av *BOLE* BL2 ....29 G1
...ia Wy *BOL* BL1 ....19 E5
...y Rd East *SWIN* M27 ....55 G2
...t St *BOLS/LL* BL3 ....36 C1
...ent St *HOR/BR* BL6 ....15 H4
...ord Rd *BOLS/LL* BL3 ....27 F5
...gate Meadow
...(off Eccles Rd)
...reen Gdns *FWTH* * BL4....37 H3
...ead Rd *EDGW/EG* BL7....4 A1
...eth St *WHTN* BL5 ....34 A4
...hurst Av *SWIN* M27 ....47 H5
...hurst Ct *BOLS/LL* BL3 ....36 B1
...hurst St *BOLS/LL* * BL3 ....36 B1
...ands Rd *SWIN* M27 ....55 E5
...meadow *EDGW/EG* BL7 ....9 F4
...bak Av *WALK* M28 ....52 D4
...Oak Cl *CHLYE* PR6 ....6 A4
...Oak Pk *WALK* M28 ....54 D5
...Oak Rd *FWTH* BL4 ....38 C5
...to' th' La *BOL* BL1 ....18 C3
...stone Rd *BOLE* BL2 ....19 H2
...Wk *WHTN* BL5 ....41 G1
...way *ATH* M46 ....43 F3
... BL4 ....37 E3
...'BR BL6 ....15 F4
... M28 ....53 H2
...E/HIN WN2 ....40 C3
...wood *HOR/BR* BL6 ....26 C3
... BL2 ....30 B3
...nhurst Dr *BOLE* BL2....20 B4
...Mill La *WGN* WN1 ....22 A5
...x Dr *BOLE* BL2 ....30 B4
...y Cross Rd *EDGW/EG* BL7...9 F5
...y Dr *LEIGH* WN7 ....49 F3
...ich St *BOLE* BL2 ....3 H5
...ate Meadow *SWIN* M27 ...55 H4
...CI *BOL* BL1 ....28 B1
...Av *SWIN* M27 ....55 H1
...Bank
...(off Longsight La) BL2 ....19 H4
...Bottom Rd *RAD* M26 ....43 F2
...ale *ATH* M46 ....43 F2
...t PR6 ....6 A3
...ale Cl BL2 ....3 H4
...ale Pk
...T (off Ravenscraig Rd) M38 ...45 F2
...ale Rd *WGNE/HIN* WN2 ....40 B3
...ean Cl *BOL* BL1 ....18 A4
...or *TYLD* M29 ....52 A5
...CI *BOLE* BL2 ....31 E1
...eld Dr *SWIN* M27 ....55 G2
... M28 ....52 D5
...eld St *BOLE* BL2 ....3 J3
... WN7 ....50 A5
...old La *BOLE* BL2 ....20 B3
...Gdns *BOLE* BL2 ....20 A3
...ey Av *BOLS/LL* BL3 ....36 D2
...ouse Av *FWTH* BL4 ....37 H5
...House Cl *BOLS/LL* BL3 ....11 G4
...BURYW BL8 ....11 H2
...hurst La *LHULT* M38 ....45 G1
...and Av *FWTH* BL4 ....45 G1
...and Gv *BOL* BL1 ....17 G5
...ands *HOR/BR* BL6 ....15 E4
...ands Rd *SWIN* M27 ....55 F5
...BURYW BL8 ....11 H2

Brooklyn St *BOL* BL1 ....28 C1
Brook Meadow *WHTN* * BL5...34 A5
Brooks Av *RAD* M26 ....31 H4
Brooks Houses *LEIGH* WN7 ...49 G3
Brookside Av *FWTH* BL4 ....45 G1
Brookside Cl *ATH* M46 ....43 E4
  BOLE BL2 ....19 H4
Brookside Crs *TOT/BURYW* BL8 ...11 H4
  WALK M28 ....46 A5
Brookside Rd *BOLE* BL2 ....29 H2
Brook St *ATH* M46 ....42 B5
  BOL BL1 ....2 E3
  CHLYE PR6 ....6 A3
  FWTH BL4 ....38 A4
  RAD M26 ....46 C1
  SWIN M27 ....55 F3
  WHTN * BL5 ....33 H4
Brookwater Cl *TOT/BURYW* BL8 ...21 H1
Brooky Moor
  EDGW/EG (off Bury Rd) BL7 ....4 A3
Broom Av *LEIGH* WN7 ....49 G4
Broomfield Cl *BOLE* BL2 ....31 E2
Broomfield Rd *BOLS/LL* BL3 ....28 A5
Broomhey Av *WGNW* WN1 ....22 A5
Broom St *SWIN* M27 ....55 H4
Broom Wy *BOL* BL1 ....19 H2
Brougham St *WALK* M28 ....45 G5
Brough Cl *WGNE/HIN* WN2 ....40 A5
Broughton Av *LHULT* M38 ....45 E4
Broughton St *BOL* BL1 ....18 B5
Brow East *BOLE* BL2 ....19 G3
Browning Av *ATH* M46 ....42 D3
Browning Cl *BOL* BL1 ....28 B1
Browning Rd *SWIN* M27 ....55 G3
Browning St *LEIGH* WN7 ....49 F5
Brownlow Rd *HOR/BR* BL6 ....14 D3
Brownlow Wy *BOL* BL1 ....28 C1
Browns Rd *BOLE* BL2 ....30 D4
Brown St *BOL* BL1 ....3 F3
  HOR/BR BL6 ....13 H5
  RAD M26 ....31 H4
  TYLD * M29 ....51 H4
  WGNE/HIN WN2 ....48 A2
Broxton Av *BOLS/LL* BL3 ....35 H4
Brunel St *BOL* BL1 ....18 B4
  HOR/BR BL6 ....15 E5
Brunswick Av *HOR/BR* BL6 ....15 F5
Brunswick Ct *BOL* BL1 ....28 C1
Bryantsfield *BOL* BL1 ....26 D4
Bryngs Dr *BOLE* BL2 ....20 B3
Brynhall Cl *RAD* M26 ....31 G5
Brynheys Cl *LHULT* M38 ....45 E3
Bryn Lea Ter *BOL* BL1 ....17 F3
Bryn Wk *BOL* BL1 ....2 E1
Buchanan Dr *WGNE/HIN* WN2 ....40 A5
Buchanan St *SWIN* M27 ....55 H2
Buckingham Av *HOR/BR* BL6 ....15 G5
Buckley La *FWTH* BL4 ....45 G1
Buckley Sq *FWTH* BL4 ....45 G5
Buckthorn Cl *WHTN* BL5 ....33 H3
Bude Av *TYLD* M29 ....52 A3
Buile Hill Av *LHULT* M38 ....45 F4
Buile Hill Gv *LHULT* M38 ....45 F4
Bullcroft Dr *TYLD* M29 ....52 A5
Buller St *BOLS/LL* BL3 ....37 G3
Bullough St *ATH* M46 ....42 C5
Bullows Rd *LHULT* M38 ....44 D2
Bulteel St *BOLS/LL* BL3 ....36 A4
  WALK M28 ....52 C5
Bunting Ms *WALK* M28 ....53 F5
Burford Dr *BOLS/LL* BL3 ....27 G4
  SWIN M27 ....55 G1
Burghley Cl *BOLE* BL2 ....30 D5
Burghley Dr *BOLS/LL* BL3 ....30 D5
Burgundy Dr *TOT/BURYW* BL8 ....11 H5
Burke St *BOL* BL1 ....18 B5
Burlington St *WGNE/HIN* WN2 ....40 A4
Burnaby St *BOLS/LL* BL3 ....28 B5
Burden Rd *BOLS/LL* BL3 ....29 F5
Burden Wy *HOR/BR* BL6 ....25 G3
Burnet Cl *TYLD* M29 ....51 H4
Burnham Av *BOL* BL1 ....27 G1
Burnmoor Rd *BOLE* BL2 ....30 B2
Burns Av *ATH* M46 ....42 D3
  LEIGH WN7 ....49 E3
  SWIN M27 ....55 F2
Burnside Cl *RAD* M26 ....31 H3
  TYLD M29 ....51 H4
Burnside Rd *BOL* BL1 ....17 H5
Burns Rd *LHULT* M38 ....44 D3
Burns St *BOLS/LL* BL3 ....3 F5
Burnt Edge La *BOL* BL1 ....16 B2
Burrington Dr *LEIGH* WN7 ....49 F4
Burton Av *TOT/BURYW* BL8 ....21 H3
Burton Gv *WALK* M28 ....55 G3
Burwell Cl *BOLS/LL* BL3 ....36 B1
Bury And Bolton Rd *RAD* M26 ....31 H3
Bury New Rd *BOL* BL1 ....3 G2
  BOLE BL2 ....3 H3
Bury Old Rd *BOLE* BL2 ....30 C1
  BOLE BL2 ....3 H3
Bury Rd *BOLE* BL2 ....30 A3
  EDGW/EG BL7 ....4 B3
  TOT/BURYW BL8 ....21 H1
Bushell St *BOLS/LL* BL3 ....35 H5
Bute St *BOL* BL1 ....27 H1
Buttercup Av *WALK* * M28 ....44 D5
Buttercup Cl *ATH* M46 ....42 D3
Butterfield Rd *WHTN* BL5 ....35 H4
Buttermere Av *SWIN* M27 ....55 H5

Buttermere Cl *BOLS/LL* BL3 ....38 B1
Buttermere Rd *FWTH* BL4 ....36 C5
Buxton Cl *ATH* M46 ....43 E4
Byland Cl *BOL* BL1 ....28 D1
Byng St *FWTH* BL4 ....37 H5
Byrness Cl *ATH* M46 ....42 D3
Byron Av *RAD* M26 ....39 F1
Byron Gv *LEIGH* WN7 ....49 G4
Byron Rd *TOT/BURYW* BL8 ....11 H2
Byron St *LEIGH* WN7 ....49 H5
Byron Wk *FWTH* BL4 ....45 F2

C

Cable St *BOL* BL1 ....3 F1
Caernarvon Cl *TOT/BURYW* BL8 ....11 H3
Caernarvon Rd *WGNE/HIN* WN2 ....40 C5
Cairngorm Dr *BOLS/LL* BL3 ....27 E5
Caithness Dr *BOLS/LL* BL3 ....27 E5
Caldbeck Av *BOL* BL1 ....27 F1
Caldbeck Dr *FWTH* BL4 ....44 C1
Calder Av *BOLS/LL* BL3 ....41 E5
Calder Dr *FWTH* BL4 ....46 D3
  SWIN M27 ....55 G3
  WALK M28 ....53 E1
Calder Rd *BOLS/LL* BL3 ....36 C2
Calderwood Cl *TOT/BURYW* BL8 ....21 H1
Caldew Cl *WGNE/HIN* WN2 ....40 A4
Caldford Cl *WGNE/HIN* WN2 ....23 G4
Caldwell St *WHTN* BL5 ....41 H3
Caleb Cl *TYLD* M29 ....51 F2
Caledonia St *BOLS/LL* BL3 ....28 A5
Caley St *BOL* BL1 ....17 F5
Calf Hey Cl *RAD* M26 ....39 F2
Callis Rd *BOLS/LL* BL3 ....28 A5
Calver Hey Cl *WHTN* BL5 ....34 C3
Calverleigh Cl *BOLS/LL* BL3 ....35 G3
Calvert Rd *BOLS/LL* BL3 ....36 C2
Calvin St *BOL* BL1 ....28 D1
Cambourne Dr *BOLS/LL* BL3 ....27 G5
  WGNE/HIN WN2 ....49 E1
Cambria Sq *BOLS/LL* * BL3 ....28 A5
Cambria St *BOLS/LL* BL3 ....28 A5
Cambridge Cl *FWTH* BL4 ....44 D3
Cambridge Dr *BOLS/LL* BL3 ....38 D1
Cambridge Rd *HOR/BR* BL6 ....25 H2
Cambridge St *ATH* M46 ....50 C1
Camden Cl *BOLE* BL2 ....31 E1
Camellia Cl *BOL* BL1 ....17 H3
Cameron St *BOL* BL1 ....18 B2
  LEIGH WN7 ....49 H5
Campbell Cl *TOT/BURYW* BL8 ....21 G3
Campbell Ct *FWTH* BL4 ....37 G5
Campbell Rd *BOLS/LL* * BL3 ....35 G5
  SWIN M27 ....55 G5
Campbell St *FWTH* BL4 ....37 F4
Campbell Wy *LHULT* * M38 ....45 G5
  WALK M28 ....45 G5
Camrose Gdns *BOL* BL1 ....28 C1
Cams Acre Cl *RAD* M26 ....39 G2
Cams La *RAD* M26 ....39 G2
Canada St *BOL* BL1 ....18 A5
  HOR/BR BL6 ....14 D5
Canal St *CHLYE* PR7 ....13 E1
Candahar St *BOLS/LL* BL3 ....37 E2
Canmore Cl *BOLS/LL* BL3 ....35 G2
Cannel Fold *WALK* M28 ....53 F4
Canning Dr *BOL* BL1 ....18 C5
Canning St *BOL* * BL1 ....18 C5
Cannon Gv *BOLS/LL* BL3 ....2 A7
Cannon St *ATH* M46 ....42 D5
  BOLS/LL BL3 ....2 B7
  RAD M26 ....31 H5
Cannon St North *BOLS/LL* * BL3 ....2 B6
Cann St *TOT/BURYW* BL8 ....11 F4
Canons Cl *BOL* BL1 ....17 H5
Canonsway *SWIN* M27 ....55 G4
Canterbury Cl *ATH* M46 ....43 E4
Canterbury Gv *BOLS/LL* BL3 ....36 B2
Canute St *BOLE* BL2 ....29 G1
  RAD M26 ....39 G2
Captain Fold Rd *LHULT* M38 ....44 D3
Captain Lees Gdns *WHTN* BL5 ....34 A5
Captain Lees Rd *WHTN* BL5 ....34 A5
Captain's Clough Rd *BOL* BL1 ....17 G5
Captain St *HOR/BR* BL6 ....14 D3
Car Bank Av *ATH* M46 ....42 D4
Car Bank Sq *ATH* M46 ....42 D4
Car Bank St *ATH* M46 ....42 D4
Carden Av *SWIN* M27 ....55 H4
Carder Cl *SWIN* M27 ....55 H4
Cardwell Gdns *BOL* * BL1 ....18 C5
Carisbrooke Dr *BOL* BL1 ....18 D4
Carisbrooke Rd *LEIGH* WN7 ....50 D5
Carlisle Cl *BOLS/LL* BL3 ....38 C3
Carlisle Pl *CHLYE* PR6 ....6 A4
Carlisle St *EDGW/EG* BL7 ....9 A4
  SWIN M27 ....55 H1
  WGNE/HIN WN2 ....40 A2
Carl St *BOL* * BL1 ....18 B5
Carlton Av *BOLS/LL* BL3 ....35 G1
Carlton Cl *BOLE* BL2 ....20 A4
  HOR/BR BL6 ....13 H5
  WALK M28 ....53 G2
Carlton Gv *HOR/BR* BL6 ....25 F1
  WGNE/HIN WN2 ....40 B5

Carlton Pl *FWTH* * BL4 ....37 H4
Carlton Rd *BOL* BL1 ....27 G2
  WALK M28 ....53 G2
Carlton St *BOLE* BL2 ....37 H4
  FWTH BL4 ....37 H4
Carlyle Gv *LEIGH* WN7 ....49 E3
Carnation Rd *FWTH* BL4 ....37 E4
Carnforth Av *WGNE/HIN* WN2 ....40 C3
Carnoustie *BOLS/LL* BL3 ....35 G2
Caroline St *BOLS/LL* BL3 ....36 B1
Carr Brook Dr *ATH* M46 ....43 E4
Carr Common Rd
  WGNE/HIN WN2 ....41 F5
Carrfield Av *LHULT* M38 ....44 C4
Carrfield Gv *LHULT* M38 ....44 C4
Carrie St *BOL* BL1 ....27 H2
Carrington Dr *BOLS/LL* BL3 ....28 D5
Carrington Gv *LEIGH* * WN7 ....49 H4
Carrington St *LEIGH* WN7 ....49 H4
Carron Gv *BOLE* BL2 ....30 B3
Carr Rd *HOR/BR* BL6 ....14 D2
Carrslea Cl *RAD* M26 ....31 G5
Carr St *SWIN* M27 ....55 F4
Carslake Av *BOL* BL1 ....28 A2
Carswell Cl *TYLD* M29 ....52 A2
Carter St *BOLS/LL* BL3 ....37 E1
  FWTH * BL4 ....46 A1
Cartleach Gv *WALK* M28 ....53 E4
Cartleach La *WALK* M28 ....52 D1
Cartmel Cl *BOLS/LL* BL3 ....34 D3
Cartmel Crs *BOLE* BL2 ....19 G5
Cartmel Gv *WALK* M28 ....54 D4
Cartwright Gv *LEIGH* WN7 ....49 F2
Carwood Gv *HOR/BR* BL6 ....25 F1
Castle Crs *HOR/BR* BL6 ....15 E2
Castle Cft *BOLE* BL2 ....19 H4
Castlecroft Av *HOR/BR* BL6 ....13 H5
Castle Dr *CHLY/EC* PR7 ....12 C1
Castleford Cl *BOL* * BL1 ....2 B1
Castle Gv *LEIGH* WN7 ....50 B1
Castle Hill Pk *WGNE/HIN* WN2 ....40 B1
Castle Hill Rd *WGNE/HIN* WN2 ....40 A2
Castle Hill St *BOLE* BL2 ....19 H4
Castle House La *CHLY/EC* PR7 ....12 C1
Castle Ri *WGNE/HIN* WN2 ....40 A3
Castle St *BOLE* BL2 ....3 H4
  FWTH * BL4 ....45 H1
  TYLD M29 ....51 F2
  WGNE/HIN WN2 ....40 A2
Castleton St *BOLE* BL2 ....19 F5
Castleway *WGNE/HIN* WN2 ....40 B1
Castlewood Sq *BOLE* BL2 ....29 G1
Catherine St *SWIN* M27 ....55 E4
Catherine St *BOLS/LL* BL3 ....35 H3
  LEIGH WN7 ....49 H5
Catherine St East *HOR/BR* BL6 ....14 D2
Catherine St West *HOR/BR* BL6 ....14 D2
Catterall Crs *BOLE* BL2 ....19 H1
Catterick Dr *BOLS/LL* BL3 ....38 C2
Cavendish Gdns *BOLS/LL* BL3 ....36 A2
Cavendish Rd *WALK* M28 ....54 D5
Cavendish St *LEIGH* WN7 ....49 H4
Cavenham Gv *BOL* BL1 ....28 A2
Cawdor Av *FWTH* BL4 ....37 F3
Cawdor Ct *FWTH* BL4 ....37 G3
Cawdor St *FWTH* BL4 ....37 F3
  SWIN M27 ....55 F3
  WALK M28 ....54 A1
  WGNE/HIN WN2 ....40 A3
Cecilia St *BOLS/LL* BL3 ....37 E1
Cecil St *BOLE* BL2 ....3 H4
  WALK M28 ....45 H5
Cedar Av *ATH* M46 ....42 B4
  BOLS/LL BL3 ....38 D3
  HOR/BR BL6 ....25 G1
  WGNE/HIN WN2 ....40 B5
Cedar Dr *SWIN* M27 ....47 F4
Cedar Gv *FWTH* BL4 ....37 F5
  WHTN BL5 ....41 G1
Cedar Rd *LEIGH* WN7 ....49 G3
Cedar Wood Ct
  BOL (off Chorley New Rd) BL1 ....27 F2
Cellini St *BOLS/LL* BL3 ....2 B3
Cemetery Rd *BOLE* BL2 ....38 B4
  FWTH BL4 ....38 B4
  RAD M26 ....39 H1
  SWIN M27 ....55 G2
Cemetery Rd North *SWIN* M27 ....55 G1
Cemetery St *WHTN* BL5 ....33 G4
Cemetery Vw *CHLY/EC* PR7 ....12 D1
Centaur Cl *SWIN* M27 ....55 H1
Centenary Ct *BOLS/LL* BL3 ....36 D1
Central Av *ATH* M46 ....43 E4
  FWTH BL4 ....37 E5
  WALK M28 ....45 E3
Central Dr *WHTN* BL5 ....33 G4
Central St *BOL* BL1 ....2 D3
Centre Gdns *BOL* BL1 ....28 B1
Centre Park Rd *BOL* BL1 ....28 B3
Century Ldg *FWTH* BL4 ....37 G5
Cestrian St *BOLS/LL* BL3 ....36 C2
Chadbury Cl *HOR/BR* BL6 ....34 C2
Chaddock La *TYLD* M29 ....52 B5
Chadwick St *BOLE* BL2 ....3 H5
  BOLS/LL BL3 ....38 D2
  LEIGH WN7 ....49 H5
  SWIN M27 ....55 H3
  WGNE/HIN WN2 ....40 A3
Chale Gn *BOLE* BL2 ....20 A4

Chalfont Dr TYLD M29 51 G4
WALK M28 54 A3
Chalfont St BOL BL1 18 D5
Chamberlain St BOLS/LL BL3 2 B6
Chancery Cl TYLD M29 51 H3
Chancery La BOL BL1 3 F4
Chanters Av ATH M46 43 E5
The Chanters WALK M28 53 G4
Chantry Cl WHTN BL5 41 H3
Chapel Aly BOL * BL1 2 E3
Chapelfield Dr WALK M28 45 F5
Chapel Fields La
WGNE/HIN WN2 40 A3
Chapelfield St BOL BL1 18 C4
Chapel Gdns
TOT/BURYW
(off Hollymount La) BL8 11 G3
Chapel Green Rd
WGNE/HIN WN2 40 A2
Chapel Meadow WALK M28 53 F4
Chapel Pl BOLS/LL BL3 29 G5
Chapel Rd SWIN M27 55 E4
Chapelstead WHTN BL5 41 H3
Chapel St ATH M46 42 D5
BOL BL1 3 G2
BOLS/LL* BL3 38 C2
CHLY/EC PR7 12 D1
EDGW/EG BL7 8 B1
FWTH* BL4 38 A5
HOR/BR BL6 13 H5
HOR/BR BL6 15 E4
TOT/BURYW BL8 11 H5
TYLD* M29 51 G2
WALK M28 52 D5
WGNE/HIN WN2 48 A2
Chapeltown Rd EDGW/EG BL7 9 F4
Chapman St BOL BL1 27 H1
Chappeltown Rd RAD M26 39 H4
Charles Ct
BOL (off Charles St) BL1 3 F2
Charles Holden St BOL BL1 2 A5
Charles St BOL BL1 3 F2
EDGW/EG BL7 8 B2
FWTH BL4 38 A4
LEIGH WN7 49 H4
SWIN M27 55 F2
TYLD M29 51 F2
WGNE/HIN WN2 40 A1
Charlesworth Av BOLS/LL BL3 37 F3
WGNE/HIN WN2 40 B4
Charlock Av WHTN BL5 41 F2
Charlotte St BOL BL1 18 C5
Charlton Dr SWIN M27 55 F1
Charnock Dr BOL BL1 28 C1
Charnwood Cl TYLD M29 51 G3
WALK M28 53 G1
Chassen Rd BOL BL1 27 H3
Chatburn Rd BOL BL1 17 F4
Chatham Gdns BOLS/LL BL3 2 B7
Chatham Pl BOLS/LL BL3 2 B7
Chatham St LEIGH WN7 49 H4
Chatsworth Dr LEIGH WN7 50 D4
Chatsworth Rd RAD M26 31 G5
Chatteris Cl WGNE/HIN WN2 40 A4
Chatton Cl TOT/BURYW BL8 21 H5
Chaucer Gv LEIGH WN7 49 E3
Chaucer St BOL BL1 28 B1
Cheadle Sq BOL * BL1 2 D4
Cheapside Sq BOL * BL1 2 E4
Chedworth Crs LHULT M38 45 E2
Chedworth Gv BOLS/LL BL3 2 C7
The Cheethams HOR/BR BL6 24 A3
Chelburn Cl WGNE/HIN WN2 48 A2
Chelford Av BOL BL1 18 C2
Chelford Dr SWIN M27 55 G1
TYLD M29 52 A5
Chelmer Cl WHTN BL5 33 H4
Chelsea Av RAD M26 39 F1
Chelsea Ct
WHTN (off Wigan Rd) BL5 41 F3
Chelsea Rd BOLS/LL BL3 36 A2
Chelwood Cl BOL BL1 8 B5
Chelwood Ms
HOR/BR
(off Chorley New Rd) BL6 26 B3
Chepstow Gv LEIGH WN7 51 E4
Cherington Dr TYLD M29 52 A2
Cheriton Dr BOLE BL2 30 A4
Cherry Gv LEIGH WN7 49 H3
Cherry Tree Av FWTH BL4 36 D5
Cherry Tree Gv LEIGH WN7 49 F5
ATH M46 42 B4
Cherry Tree Wy BOLE BL2 19 F3
Cherrywood Av WHTN BL5 43 G1
Cherrywood Cl WALK M28 53 F3
Cherwell Cl WGNE/HIN WN2 23 G4
Cherwell Rd WHTN BL5 33 H3
Chesham Av BOL BL1 18 C5
Chester Av BOLS/LL BL3 38 D1
Chester Cl BOLS/LL BL3 38 D1
Chester Pl CHLYE PR6 6 A4
Chester Rd TYLD M29 52 B3
Chester St ATH M46 51 E1
SWIN M27 55 G4
Chesterton Dr BOLS/LL BL3 27 E5
Chester Wk BOL BL1 18 C5
Chestnut Av ATH * M46 42 C4
WALK M28 53 H1
Chestnut Cl BOLS/LL BL3 35 H1
Chestnut Dr WHTN BL5 41 H1
Chestnut Gv RAD M26 39 H5
WGNE/HIN WN2 40 C4
Chetwyn Av EDGW/EG BL7 9 E5
Cheviot Cl BOL BL1 18 B2
HOR/BR BL6 15 E2
Chew Moor La WHTN BL5 34 A3
Chichester Av ATH M46 50 A1
Childwall Cl BOLS/LL BL3 36 C3
Chilgrove Av HOR/BR BL6 23 H1
Chilham Rd WALK M28 54 A1
Chilham St BOLS/LL BL3 35 H3
SWIN M27 55 G5
Chiltern Av ATH M46 43 F3
Chiltern Cl HOR/BR BL6 15 E2
WALK M28 54 A3
Chiltern Dr BOLE BL2 29 G3
SWIN M27 55 H5
Chiltern Wy TYLD M29 51 H3
Chilton Cl LEIGH WN7 49 H4
Chinnor Cl LEIGH WN7 49 H4
Chip Hill Rd BOLS/LL BL3 35 G1
Chipping Rd BOL BL1 17 F5
Chisholme Cl TOT/BURYW BL8 11 H2
Chiswick Dr BOLS/LL BL3 30 D5
Chisworth Cl LEIGH WN7 49 G4
Chisworth St BOLE BL2 19 F4
Chorley Cl TOT/BURYW BL8 31 H1
Chorley New Rd HOR/BR BL6 14 D4
HOR/BR BL6 26 A2
Chorley Old Rd BOL BL1 17 E5
HOR/BR BL6 15 G4
Chorley Rd CHLY/EC PR7 13 E2
CHLYE PR6 6 A3
HOR/BR BL6 13 G4
SWIN M27 55 F2
WGN WN1 12 A2
WHTN BL5 24 B4
Chorley St BOL BL1 2 B2
CHLYE PR6 6 B4
Chowbent Cl ATH M46 43 E5
Christ Church Cl BOLE * BL2 20 B5
Christ Church La BOLE BL2 20 B4
Chronnell Dr BOLE BL2 30 A2
Chulsey Gate La HOR/BR BL6 34 A1
Chulsey St BOLS/LL BL3 35 H2
Church Av BOLS/LL BL3 36 A1
WGNE/HIN WN2 48 B3
Church Bank BOL BL1 3 F3
Church Cl RAD M26 38 D5
Churchfield Cl RAD M26 39 H4
Churchgate BOL BL1 3 F3
Churchill Av BOLE BL2 31 F1
Churchill Dr BOLS/LL BL3 39 E2
Churchill St BOLE BL2 29 G3
Church La WHTN BL5 33 G2
Church Mdw BOLE BL2 20 B4
Church Rd BOL BL1 17 H5
BOL BL1 18 A5
FWTH BL4 38 A5
RAD M26 38 C5
TYLD M29 52 A5
WALK M28 45 H5
Churchside FWTH BL4 45 F1
Church St BOLE BL2 19 H2
BOLE BL2 31 E1
BOLS/LL BL3 38 B2
CHLYE PR6 6 A5
FWTH BL4 38 A5
HOR/BR BL6 13 G5
HOR/BR BL6 15 E3
SWIN M27 55 G3
TOT/BURYW BL8 21 H2
WGNE/HIN WN2 23 F4
WHTN BL5 33 G4
Churchtown Av BOLE BL2 30 B3
Church Wk FWTH * BL4 37 G5
SWIN M27 47 H4
TOT/BURYW
(off Hollymount La) BL8 11 F3
Churchward Sq HOR/BR BL6 15 E5
Churnett Cl WHTN BL5 33 H3
Cinnamon Av WGNE/HIN WN2 40 B4
Cirencester Cl LHULT M38 45 E2
City Rd WALK M28 53 E3
Clammerclough Rd FWTH BL4 38 B5
Claremont Av WGNE/HIN WN2 40 B3
Claremont Ct BOL * BL1 28 C1
Claremont Dr LHULT M38 45 F3
Clarence Ct BOL * BL1 2 C2
Clarence Rd SWIN M27 55 E4
Clarence St ATH M46 51 E2
BOL BL1 2 E2
FWTH BL4 38 A4
Clarendon Gv BOLE BL2 3 J6
Clarendon Rd BOLE BL2 29 G3
SWIN M27 55 H3
Clarendon St BOLS/LL BL3 36 C1
Clarke Crs LHULT M38 44 B2
Clarke St BOL BL1 28 A2
Claude Av SWIN M27 55 F3
Claude St SWIN M27 55 F3
Claughton Av BOLE BL2 30 B3
WALK M28 53 G3
Claughton Rd TOT/BURYW BL8 21 H2
Claybank Dr TOT/BURYW BL8 11 F5
Claydon Dr BOLS/LL BL3 30 D5
Claymore St BOLS/LL * BL3 36 D2
Claypool Rd HOR/BR BL6 25 G1
Clay St EDGW/EG BL7 9 E5
Clayton Av BOLS/LL BL3 29 F5
Clayton Cl TOT/BURYW BL8 31 H1
Clayton St BOLS/LL BL3 29 F5
Clegg's Buildings BOL * BL1 2 C2
Clegg's La LHULT M38 45 E3
Clegg St BOLE BL2 29 G3
TYLD M29 51 G5
Clelland St FWTH BL4 46 A1
Clement Av ATH M46 50 A1
Cleveland Gdns BOLS/LL BL3 35 H1
Cleveland St BOLS/LL * BL3 35 H1
Cleveleys Av BOLE BL2 29 G2
Cliff Av TOT/BURYW BL8 11 G5
Clifford Rd BOLS/LL * BL3 35 G3
Clifton Av TYLD M29 52 A5
Clifton Ct FWTH BL4 37 F3
Clifton Dr HOR/BR BL6 13 F4
SWIN M27 55 F1
Clifton Gv SWIN M27 55 E1
Clifton House Rd SWIN M27 47 F3
Clifton St BOL * BL1 2 C2
FWTH BL4 46 B1
TYLD M29 52 C3
Clifton Vw SWIN M27 47 G4
Clitheroe Dr TOT/BURYW BL8 21 H5
Clivedale Pl BOL BL1 3 F4
Clive Rd WHTN BL5 41 G2
Clive St BOLE BL2 3 F4
Clock Tower Cl WALK M28 44 D5
Cloister Av LEIGH WN7 49 F2
The Cloisters WHTN BL5 41 G3
Cloister St BOL BL1 18 A5
Close La WGNE/HIN WN2 40 B5
Closes Farm BOLS/LL BL3 35 H3
Close St WGNE/HIN WN2 40 B2
The Close ATH M46 43 F3
BOLE BL2 19 F4
Cloudstock Gv LHULT M38 44 C3
Clough Av WHTN BL5 33 H5
Cloughbank RAD M26 47 E1
Cloughfold RAD M26 46 D1
Clough Fold WHTN BL5 33 H5
Clough Meadow BOL BL1 26 D4
Clough Meadow Rd RAD M26 39 G2
Clough St FWTH BL4 46 B1
The Clough
BOL (off Chorley New Rd) BL1 27 E2
Clovelly Av LEIGH WN7 49 H3
Clovelly Rd SWIN M27 55 E4
Cloverdale Sq BOL BL1 27 G1
Clunton Av BOLS/LL BL3 35 H1
Clyde Rd RAD M26 31 H5
TYLD M29 52 A4
Clyde St BOL * BL1 18 C5
Clyde Ter RAD * M26 31 H5
Coach Rd TYLD M29 52 A5
Coach St ATH M46 42 D5
Coal Pit La ATH M46 42 B5
LEIGH WN7 49 G3
WGNE/HIN WN2 48 D2
Cobden St BOL BL1 18 B4
EDGW/EG* BL7 8 B2
RAD M26 31 H4
TYLD M29 51 G2
Cobham Av BOLS/LL BL3 36 B2
Cochrane St BOLS/LL BL3 28 D5
Cockerell Springs BOLE * BL2 3 G5
Cocker St LHULT M38 45 E4
Cockey Moor Rd BOLE BL2 31 F1
Codale Dr BOLE BL2 30 B1
Code La WHTN BL5 32 D1
Coe St BOLS/LL BL3 2 E7
Colchester Av BOLE BL2 30 A2
Colchester Dr FWTH BL4 37 E4
Coleford Gv BOL BL1 2 C5
Colenso Ct BOLE * BL2 29 G3
Coleridge Av RAD M26 39 G2
Coleridge Rd TOT/BURYW BL8 11 H2
Colesbourne Cl LHULT M38 45 E2
Colindale Cl BOLS/LL * BL3 28 A5
Colinton Cl BOL BL1 28 B1
Collard St ATH M46 42 B4
College Cl BOLS/LL BL3 2 D6
College Wy BOLS/LL BL3 2 B5
Colliers Row Rd BOL BL1 16 D2
Collier St SWIN M27 55 G4
Colliery La ATH M46 42 A4
Collingwood Wy WHTN BL5 33 G4
Collins La WHTN BL5 41 H2
Collins St TOT/BURYW BL8 21 H3
Collyhurst Av WALK M28 54 A1
Colmore Gv BOLE BL2 19 F3
Colmore St BOLE BL2 19 F4
Columbia Rd BOL BL1 28 A2
Colwith Av BOLE BL2 30 A1
Colwyn Dr WGNE/HIN WN2 49 E1
Colwyn Gv ATH M46 42 C3
Colwyn Rd SWIN M27 55 E5
Combermere Cl TYLD M29 51 H2
Common End CHLY/EC PR7 12 C3
Common La TYLD M29 51 G2
Common Side Rd WALK M28 52 D4
Common St WHTN BL5 40 D1
The Common CHLY/EC PR7 12 C2
Como St BOLS/LL * BL3 36 A1
Congresbury Rd LEIGH WN7 49 F4
Conisber Cl EDGW/EG BL7 8 C3
Coniston BOL * BL1 18 D4
Coniston Av ATH M46 42 D3
CHLYE PR6 6 B4
FWTH BL4 44 C1
LHULT M38
Coniston Cl BOLS/LL BL3
Coniston Gv LHULT M38
Coniston Rd HOR/BR BL6
SWIN M27
TYLD M29
WGNE/HIN WN2
Connaught Sq BOLE BL2
Connel Cl BOLE BL2
Conningsby Cl EDGW/EG BL7
Constable Cl BOL BL1
Constance Rd BOLS/LL BL3
Conway Av BOL BL1
Conway Cl LEIGH WN7
Conway Crs TOT/BURYW BL8
Conway Rd WGNE/HIN WN2
Conway St FWTH BL4
Cooke St FWTH BL4
HOR/BR BL6
Cooling La TYLD M29
Coombe Cl TYLD M29
Co-operative St LHULT * M38
Cooper St HOR/BR BL6
Coop St BOL BL1
Cope Bank BOL BL1
Cope Bank West BOL * BL1
Copeland Ms BOL BL1
Copesthorne Cl
WGNE/HIN WN2
Coplow Dl WGNE/HIN WN2
Copperas La HOR/BR BL6
WGNE/HIN WN2
Copperfields HOR/BR BL6
The Coppice BOLE BL2
WALK M28
The Copse EDGW/EG BL7
Copthorne Dr BOLE BL2
Corfe Cl WGNE/HIN WN2
Corhampton Crs ATH M46
Cornbrook Cl WHTN BL5
Cornergate WHTN BL5
Corner La WGNE/HIN WN2
Cornlea Dr WALK M28
Cornwall Av TYLD M29
WHTN BL5
Cornwall Dr WGNE/HIN WN2
Coronation Av ATH M46
Coronation Dr LEIGH WN7
Coronation Gdns RAD M26
Coronation Rd RAD M26
Coronation St BOL BL1
Corporation St BOL BL1
Corranstone Cl HOR/BR BL6
Corrie Crs FWTH BL4
Corrie Dr FWTH BL4
Corrie St LHULT M38
Corring Wy BOL BL1
Corrin Rd BOLE BL2
Corsey Rd WGNE/HIN WN2
Corson St FWTH BL4
Corston Gv HOR/BR BL6
Cotefield Av BOLS/LL BL3
Cotford Rd BOL BL1
Cotswold Dr HOR/BR BL6
Cottage Cft BOLE BL2
Cottingley Cl BOL BL1
Cotton St BOL BL1
Coucill Sq FWTH BL4
Countess La RAD M26
County Rd WALK M28
Coupes Gn WHTN BL5
Coupland Rd WGNE/HIN WN2
Court St BOLE BL2
Courtyard Dr WALK M28
The Courtyard
BOL (off Calvin St) BL1
Cousin Flds BOLE BL2
Coventry Rd RAD M26
Coverdale Av BOL BL1
Coverdale Rd WHTN BL5
Cowburn St WGNE/HIN WN2
Cowdals Rd HOR/BR BL6
Cow La BOLS/LL BL3
Cow Lees WHTN BL5
Cowley Rd BOL BL1
Cox Green Cl EDGW/EG BL7
Cox Wy ATH M46
Crab Tree La ATH M46
Craighall Rd BOL BL1
Cramond Cl BOL BL1
Cramond Wk BOL BL1
Cranark Cl BOL BL1
Cranberry Dr BOLS/LL BL3
Cranborne Cl HOR/BR BL6
Crane St BOLS/LL * BL3
Cranfield Rd HOR/BR BL6
Cranford St BOLS/LL BL3
Cranham Close Crs
LHULT * M38
Cranleigh Cl HOR/BR BL6
Cranleigh Dr TYLD M29
WALK M28
Cranshaw St TYLD M29
Cranstal Dr WGNE/HIN WN2
Cranworth Av TYLD M29
Crathie Ct BOL BL1
Craven Pl BOL BL1
Craven St East HOR/BR BL6
Crawford Av BOLE BL2
CHLY/EC PR7

M29 .....51 F1
M28 .....54 B3
...WN2 .....23 F5
rd St BOLE BL2 .....3 H4
Cl TYLD M29 .....52 A2
n Dr BOLE BL2 .....30 C5
...Av BOL BL1 .....2 B2
BL4 .....45 G2
t Dr LHULT M38 .....45 F3
t Rd BOLS/LL BL3 .....37 F2
BL4 .....46 B2
BR BL6 .....25 G2
scent BOLE BL2 .....20 B3
LL BL3 .....38 D3
EG BL7 .....9 E4
BR BL6 .....25 F1
126 .....31 F5
BL5 .....41 G1
gham Rd BOLS/LL BL3 .....35 F2
d WALK M28 .....45 E4
n Av WGNE/HIN WN2 .....23 H5
ers Wy WHTN BL5 .....33 G5
ield La WALK M28 .....45 G5
BOLS/LL BL3 .....28 C5
Cl BOLS/LL BL3 .....35 E1
St ATH M46 .....50 A2
BOL BL1 .....2 A5
le St BOL BL1 .....28 D1
ATH M46 .....50 D1
TOT/BURYW BL8 .....21 G1
Wk BOLE BL2 .....19 G1
BOLE BL2 .....20 A3
LHULT M38 .....44 D3
BOLS/LL BL3 .....29 F5
TYLD M29 .....51 F3
e Av WALK M28 .....46 A5
e La WALK M28 .....46 A5
e Gv WALK M28 .....46 A5
BOLS/LL BL3 .....37 F1
M38 .....44 D3
BL5 .....33 G2
ank TOT/BURYW BL8 .....10 D2
uke Dr LEIGH WN7 .....49 G2
uke Fold WALK M28 .....53 F4
le Av BOL BL1 .....27 H2
AV BOLE BL2 .....29 G1
Dr ATH M46 .....50 A1
rd Gdns BOL BL1 .....18 D5
on Av BOLE BL2 .....30 A2
on Pl BOL * BL1 .....3 F4
on Rd HOR/BR BL6 .....25 H2
126 .....38 C5
on St BOL BL1 .....3 G2
BL4 .....46 A1
M27 .....55 G3
on St BOL BL1 .....54 B1
on V BOLE BL2 .....29 H2
on Wy BOLE BL2 .....19 G4
ell Rd SWIN M27 .....55 G2
ell St BOLS/LL BL3 .....2 B5
BOLS/LL BL3 .....2 E6
e Wy WGNE/HIN WN2 .....40 B5
V WALK M28 .....54 B1
rd Rd BOL BL1 .....27 H2
126 .....31 G3
ATH M46 .....43 E4
le Rd BOLE BL2 .....30 B2
HIN WN2 .....40 B3
on St BOLS/LL BL3 .....29 G5
d Dr RAD M26 .....39 G2
M27 .....55 G2
M28 .....54 B4
rd Dr BOLS/LL BL3 .....27 E5
ds Rd WALK M28 .....52 D4
BOLS/LL BL3 .....38 C1
oor Dr BOLE BL2 .....3 K1
mrod St BOLS/LL BL3 .....2 A6
ATH M46 .....42 B4
.1 .....3 F1
BL3 .....38 D2
EG BL7 .....8 D5
BL4 .....37 H4
BL4 .....46 D3
M29 .....51 F3
s
URYW (off High St) BL8 .....21 H1
Av CHLYE PR6 .....6 A4
St BOLS/LL BL3 .....36 A1
rough Cl HOR/BR BL6 .....25 H1
d Rd BOLE BL2 .....19 G5
v LEIGH WN7 .....50 D5
a HOR/BR BL6 .....14 B4
ATH M46 .....42 C5
.1 .....3 F1
Nest BOLS/LL BL3 .....30 B5
Cl BOLE BL2 .....20 B4
WIGN WN7 .....49 H3
ck Cl BOLS/LL BL3 .....38 C5
ck Rd FWTH BL4 .....44 C1
all St BOL BL1 .....18 C5
k Rd EDGW/EG BL7 .....18 D1
Cl BOL * BL1 .....18 B5

Cumberland Rd ATH M46 .....43 E4
Cumbermere La TYLD M29 .....51 H1
Cundey St BOL BL1 .....28 A1
Cunliffe Brow BOL BL1 .....17 H5
Cunningham Rd WHTN BL5 .....41 E1
Curtels St HOR/BR BL6 .....14 D3
Curtels Cl WALK M28 .....55 E4
Curtis St BOLS/LL BL3 .....36 A3
Curzon Rd BOL BL1 .....28 A3
Cuthbert St BOLS/LL BL3 .....35 G3
Cypress Gv FWTH * BL4 .....46 B1
Cyril St BOLS/LL BL3 .....29 E5

D

Daccamill Dr SWIN M27 .....55 H5
Daffodil Rd FWTH BL4 .....37 E4
Daffodil St BOL BL1 .....18 D2
Dagmar St WALK M28 .....45 G4
Daisy Av FWTH BL4 .....37 E4
Daisyfield
  HOR/BR
  (off Chorley New Rd) BL6 .....25 F1
Daisy Hall Dr WHTN BL5 .....41 G3
Daisyhill Ct WHTN BL5 .....41 H3
Daisy Hill Dr CHLYE PR6 .....6 A4
Daisy St BOLS/LL BL3 .....36 A1
Dalby Av SWIN M27 .....55 G4
Dalby Rd WGNE/HIN WN2 .....40 D3
Dalebank ATH M46 .....42 C3
Dalebank Ms
  SWIN
  (off Clifton House Rd) M27 .....47 F3
Dalegarth Av HOR/BR BL6 .....26 C3
Dale Lee WHTN BL5 .....34 A5
Dales Brow EDGW/EG BL7 .....18 D1
  SWIN* M27 .....55 F5
Dales Gv WALK M28 .....54 B2
Dales Park Dr SWIN * M27 .....55 F5
Dale St FWTH * BL4 .....38 A4
  SWIN M27 .....55 G5
  WHTN BL5 .....41 H3
Dale St East HOR/BR BL6 .....25 F1
Dale St West HOR/BR BL6 .....15 F5
Dalkeith Av BOLS/LL BL3 .....27 F5
Dalkeith Rd WGNE/HIN WN2 .....40 C3
Dalton Fold WHTN BL5 .....33 H5
Dalymount Cl BOLE BL2 .....19 F5
Dams Head Fold WHTN BL5 .....33 H4
Danby Rd BOLS/LL BL3 .....36 C2
Danebridge Cl FWTH * BL4 .....38 A5
Danes Av WGNE/HIN WN2 .....40 A2
Danes Brook Cl
  WGNE/HIN WN2 .....40 A2
Danesbury Rd BOL BL1 .....19 F3
Danes Gn WGNE/HIN WN2 .....40 A1
Dane St BOLS/LL * BL3 .....36 A1
Darbishire St BOL BL1 .....29 E1
Darbyshire Cl BOL BL1 .....29 E1
Darcy St BOLE BL2 .....29 G5
Dark La HOR/BR BL6 .....13 F3
Darley Av FWTH BL4 .....38 A4
Darley Gv FWTH BL4 .....38 A4
Darley St BOL BL1 .....28 B3
  FWTH BL4 .....38 A5
  HOR/BR BL6 .....14 D2
Darley Ter BOL * BL1 .....28 B1
Darlington St TYLD M29 .....51 G2
Darlington St East TYLD M29 .....51 H2
Darnley Av WALK M28 .....53 G2
Darvel Cl BOLE BL2 .....30 B4
Darwen Rd EDGW/EG BL7 .....8 D4
Darwin St BOL BL1 .....18 B5
Davenport Fold Rd BOLE * BL2 .....20 C3
Davenport Gdns BOL * BL1 .....2 C2
Davenport St BOL BL1 .....2 C2
David Brow BOLS/LL BL3 .....35 G3
Davies St FWTH BL4 .....46 C1
Dawes St BOL BL1 .....2 E5
Dawson La BOL BL1 .....2 C3
Dawson St ATH * M46 .....42 C5
Dealey Rd BOLS/LL BL3 .....35 G1
Deal St BOLS/LL BL3 .....36 D2
Dean Cl FWTH BL4 .....36 D5
Dean Ct BOL BL1 .....3 F1
Deane Av BOLS/LL BL3 .....27 H5
Deane Church La BOLS/LL BL3 .....35 H1
Deane Rd BOLS/LL BL3 .....28 A5
Deane Wk BOLS/LL BL3 .....2 C4
Deanscourt Av SWIN M27 .....55 G4
Deansgate BOL BL1 .....2 C3
  WGNE/HIN WN2 .....40 A2
Deans Rd SWIN M27 .....55 G4
Dean St RAD M26 .....39 H2
Deansway SWIN M27 .....55 G5
Dearden Av LHULT M38 .....45 G3
Dearden St BOLS/LL BL3 .....38 C1
Debenham Ct FWTH * BL4 .....45 H1
Dee Dr FWTH BL4 .....46 D3
Deepdale Rd BOLE BL2 .....30 A2
Dee Rd TYLD M29 .....52 A4
Defence St BOLS/LL BL3 .....2 D4
Defiance St ATH M46 .....42 C5
De Lacy Dr BOLE BL2 .....29 F1
Delaford Av WALK M28 .....54 A4
Dellside Gv WALK M28 .....46 A5
Dell St BOLE BL2 .....19 G2

Delph Av EDGW/EG BL7 .....8 B1
Delph Brook Wy EDGW/EG BL7 .....8 B2
Delph Gv LEIGH WN7 .....49 H4
Delph Hill BOL BL1 .....17 E5
Delph Hill Cl BOL BL1 .....17 E5
Delphi Av WALK M28 .....53 H1
Delph La BOLE BL2 .....31 E1
Delph St BOLS/LL BL3 .....28 B5
The Delph
  WALK (off Worsley Rd) M28 .....54 B5
Denbigh Gv ATH M46 .....42 C3
Denbigh Rd BOLE BL2 .....3 J7
Dene Bank BOLE BL2 .....19 G2
Dene St BOLE BL2 .....19 G2
Denham Cl BOL BL1 .....19 E2
Denstone Crs BOLE BL2 .....19 H5
Dentdale Cl BOL BL1 .....26 D4
Denton Rd BOLS/LL BL3 .....30 D4
Derby Pl CHLYE PR6 .....6 A4
Derby Rd RAD M26 .....38 C5
Derbyshire Rw BOL * BL1 .....18 C4
Derby St ATH M46 .....42 C4
  BOLS/LL BL3 .....2 C7
  HOR/BR BL6 .....25 F1
  WHTN BL5 .....33 H4
Derwent Cl BOLS/LL BL3 .....38 B2
  WALK M28 .....53 F1
Derwent Dr FWTH BL4 .....46 D3
Derwent Rd FWTH BL4 .....36 D5
  WGNE/HIN WN2 .....40 A3
Derwent St TYLD M29 .....51 G4
Design St BOLS/LL BL3 .....35 H2
Desmond St ATH M46 .....50 A1
Devoke Av WALK M28 .....54 A1
Devoke Gv FWTH BL4 .....36 C5
Devon Cl BOLS/LL BL3 .....38 D1
  WGNE/HIN WN2 .....23 H5
Devon Dr BOLE BL2 .....31 E1
Devon Rd TYLD M29 .....51 F1
Devonshire Dr WALK M28 .....52 C5
Devonshire Rd ATH M46 .....42 C3
  BOL BL1 .....27 H2
  WALK M28 .....45 G2
Devon St BOLE BL2 .....3 H4
  FWTH BL4 .....37 H3
  SWIN M27 .....55 H1
  WGNE/HIN WN2 .....40 A3
Dewberry Cl TYLD M29 .....52 C2
Dewhurst Clough Rd
  EDGW/EG BL7 .....8 B2
Dewhurst Ct EDGW/EG BL7 .....8 B2
Dewhurst Rd BOLE BL2 .....20 A4
Dial Ct FWTH * BL4 .....37 H4
Dicconson La WHTN BL5 .....32 C1
Dickenson St WGNE/HIN WN2 .....40 A4
Dickinson Cl BOL * BL1 .....28 C1
Dickinson St BOL BL1 .....28 C1
Dickson St West HOR/BR BL6 .....14 C3
Dijon St BOLS/LL BL3 .....36 A1
Dilham Ct BOL BL1 .....28 A2
Dimple Pk EDGW/EG BL7 .....8 B1
Dingle Wk BOL BL1 .....2 E1
Dinsdale Dr BOLS/LL BL3 .....2 A7
Ditchcocker Brow BOL BL1 .....27 F1
Division St BOLS/LL BL3 .....36 D2
Dixey St HOR/BR BL6 .....14 C4
Dixon Dr SWIN M27 .....47 G4
Dixon Green Dr FWTH BL4 .....37 G5
Dixon St HOR/BR BL6 .....14 C3
  WHTN BL5 .....33 G2
Dobb Brow Rd WHTN BL5 .....41 F1
Dobhill St FWTH BL4 .....37 H5
Dobson Rd BOL BL1 .....28 A3
Dobson St BOL BL1 .....18 B5
Dodd La WHTN BL5 .....32 D2
Dodd's Farm La
  WGNE/HIN WN2 .....32 A2
Dodhurst Rd WGNE/HIN WN2 .....40 B2
Doe Brow SWIN M27 .....47 G4
Doefield Av WALK M28 .....53 G3
Doe Hey Gv FWTH BL4 .....37 F3
Doe Hey Rd BOLS/LL BL3 .....37 F3
Doffcocker Brow BOL BL1 .....27 F1
Doffcocker La BOL BL1 .....27 F1
Doman St BOLS/LL BL3 .....28 D5
Doncaster Cl BOLS/LL BL3 .....38 B2
Donnington Gdns
  WALK (off Wilbraham Rd) M28 .....45 H5
Donnington Rd RAD M26 .....31 E5
Don St BOLE BL2 .....36 B2
Doodson Sq FWTH BL4 .....37 H5
Dootson St WGNE/HIN WN2 .....40 C2
Dorchester Av BOLE BL2 .....30 A1
Dorchester Rd SWIN M27 .....55 H3
Doris Av BOLE BL2 .....29 H3
Dorket Gv WHTN BL5 .....41 F2
Dorking Cl BOL BL1 .....18 D5
Dormer St BOL BL1 .....18 D4
Dorning St ATH M46 .....51 F2
  FWTH BL4 .....38 B5
  HOR/BR BL6 .....24 A3
Dorris St BOLS/LL * BL3 .....36 A2
Dorset Av FWTH BL4 .....37 G5
  TYLD M29 .....43 F5
Dorset Cl FWTH BL4 .....37 G5
Dorset Rd BOLS/LL BL3 .....36 A1
Dorset St BOLE BL2 .....3 H4
  SWIN M27 .....55 H1
  WGNE/HIN WN2 .....40 A1
Dorstone Cl WGNE/HIN WN2 .....40 D3
Dotterel St LEIGH WN7 .....50 A5

Dougill St BOL BL1 .....27 H1
Douglas Av HOR/BR BL6 .....15 E2
Douglas Cl HOR/BR BL6 .....15 E3
Douglas Pk ATH M46 .....43 E5
Douglas Rd ATH M46 .....51 E1
  LEIGH WN7 .....49 E4
  SWIN M27 .....55 E4
Douglas St ATH M46 .....43 E5
  BOL* BL1 .....18 C2
Dove Bank Rd BOLS/LL BL3 .....38 B1
Dovecote Cl EDGW/EG BL7 .....9 F4
Dovecote La LHULT M38 .....44 C5
Dovedale Rd BOLE BL2 .....20 B5
Dover Gv BOLS/LL BL3 .....2 B7
Dove Rd BOLS/LL BL3 .....35 H1
Dover St BOL BL1 .....37 G3
Dove St BOL BL1 .....18 C3
Dovey Cl TYLD M29 .....52 A4
Dow Fold TOT/BURYW BL8 .....21 H4
Dow La TOT/BURYW BL8 .....21 H4
Downgreen Rd BOLE BL2 .....2 E1
Downhall Gn BOL * BL1 .....2 E1
Downham Av BOLE BL2 .....29 G2
Dowson St BOLE BL2 .....3 H4
Doyle Rd BOLS/LL BL3 .....35 E2
Drake Av FWTH BL4 .....45 H2
Drake Hall WHTN BL5 .....40 A5
Drake St ATH M46 .....50 C1
Draycott Dr WGNE/HIN WN2 .....40 A5
Draycott St BOL BL1 .....18 C5
Draycott St East BOL BL1 .....18 B5
Drayton Cl BOL BL1 .....18 B5
The Drive
  WHTN (off Everest Rd) BL5 .....42 C2
Droxford Gv ATH M46 .....43 E3
Druids Cl EDGW/EG BL7 .....8 B1
Drummond St BOL * BL1 .....18 C3
Dryad Cl SWIN M27 .....55 H1
Dryburgh Av BOL BL1 .....18 B4
Dryden Av SWIN M27 .....55 H4
Dryfield La HOR/BR BL6 .....14 C2
Duchess Wk BOLS/LL BL3 .....35 H1
Duchy Av WALK M28 .....53 H3
  WHTN BL5 .....35 G5
Ducie Av BOL BL1 .....28 A3
Ducie St RAD M26 .....31 H5
Duckshaw La FWTH BL4 .....37 G5
Duddon Av BOLE BL2 .....30 B1
Dudley Av BOLE BL2 .....29 G1
Dudley Rd WGNE/HIN WN2 .....55 H2
Dudwell Cl BOL BL1 .....28 A1
Duerden St BOLS/LL * BL3 .....35 G3
Duke Rd BOLE BL2 .....31 E1
Duke St BOL BL1 .....2 D1
  LHULT M38 .....45 E3
  TYLD M29 .....52 A5
  WALK M28 .....54 C1
Duke St North BOL BL1 .....2 D1
Dulverton Gdns
  BOLS/LL (off Boscow Rd) BL3 .....38 D3
Dunbar Dr BOL BL1 .....28 A2
Dunbar St SWIN M27 .....55 H1
Dunblane Av BOLS/LL BL3 .....27 E5
Duncan St HOR/BR BL6 .....15 E4
Dunchurch Cl HOR/BR BL6 .....26 D4
Duncombe Rd BOLS/LL BL3 .....36 C2
Dunedin Rd TOT/BURYW BL8 .....11 H2
Dunham Cl WHTN BL5 .....41 F3
Dunlin Cl BOLE BL2 .....3 H7
Dunmail Cl TYLD M29 .....52 A5
Dunoon Dr BOL BL1 .....18 A2
Dunoon Rd WGNE/HIN WN2 .....23 H5
Dunsop Dr BOL BL1 .....17 F4
Dunstan St BOLE BL2 .....29 G3
Dunster Pl WALK M28 .....52 D4
Dunster Rd WALK M28 .....52 D4
Durban Rd BOL BL1 .....18 C2
Durban St ATH M46 .....50 A1
Durham Cl BOLS/LL BL3 .....38 D1
  TYLD M29 .....43 G5
Durham Rd WGNE/HIN WN2 .....40 A4
Durham St BOL BL1 .....18 D5
Duty St BOL BL1 .....18 C4
Duxbury Av BOLE BL2 .....20 A2
  BOLS/LL BL3 .....30 C5
Duxbury St BOL BL1 .....18 B5
Dymchurch Av RAD M26 .....47 E1
Dyson Cl FWTH BL4 .....37 H5
Dyson St FWTH * BL4 .....45 H1

E

Eagle St BOLE BL2 .....3 H3
Eagley Brook Wy BOL BL1 .....18 D4
Eagley Wk BOLS/LL BL3 .....18 D1
Eagley Brow EDGW/EG BL7 .....18 D1
Ealinger Wy SWIN M27 .....55 H1
Eames Av RAD M26 .....38 C5
Earl St ATH M46 .....50 B1
Earlswood Wk BOLS/LL BL3 .....36 D1
Earnshaw St BOLS/LL * BL3 .....36 A2
Easedale Rd BOL BL1 .....27 G2
Eastbank St BOL BL1 .....18 D5
Eastbourne Gv BOL BL1 .....27 G2
Eastchurch Cl FWTH BL4 .....45 H1
Eastfields RAD M26 .....31 G5
Eastgrove Av BOL BL1 .....18 C1

Eastham Wy *LHULT* M38 ....**45** F3
East Lancashire Rd *WALK* M28.....**52** D4
East Lynn Dr *WALK* M28 ....**54** C1
East Meade *BOLS/LL* BL3..............**36** C3
SWIN M27 ....**55** G5
East Moor *WALK* M28.......................**53** E4
Eastmoor Gv *WHTN* BL5 ....**35** H3
East Rd *BOL* BL1 ....**18** C3
East St *ATH* M46 ....**51** F2
WGNE/HIN WN2 ....**40** D5
East Wk *EDGW/EG* BL7 ....**8** B2
East Wy *BOL* BL1 ....**19** F4
Eastwood Av *WALK* M28.................**45** E5
Eastwood Dr *BOLS/LL* BL3 ....**35** G2
Eastwood Ter *BOL* BL1 ....**27** F2
Eatock Wy *WHTN* BL5 ....**41** F2
Eaton St *WGNE/HIN* WN2 ....**40** A2
Ebury St *RAD* M26 ....**39** H1
Eccles Rd *SWIN* M27 ....**55** H5
Eccleston Av *BOLE* BL2 ....**29** F1
SWIN M27 ....**55** H4
Eckersley Fold La *ATH* M46 ....**50** A2
Eckersley St *BOL* BL1 ....**18** C4
Eckersley St *BOLS/LL* BL3 ....**36** A1
Edale Cl *ATH* M46 ....**42** C5
Edale Rd *BOLS/LL* BL3 ....**35** G1
FWTH BL4 ....**37** G3
Eddith Gv *BOLE* BL2 ....**29** G3
Eden Av *BOL* BL1 ....**18** C4
Eden Bank *LEIGH* WN7 ....**50** B5
Edenbridge Dr *RAD* M26 ....**46** D1
Eden Gv *BOL* BL1 ....**18** C4
Eden St *BOL* BL1 ....**18** C4
Edenvale *WALK* M28 ....**53** E3
Edgar St *BOLS/LL* BL3 ....**2** D6
Edge Fold
   FWTH (off Plodder La) BL4....**36** A4
Edge Fold Crs *WALK* M28 ....**53** H3
Edge Fold Rd *WALK* M28 ....**53** H2
Edge Gn *WALK* * M28 ....**53** G3
Edge Hill Rd *BOLS/LL* BL3 ....**35** H2
Edge La *BOL* BL1 ....**16** C2
Edgemoor Cl *RAD* M26 ....**31** G5
Edgeworth Av *BOLE* BL2.................**31** F4
Edgeworth Rd *WGNE/HIN* WN2 ....**40** C5
Edgmont Av *BOLS/LL* BL3 ....**36** B1
Edinburgh Dr *WGNE/HIN* WN2 .....**40** D5
Edinburgh Rd *BOLS/LL* BL3 ....**38** C3
Edith St *BOL* BL1 ....**28** A4
   FWTH BL4 ....**45** H1
Edmunds Ct *BOLS/LL* * BL3 ....**2** B6
Edna St *LEIGH* WN7 ....**49** E4
Edstone Cl *BOLS/LL* BL3 ....**35** F1
Edward St *BOLS/LL* BL3 ....**2** A7
   FWTH BL4 ....**37** F3
   HOR/BR BL6 ....**14** C4
   RAD M26 ....**38** D5
   WHTN BL5 ....**33** G5
Egerton Ct
   WALK (off Glen Av) M28 ....**54** C3
Egerton Gv *WALK* M28 ....**45** H5
Egerton Ldg *EDGW/EG* BL7 ....**8** C3
Egerton Pk *WALK* M28 ....**54** D4
Egerton Rd *WALK* M28 ....**45** H5
Egerton St *FWTH* BL4 ....**37** G4
Egerton V *EDGW/EG* BL7 ....**8** B2
Eggar Ct *TYLD* M29 ....**51** H4
Egham Ct
   BOLE (off Horsa St) BL2 ....**29** F1
Egyptian St *BOL* BL1 ....**28** D1
Eldercot Gv *BOLS/LL* BL3 ....**35** G1
Eldercot Rd *BOLS/LL* BL3 ....**35** G1
Eldon St *BOLE* BL2 ....**29** F1
   LEIGH WN7 ....**49** F5
Eleanor St *BOL* BL1 ....**19** E2
Elgin St *BOL* BL1 ....**18** A1
Elgol Dr *BOLS/LL* BL3 ....**27** E5
Elham Cl *RAD* M26 ....**47** E1
Elizabeth Av *WGNE/HIN* WN2 ......**48** A2
Elizabeth St *ATH* M46 ....**42** D5
   SWIN M27 ....**55** H2
Elkstone Av *LHULT* M38 ....**45** E2
Ellenbrook Rd *WALK* M28 ....**53** F3
Ellendale Gra *WALK* M28 ....**53** F3
Ellen Gv *FWTH* BL4 ....**47** E4
Ellenor Dr *TYLD* M29 ....**52** A4
Ellen St *BOL* BL1 ....**18** A4
Elleray Cl *BOLS/LL* BL3 ....**39** E2
Ellerbeck Cl *BOLE* BL2 ....**31** G5
Ellerbeck Crs *WALK* M28 ....**53** G4
Ellesmere Av *WALK* M28 ....**45** G5
Ellesmere Gdns *BOLS/LL* BL3 .....**36** B2
Ellesmere Rd *BOLS/LL* BL3 ....**36** A2
Ellesmere St *BOLS/LL* BL3 ....**2** A6
   FWTH BL4 ....**37** H5
   LHULT M38 ....**45** G5
   SWIN M27 ....**55** F4
   TYLD M29 ....**51** F2
Elliot St *BOL* BL1 ....**18** A4
Elliott St *FWTH* BL4 ....**45** G1
   TYLD M29 ....**51** E3
Ellis Crs *WALK* M28 ....**45** F5
Ellis St *BOLS/LL* BL3 ....**28** C5
Elm Av *RAD* M26 ....**39** H5
Elmbridge Wk *BOLS/LL* BL3 ....**2** A7
Elmfield Av *WALK* M28 ....**54** C4
Elmfield Av *ATH* M46 ....**42** B4
Elmfield St *BOL* BL1 ....**18** D4
   FWTH BL4 ....**45** F4

Elmridge *LEIGH* WN7 ....**50** B5
Elm Rd *BOLS/LL* BL3 ....**38** D3
   FWTH BL4 ....**46** B3
   WHTN BL5 ....**41** C1
Elmstone Gv *BOL* * BL1 ....**28** D1
Elm St *FWTH* BL4 ....**37** H4
   SWIN M27 ....**55** G2
   TYLD * M29 ....**51** G2
Elmwood Cl *WHTN* BL5 ....**43** G1
Elmwood Gv *BOL* * BL1 ....**28** A2
   BOLS/LL * BL3 ....**45** G2
Elsdon Dr *ATH* M46 ....**43** E4
Elsdon Gdns *BOLE* BL2 ....**29** F1
Elsfield Cl *BOL* * BL1 ....**18** B5
Elsham Cl *BOLE* BL2 ....**18** C2
Elsham Dr *WALK* M28 ....**45** F5
Elsinore St *FWTH* BL4 ....**37** G5
Elsinore St *BOLE* BL2 ....**19** F4
Elswick Av *BOLS/LL* BL3 ....**27** H5
Elsworth Dr *BOL* BL1 ....**18** D3
Elterwater Rd *FWTH* BL4 ....**44** C1
Elton Av *BOLS/LL* BL3 ....**36** D5
Elton St *BOLE* BL2 ....**3** H3
Elvington Crs *WALK* M28 ....**53** C3
Ely Cl *WALK* M28 ....**53** F5
Ely Dr *TYLD* M29 ....**52** A4
Ely Gv *BOL* BL1 ....**28** C1
Emblem St *BOLS/LL* BL3 ....**2** B7
Embleton Cl *BOLE* BL2 ....**30** A1
Embsay Cl *BOL* BL1 ....**18** B2
Emerald St *BOL* BL1 ....**18** D4
Emlyn St *FWTH* BL4 ....**37** G4
   SWIN M27 ....**55** F3
Emmanuel Cl *BOLS/LL* BL3 ....**2** B7
Emmanuel Pl *BOLS/LL* BL3 ....**2** B7
Emmett St *HOR/BR* BL6 ....**14** D4
Empire Rd *BOLE* BL2 ....**29** H2
Empress Dr *LEIGH* WN7 ....**51** E5
Empress St *BOL* * BL1 ....**27** H1
Ena Crs *LEIGH* WN7 ....**49** E4
Ena St *BOLS/LL* BL3 ....**37** E2
Endon St *BOL* BL1 ....**27** H1
Endsley Av *WALK* M28 ....**53** G2
Enfield Cl *BOL* BL1 ....**28** C1
   SWIN M27 ....**55** G5
Enfield St *WALK* M28 ....**45** H3
Engine Fold Rd *WALK* M28 ....**45** G4
Engine La *TYLD* M29 ....**43** C4
Engledene *BOL* BL1 ....**18** B1
Ennerdale Av *BOLE* * BL2 ....**30** A1
   SWIN M27 ....**55** H5
Ennerdale Cl *BOLS/LL* BL3 ....**38** B2
Ennerdale Gv *FWTH* BL4 ....**36** C5
Ennerdale Rd *TYLD* M29 ....**51** H4
   WGNE/HIN WN2 ....**40** A3
Enstone Wy *TYLD* M29 ....**52** A2
Enterprise Pk *HOR/BR* BL6 ....**25** E2
Entwisle Rw *FWTH* BL4 ....**37** H5
Entwisle St *FWTH* * BL4 ....**37** H4
   SWIN M27 ....**55** F2
Entwistle St *BOLE* BL2 ....**3** K1
Ephraim's Fold *WGNE/HIN* WN2 ...**23** H4
Epsom Cft *CHLYE* PR6 ....**6** C5
Era St *BOLE* BL2 ....**29** H3
Ernest St *BOLE* BL2 ....**2** A4
Ernlouen Av *BOL* BL1 ....**27** G2
Errington Cl *BOLS/LL* BL3 ....**27** F5
Erskine Cl *BOLS/LL* BL3 ....**27** E5
Eskdale Av *BOLE* BL2 ....**20** B5
   HOR/BR BL6 ....**24** A3
Eskdale Rd *WGNE/HIN* WN2 ....**40** A3
Eskrick St *BOL* BL1 ....**18** B5
Essex Pl *TYLD* M29 ....**43** F5
Essex St *HOR/BR* BL6 ....**25** F1
Essingdon St *BOLS/LL* BL3 ....**36** B1
Esthwaite Dr *TYLD* M29 ....**51** C4
Ethel St *BOLS/LL* BL3 ....**2** A6
Europa Wy *RAD* M26 ....**46** C1
Eustace St *BOLS/LL* BL3 ....**37** E2
Evanstone Cl *HOR/BR* BL6 ....**14** C4
Eva St *LEIGH* WN7 ....**49** E4
Everard Cl *WALK* M28 ....**53** G3
Everbrom Rd *BOLS/LL* BL3 ....**35** G3
Everest Rd *ATH* M46 ....**42** C3
Everleigh Cl *BOLE* BL2 ....**20** A2
Everton St *SWIN* M27 ....**55** G5
Evesham Cl *BOLS/LL* BL3 ....**2** B6
Evesham Dr *FWTH* * BL4 ....**37** F5
Evesham Wk *BOLS/LL* BL3 ....**27** F5
Ewart St *BOL* BL1 ....**18** C5
Ewhurst Av *SWIN* M27 ....**55** F5
Exchange St *BOL* * BL1 ....**2** E4
Exeter Av *BOLE* BL2 ....**19** F5
   FWTH BL4 ....**36** D4
   RAD M26 ....**38** A1
Exeter Dr *WGNE/HIN* WN2 ....**23** H5
Exeter Rd *WGNE/HIN* WN2 ....**40** A3
Exford Dr *BOLE* BL2 ....**30** C4

Factory St *TYLD* M29 ....**51** F2
Factory St East *ATH* M46 ....**42** C5
Factory St West *ATH* M46 ....**42** C5
Fair Acres *BOLE* BL2 ....**20** A4
Fairbairn St *HOR/BR* BL6 ....**14** D5
Fairclough St *BOLS/LL* BL3 ....**36** D1
Fairfield Rd *FWTH* BL4 ....**45** G1
Fairford Dr *BOLS/LL* BL3 ....**28** C5
Fairhaven Av *WHTN* BL5 ....**34** B4
Fairhaven Rd *BOL* BL1 ....**18** D4
Fairhurst Dr *WALK* M28 ....**52** D1
Fairlie Av *BOLS/LL* BL3 ....**27** F5
Fairlyn Cl *WHTN* BL5 ....**43** G1
Fairlyn Dr *WHTN* BL5 ....**43** G1
Fairmount Av *BOLE* BL2 ....**30** A2
Fairmount Rd *SWIN* M27 ....**54** D5
Fairoak Ct *BOLS/LL* BL3 ....**2** A7
Fair St *BOLS/LL* * BL3 ....**36** A3
Fairway Av *BOL* BL2 ....**20** C3
Fairways *HOR/BR* BL6 ....**15** E4
The Fairways *WHTN* BL5 ....**33** F5
Faith St *BOL* BL1 ....**27** F1
Falcon Dr *LHULT* M38 ....**45** E3
Falconwood Cha *WALK* M28 ....**53** F5
Falkirk Dr *BOLE* BL2 ....**30** B4
Falkland Cl *BOLE* BL2 ....**30** C3
Fall Birch Rd *HOR/BR* BL6 ....**25** H2
Fallow Cl *WHTN* BL5 ....**33** G3
Fallowfield Wy *ATH* M46 ....**51** E2
Faraday Dr *BOL* BL1 ....**18** A5
Far Hey Cl *RAD* M26 ....**39** G2
Faringdon Wk *BOLS/LL* * BL3 ....**2** C7
Farland Pl *BOLS/LL* BL3 ....**27** F5
Farleigh Cl *WHTN* BL5 ....**34** A3
Farman St *BOLS/LL* * BL3 ....**36** B2
Farm Av *CHLYE* PR6 ....**6** A4
Farm Cl *TOT/BURYW* BL8 ....**21** H1
Farnborough Rd *BOL* BL1 ....**18** C1
Farndale Sq *LHULT* M38 ....**45** G5
Farnham Cl *BOL* BL1 ....**28** C1
   LEIGH WN7 ....**49** H5
Farnworth St *BOLS/LL* * BL3 ....**36** A1
Faulkner St *BOLS/LL* BL3 ....**28** C5
Fawcetts Fold *WHTN* BL5 ....**33** G1
Fawcett St *BOLE* * BL2 ....**3** K3
Fearney Side *BOLS/LL* BL3 ....**38** B2
Fearnhead Av *HOR/BR* BL6 ....**14** D2
Fearnhead St *BOLS/LL* BL3 ....**36** A1
Felbridge Cl *WHTN* BL5 ....**34** A4
Fells Gv *WALK* M28 ....**54** B2
Fellside *BOLE* BL2 ....**20** C4
Fellside Cl *TOT/BURYW* * BL8 ....**11** H5
Felsted Cl *BOL* BL1 ....**27** E2
Felton Wk *BOL* BL1 ....**18** C5
Fenners Cl *BOLS/LL* BL3 ....**36** B2
Fenwick Cl *WHTN* BL5 ....**41** H2
Fereday St *WALK* M28 ....**45** G4
Fernbray Rd *WGNE/HIN* WN2 ......**40** G4
Fern Cl *ATH* M46 ....**50** D1
Fern Clough *BOL* BL1 ....**27** F3
Ferndown Rd *BOLE* BL2 ....**20** A4
Fernhill Av *BOLS/LL* BL3 ....**35** G1
Fernhills *EDGW/EG* BL7 ....**8** C2
Fernlea Crs *SWIN* M27 ....**55** G4
Fern Lea Gv *LHULT* M38 ....**44** D4
Fernleigh
   HOR/BR
   (off Chorley New Rd) BL6 ....**25** F1
Ferns Gv *BOL* BL1 ....**27** H3
Fernside *RAD* M26 ....**46** D2
Fernside Gv *WALK* * M28 ....**46** A2
Fernstead *BOLS/LL* BL3 ....**28** A4
Fernstone Cl *HOR/BR* BL6 ....**14** C4
Fern St *BOLS/LL* BL3 ....**28** A4
   FWTH BL4 ....**38** A4
Fettler Cl *SWIN* M27 ....**55** G4
Fewston Cl *BOL* BL1 ....**18** C2
Fielders Wy *SWIN* M27 ....**47** G4
Fielding Pl *CHLYE* PR6 ....**6** B4
Field St *WGNE/HIN* WN2 ....**40** A4
Fifth Av *BOL* BL1 ....**27** H5
Fifth St *BOL* BL1 ....**17** F3
Filton Av *BOLS/LL* BL3 ....**2** B7
Finch Av *FWTH* BL4 ....**44** D1
Finlay St *FWTH* * BL4 ....**37** H5
Finney St *BOLS/LL* * BL3 ....**36** D1
Firecrest Cl *WALK* M28 ....**53** F3
Firethorn Cl *WHTN* BL5 ....**33** H3
Firfield Gv *WALK* M28 ....**46** B5
Fir Rd *FWTH* BL4 ....**37** F5
   SWIN M27 ....**55** G5
Firs Rd *WHTN* BL5 ....**34** A3
First Av *ATH* M46 ....**42** D4
   TOT/BURYW BL8 ....**21** H1
Fir St *BOL* BL1 ....**18** D5
First St *BOL* BL1 ....**17** F3
Firswood Dr *SWIN* M27 ....**55** G5
Fir Tree Av *WALK* M28 ....**53** F5
Firwood Av *FWTH* BL4 ....**45** G2
Firwood Gv *BOLE* BL2 ....**19** F5
Firwood La *BOLE* BL2 ....**19** F4
Fitton Crs *SWIN* M27 ....**47** H5
Fitzhugh St *BOL* * BL1 ....**19** E2
Five Quarters *RAD* M26 ....**31** G5
Flapper Fold La *ATH* M46 ....**42** C4
Fleet St *BOLS/LL* BL3 ....**15** F4
Fleetwood Rd *WALK* M28 ....**45** E5
Fletcher Av *ATH* M46 ....**42** D3
Fletcher St *ATH* * M46 ....**42** C5

BOLS/LL BL3 ....**36** A1
BOLS/LL BL3 ....**3** K2
FWTH BL4 ....**38** A4
Flitcroft Ct *BOLS/LL* * BL3 ....**36** A1
Florence Av *BOL* BL1 ....**28** A1
Florence St *BOLS/LL* * BL3 ....**38** A4
Fold Rd *RAD* M26 ....**39** F1
Folds *HOR/BR* BL6 ....**15** F5
Folds Rd *BOL* BL1 ....**16** D5
   BOL BL1 ....**3** G2
Fold St *BOL* * BL1 ....**18** A4
Fold V *EDGW/EG* BL7 ....**8** D4
Fontwell Rd *BOLS/LL* BL3 ....**38** B3
Footman Cl *TYLD* M29 ....**51** H3
Forbes Cl *WGNE/HIN* WN2 ....**40** B4
Fordham Gv *BOL* BL1 ....**27** G1
Ford St *RAD* M26 ....**38** D5
Forest Dr *WHTN* BL5 ....**34** A3
Forester Hill Av *BOLS/LL* BL3 ......**36** B2
Forester Hill Cl *BOLS/LL* BL3 ....**36** B2
Forest Rd *BOL* BL1 ....**18** D3
Forest Wy *BOLE* BL2 ....**20** C4
Forfar St *BOL* BL1 ....**18** D4
Formby Av *ATH* M46 ....**51** E3
Forresters Cl *WGNE/HIN* WN2 .....**40** B4
Forrester St *WALK* M28 ....**53** H3
Forth Pl *RAD* M26 ....**38** D5
Forth Rd *RAD* M26 ....**38** D5
Forton Av *BOLE* BL2 ....**30** C4
Fortune St *BOLS/LL* BL3 ....**38** A3
Fossgill Av *BOL* BL1 ....**18** C1
Foster La *BOLE* BL2 ....**31** G5
Foster St *RAD* M26 ....**38** D5
Foundry St *BOLS/LL* BL3 ....**27** H5
   BOLS/LL BL3 ....**36** B2
Fountain Pk *WHTN* BL5 ....**33** G3
Fountains Av *BOLE* BL2 ....**20** C4
Fountains Cl *TYLD* M29 ....**51** G2
Fourth Av *BOL* BL1 ....**27** H5
Fourth St *BOL* BL1 ....**17** F3
Foxdale Cl *EDGW/EG* BL7 ....**8** D4
Foxendale Wk *BOLS/LL* BL3 ....**2** B7
Foxholes Rd *HOR/BR* BL6 ....**15** F3
Foxley Gv *BOLS/LL* BL3 ....**38** A3
Fox St *HOR/BR* BL6 ....**15** F5
Frances Pl *ATH* M46 ....**42** C4
Frances St *BOL* BL1 ....**28** D1
France St *WHTN* BL5 ....**41** F2
Francis Av *WALK* M28 ....**53** H3
Francis St *FWTH* BL4 ....**38** A4
   LEIGH WN7 ....**49** H5
   TYLD M29 ....**51** G2
Frankford Av *BOL* * BL1 ....**27** H1
Frankford Sq *BOL* * BL1 ....**27** H1
Frank St *BOL* BL1 ....**28** A4
Freckleton Dr *TOT/BURYW* BL8 ...**21** H1
Frederick St *FWTH* BL4 ....**45** G1
Freelands *TYLD* M29 ....**51** G3
Freesia Av *WALK* M28 ....**53** F3
French Gv *BOLS/LL* BL3 ....**38** C3
Freshfield Av *ATH* M46 ....**42** B5
   BOLS/LL BL3 ....**38** C3
Freshfield Gv *BOLS/LL* BL3 ....**38** C3
Freshfield Rd *WGNE/HIN* WN2 ....**40** B4
Freshfields *RAD* M26 ....**46** D2
Friars Cl *TYLD* M29 ....**51** H3
Frinton Rd *BOLS/LL* BL3 ....**38** C3
Frogley St *BOLE* * BL2 ....**29** H3
Frome Cl *TYLD* M29 ....**51** H3
Fryent Cl *HOR/BR* BL6 ....**25** H1
Fulbrook Wy *TYLD* M29 ....**52** A2
Fulmar Cl *WHTN* BL5 ....**43** H1
Fulmere Ct *SWIN* M27 ....**55** G4
Fulwell Av *TYLD* M29 ....**51** H3
Fulwood Ct *TOT/BURYW* BL8 ....**21** H1
Furness Av *BOLE* BL2 ....**20** C4
Furness Crs *LEIGH* WN7 ....**49** H5
Furness Rd *BOL* BL1 ....**27** H1
Furness Sq *BOLE* BL2 ....**20** C4
Furnival St *LEIGH* WN7 ....**49** H5
Furze Av *WHTN* BL5 ....**33** H3
Futura Pk *HOR/BR* BL6 ....**25** E2
Fylde Av *BOLE* BL2 ....**20** C4
Fylde St *FWTH* BL4 ....**37** H4
Fylde St East *FWTH* BL4 ....**37** H4

F

G

Factory Brow *HOR/BR* BL6..............**13** H4
Factory Hl *HOR/BR* BL6 ....**15** F3
Factory La *CHLYE* PR6 ....**6** B4

Gable St *BOLE* BL2 ....**29** H3
Gadbury Av *ATH* M46 ....**51** E2
Gadwall Cl *WALK* M28 ....**53** F3
Gainford Wk *BOLS/LL* BL3 ....**36** B2
Gainsborough Av *BOLS/LL* BL3 ....**36** B2
Galindo St *BOLE* BL2 ....**30** B4
Galloway Cl *BOLS/LL* BL3 ....**35** G1
Galloway Dr *SWIN* M27 ....**55** H5
Galloway Rd *SWIN* * M27 ....**55** H5
Gambleside Cl *WALK* M28 ....**53** F3
Garden La *WALK* M28 ....**45** H3
The Gardens *EDGW/EG* BL7 ....**8** D3
   EDGW/EG BL7 ....**8** D3
Garden St *FWTH* BL4 ....**45** H1
   TYLD M29 ....**51** G2
Garfield Gv *BOLS/LL* BL3 ....**36** B1
Garfield St *BOLS/LL* BL3 ....**36** B1
Gargrave Av *BOL* BL1 ....**18** C1

t St BOL BL1	18 C4
Hall Rd WALK M28	52 C4
a TYLD M29	52 B4
le La HOR/BR BL6	26 D3
e Gv BOL BL1	18 A5
t St BOL BL1	2 C4
ng Dr TOT/BURYW BL8	31 H1
Av ATH M46	42 B5
n Cl LEIGH WN7	49 G2
ood Rd BOLS/LL BL3	36 C3
ere Rd ATH M46	43 F3
k Rd BOL BL1	17 H4
St BOL BL1	2 B1
M27	55 H1
/HIN WN2	40 A1
BOL BL1	2 C4
/EC PR7	12 D1
BL4	37 H4
BR BL6	15 F4
M26...	39 H2
/HIN WN2	40 A4
BL5...	33 H5
na St FWTH BL4	37 F4
a Ct BOLS/LL BL3	35 H3
a St BOLS/LL BL3	35 H5
t St FWTH BL4	38 A5
V BL5...	33 G4
v WALK M28	54 A1
St BOLS/LL BL3	28 B5
d WALK M28	54 D4
r St BOLS/LL BL3	2 A6
Gv WALK M28	45 E5
a WALK M28	45 E5
St BOL BL1	29 C1
Av CHLYE PR6	6 A5
Pl WGNE/HIN WN2	40 B4
Cl WALK M28	53 G2
WALK M28	54 A4
ale St BOLS/LL BL3	29 E5
n WALK M28	53 G1
Gdns BOL BL1	28 A4
Gv BOL BL1	2 A4
La BOLS/LL BL3	28 A4
Rd BOL BL1	28 A4
m Brow HOR/BR BL6	15 F3
n Pk RAD M26	31 G5
Cl BOLS/LL BL3	36 A2
Av BOL BL1	17 E5
n Dr TOT/BURYW BL8	21 C4
Av HOR/BR BL6	25 H2
St BOL BL1	28 A3
e BOL BL1	28 B1
ne Cl BOL * BL1	18 C5
ne Pl FWTH BL4	37 G4
ne Rd BOL BL1	37 G4
ne St BOL BL1	18 C5
St BL5	33 G4
St FWTH BL4	19 F5
le Cl BOLE BL2	19 F5
le La BOLE BL2	29 H1
Cl LEIGH WN7	50 D5
FWTH * BL4	46 A1
bury Rd TYLD M29	51 H4
ury Dr WHTN BL5	33 H3
s Av BOLE BL2	20 C3
St BOL * BL1	3 F2
St BOLE BL2	3 G5
WN7	49 G1
E/HIN WN2	49 E1
BL5...	33 G4
Wy EDGW/EG BL7	9 E3
BOLS/LL BL3	27 H5
BL4	46 D2
M27	55 F3
ott St BOL BL1	18 B5
rk Gdns FWTH BL4	37 H5
rn St BOLS/LL BL3	35 H5
r WHTN BL5	41 F1
St BOLE BL2	30 B4
ttages	
(off Romney Rd) BL1	17 C5
le Dr BOLS/LL BL3	27 F4
le Rd WALK M28	52 D4
von Cl BOLS/LL BL3	35 E1
gles BOLS/LL BL3	35 F5
Sq FWTH BL4	37 F3
rth Dr HOR/BR BL6	26 C4
Av WALK M28	54 A4
aye Gv WGNE/HIN WN2	40 C3
re Av FWTH BL4	37 E3
re Rd TOT/BURYW BL8	11 H2
erk LEIGH WN7	50 A5
e Cl BOL BL1	18 D5
le Dr BOLS/LL BL3	27 F5

Glenside Dr BOLS/LL BL3	36 D3
Glenside Gv WALK M28	46 A4
The Glen BOL BL1	27 E3
Glenthorne St BOL BL1	28 C1
Glentrool Ms BOL BL1	27 G3
Globe La EDGW/EG BL7	8 B1
Glossop Wy WGNE/HIN WN2	40 B4
Gloster St BOLE BL2	3 H3
Gloucester Av HOR/BR BL6	15 F5
Gloucester Crs WGNE/HIN WN2	40 A2
Gloucester Pl ATH M46	42 D4
Gloucester St ATH M46	42 C5
Glover St BOL BL1	14 D3
LEIGH WN7	49 E3
Glynne St FWTH BL4	37 G5
Glynrene Dr SWIN M27	55 E1
Glynwood Pk FWTH BL4	37 G4
Godlee Dr SWIN M27	55 G4
Goldcrest Cl WALK M28	53 F4
Goldrill Av BOLE BL2	30 B2
Goldrill Gdns BOLE BL2	30 B2
Goldsmith St BOLS/LL BL3	36 B1
Gooch St HOR/BR BL6	14 D5
Goodshaw Rd WALK M28	53 G3
Goodwill Cl SWIN M27	55 H4
Goodwin St BOL BL1	18 B1
Goodwood Cl BOLS/LL BL3	38 B2
Goose Cote Hl EDGW/EG BL7	8 C2
Gordon Av BOLS/LL BL3	28 A5
Gordon Rd SWIN M27	55 E5
Gordon St LEIGH WN7	49 H5
Gorse Dr LHULT M38	44 D2
Gorsefield Dr SWIN M27	55 H4
Gorse Rd SWIN M27	55 H5
WALK M28	54 A1
Gorses Dr WGNE/HIN WN2	23 G5
Gorses Mt BOLE BL2	29 C5
Gorses Rd BOLS/LL BL3	29 H5
Gorsey Hey WHTN BL5	41 G1
Gorton Gv WALK M28	45 G3
Gorton St BOLE BL2	3 G5
FWTH BL4	45 F1
Gowanlock's St BOL BL1	18 C5
Gower St BOL BL1	2 A2
FWTH BL4	37 G4
Grace St BOL BL1	14 D3
Grafton St ATH M46	50 A2
BOL BL1	2 A1
CHLY/EC PR7	12 D1
Graham St BOL * BL1	2 E1
Granby Rd SWIN M27	55 E4
Granby St TOT/BURYW BL8	21 H3
Grange Av BOLS/LL BL3	39 E2
SWIN M27	55 F1
Grange Park Rd BOLE BL2	19 G1
Grange Rd BOLE BL2	9 G5
BOLS/LL BL3	27 H5
FWTH BL4	37 E4
WALK M28	52 C4
WGNE/HIN WN2	48 A2
The Grange WHTN BL5	33 E5
Grangewood BOLE BL2	9 G5
Grantchester Pl FWTH BL4	36 D4
Grantchester Wy BOLE BL2	30 A1
Grantham Cl BOL * BL1	28 C1
Grant St FWTH BL4	37 F3
Granville Av BOLS/LL BL3	36 D3
Granville St CHLYE PR6	6 A5
FWTH BL4	37 H4
LEIGH WN7	49 H4
WALK M28	45 G5
WGNE/HIN* WN2	40 A3
Grasmere Av BOLS/LL BL3	38 C1
FWTH BL4	44 D1
SWIN M27	55 E1
WGNE/HIN WN2	40 A4
Grasmere Rd SWIN M27	55 H5
Grasmere St BOL BL1	18 C5
Grasscroft WGNE/HIN WN2	40 C5
Grassington Ct TOT/BURYW BL8	21 G3
Grassington Pl BOLE BL2	29 E1
Grassland Ri LHULT M38	44 C4
Gratten Cl WALK M28	45 G4
Graymar Rd LHULT M38	45 E4
Grayson Rd LHULT M38	45 F4
Gray St BOL BL1	2 D1
Gray St North BOL BL1	2 D1
Graythwaite Rd BOL BL1	17 F5
Great Bank Rd WHTN BL5	33 F3
Great Boys Cl TYLD M29	52 C2
Great Holme BOLS/LL BL3	36 D2
Great Marld Cl BOL BL1	17 F5
Great Moor St BOL BL1	2 D5
Great Stone Cl RAD * M26	39 F2
Great Stones Cl EDGW/EG BL7	8 C2
Grecian St BOLS/LL BL3	36 D1
Green Acre WHTN BL5	41 H1
Green Acre Pk	
BOL (off Howard St) BL1	28 D1
Greenacres EDGW/EG BL7	4 A3
Green Av BOLS/LL BL3	37 F2
LHULT M38	44 C3
SWIN M27	55 H1
Green Bank BOLE BL2	20 A4
Greenbank Av SWIN * M27	55 F5
Greenbank Rd BOLS/LL BL3	27 H5
RAD M26	31 H5
Greenbarn Wy HOR/BR BL6	13 H5
Greenburn Dr BOLE BL2	20 A5

Green Cl ATH M46	51 E2
Green Common La WHTN BL5	42 B2
Greencourt Dr LHULT M38	44 D4
Greendale ATH M46	43 E4
Green Dr HOR/BR BL6	26 C3
Greenfield Cl WHTN BL5	33 F5
Greenfield Rd ATH M46	43 E3
CHLYE PR6	6 A4
Greenfields Cl WGNE/HIN WN2	40 B2
Greenfold Av FWTH BL4	45 F1
Green Fold La WHTN BL5	41 G1
Greengate BOLS/LL BL3	30 B2
Greenhalgh La CHLYE PR6	6 B4
Green Hall Cl ATH M46	43 F3
Greenheys BOLE BL2	20 A4
Greenheys Crs TOT/BURYW BL8	11 G3
Greenheys Rd LHULT M38	44 C2
Greenhill Av BOLS/LL BL3	27 H5
FWTH BL4	45 H3
Greenland Cl TYLD M29	51 H5
Greenland La CHLYE PR6	13 A4
Greenland Rd BOLS/LL BL3	36 D3
TYLD M29	51 H5
Green La BOLS/LL BL3	36 D2
HOR/BR BL6	14 C1
HOR/BR BL6	14 D2
LEIGH WN7	50 C5
WGNE/HIN WN2	40 D3
Greenleach La WALK M28	54 B3
Greenleaf Cl WALK M28	52 D5
Greenleas HOR/BR BL6	26 C4
Green Mdw WHTN BL5	41 F1
Greenmount Cl	
TOT/BURYW BL8	11 H2
Greenmount Ct BOL BL1	27 G2
Greenmount Dr	
TOT/BURYW BL8	11 H1
Greenmount La BOL BL1	27 G2
Greenmount Pk FWTH BL4	46 C2
Greenoak RAD M26	47 E1
Greenoak Dr WALK M28	45 G3
Greenock Cl BOLS/LL BL3	27 E5
Greenough St ATH M46	50 B2
Greenpark Cl TOT/BURYW BL8	11 G3
Greenroyd Av BOLE BL2	20 A5
Greenside Av FWTH BL4	46 B2
Greenside Cl TOT/BURYW BL8	10 D1
Greenside Dr TOT/BURYW BL8	10 D1
Greenside St BOLE BL2	31 E1
Greensmith Wy WHTN BL5	33 G3
Greenstone Av HOR/BR BL6	14 C4
Green St ATH M46	50 A1
BOL BL1	3 F3
CHLYE PR6	6 B4
FWTH BL4	37 G4
TOT/BURYW BL8	21 H3
TYLD M29	51 G2
The Green	
CHLYE (off Chorley Rd) PR6	6 A2
TOT/BURYW BL8	11 H3
Greenthorne Cl EDGW/EG BL7	4 A2
Green Wy BOL BL1	19 F4
Greenway HOR/BR BL6	15 H4
Green Way Cl BOL BL1	19 E5
Greenways LEIGH WN7	50 A5
Greenwood Av LHULT M38	45 G5
Greenwood Cl WALK M28	52 C4
Greenwood La HOR/BR BL6	25 G1
Greenwoods La BOLE BL2	20 B3
Greenwood St FWTH BL4	37 H5
Greenwood V BOL BL1	18 C4
Greenwood V South BOL * BL1	18 D4
Gregory Av ATH M46	42 C3
BOLE BL2	30 A2
Gregory St WGNE/HIN WN2	40 C3
Gregson Fld BOLS/LL * BL3	28 C5
Grenaby Av WGNE/HIN WN2	40 C3
Grendon St BOLS/LL BL3	36 A2
Gresham St BOL BL1	18 D4
Gresley Av HOR/BR BL6	15 E4
Gretna Rd ATH M46	50 A2
Greylag Crs WALK M28	53 H3
Greystoke Dr BOL BL1	18 B1
Greystone Av WGNE/HIN WN2	23 G5
Grierson St BOL BL1	18 C4
Grimeford La CHLYE PR6	13 H1
HOR/BR BL6	13 G2
Grindrod St BOL BL1	39 H1
Grindsbrook Rd RAD M26	31 H3
Grisdale Rd BOLS/LL BL3	27 E5
Grizedale Cl BOL BL1	17 F5
Grosvenor Cl WALK M28	45 G3
Grosvenor Ct WALK M28	45 G3
Grosvenor Rd LEIGH WN7	49 F5
WALK M28	45 G3
Grosvenor St BOLE BL2	3 G6
BOLS/LL BL3	38 C5
FWTH BL4	39 H5
RAD M26	39 H1
SWIN M27	55 H1
Grove Av CHLYE PR6	6 A5
Grove Crs CHLYE PR6	6 A5
Grove Hl WALK M28	52 D5
Grovehurst SWIN M27	55 E5
Grove Ms	
WALK (off Malvern Gv) M28	45 H5
Grove St BOL BL1	2 C4
FWTH BL4	38 A5
The Grove BOLE BL2	3 K7
BOLS/LL BL3	38 D2

Grundy Rd FWTH BL4	46 A1
Grundy St BOLS/LL BL3	36 B1
WALK M28	46 B5
BL5	33 C4
Guido St BOL BL1	18 B5
Guild Av WALK M28	53 H1
Guildford Rd BOL BL1	17 H5
Guild St EDGW/EG BL7	19 F1
Gunters Av WHTN BL5	41 G2

H

Habergham Cl WALK M28	53 G4
Hacken Bridge Rd BOLS/LL BL3	37 H1
Hacken La BOLS/LL BL3	37 G1
Hackford Cl BOL BL1	28 A2
Hadleigh Cl BOL BL1	19 E1
Hadwin St BOL BL1	28 D1
Haigh Rd WGNE/HIN WN2	23 F4
Haigh St BOL BL1	2 E1
Haig Rd WGNE/HIN WN2	23 F3
Haile Dr WALK M28	52 D5
Halbury Wk BOL * BL1	18 D5
Halesfield WGNE/HIN WN2	48 D1
Half Acre RAD M26	31 H4
Half Acre La HOR/BR BL6	23 G1
The Hall Coppice EDGW/EG BL7	8 B2
Hallgate WHTN BL5	41 G3
Hallington Cl BOLS/LL BL3	36 D1
Hall i' th' Wood La BOL BL1	19 E3
Halliwell Rd BOL BL1	18 A4
Halliwell St BOL * BL1	18 B5
Hall La BOLS/LL BL3	38 A2
FWTH BL4	37 H5
HOR/BR BL6	13 G2
HOR/BR BL6	25 C3
Hall Lee Dr WHTN BL5	34 A4
Hallstead Av LHULT M38	44 C4
Hallstead Gv LHULT M38	44 C4
Hall St FWTH BL4	37 H3
RAD M26	31 H4
SWIN M27	55 H1
TOT/BURYW BL8	21 G2
Halsall Dr BOLS/LL BL3	36 C2
Halshaw La FWTH BL4	46 B1
Halstead St BOLE BL2	3 K4
Halton St BOLE BL2	3 K4
Hambleden Cl BOLS/LL BL3	27 F5
Hambledon Cl ATH M46	43 E3
Hambleton Cl TOT/BURYW BL8	31 H4
Hamel St BOLE BL2	36 B2
Hamer St BOLE BL2	29 F1
Hamilton Rd TYLD M29	52 B5
WGNE/HIN WN2	40 C4
Hamilton St ATH M46	50 B1
BOL BL1	18 C3
LEIGH WN7	49 F5
SWIN M27	55 F2
Hamnet Cl BOL BL1	19 E2
Hampson Fold RAD M26	39 H1
Hampson St ATH * M46	42 C5
HOR/BR BL6	14 D3
Hampton Gv LEIGH WN7	51 E4
Hampton Rd BOLS/LL BL3	37 E2
Handel St BOL BL1	18 B4
Hanover Ct	
WALK (off Chatsworth Rd) M28	54 D5
Hanover St BOL BL1	2 C4
LEIGH WN7	50 A5
Harbern Dr LEIGH WN7	49 F1
Harbourne Av WALK M28	53 G3
Harbourne Cl WALK M28	53 G3
Harcourt St WALK M28	45 H3
Hardcastle Cl BOLE BL2	19 C1
Hardcastle Gdns BOLE BL2	19 C1
Hardcastle Rd BOL BL1	18 D5
Harden Dr BOLE BL2	19 E5
Hardie Av FWTH BL4	45 F1
Harding St CHLYE PR6	6 B4
Hardman Cl RAD M26	31 H4
Hardmans EDGW/EG BL7	8 D4
Hardman's La EDGW/EG BL7	8 D4
Hardman St FWTH BL4	46 A1
RAD M26	31 H4
Hardwick Cl BOLS/LL BL3	30 D5
Hardy Cl WHTN BL5	33 G2
Hardy Gv WALK M28	54 B3
Hardy Mill Rd BOLE BL2	20 B3
Harebell Av WALK * M28	44 D5
Harewood Wy SWIN M27	55 H1
Hargreaves St BOL * BL1	18 C5
Harlea Av WGNE/HIN WN2	40 C5
Harlech Av WGNE/HIN WN2	40 A4
Harlesden Crs BOLS/LL BL3	28 A5
Harley Av BOLE BL2	31 F1
Haroldene St BOLE BL2	19 F5
Harold St BOL BL1	18 B5
WGNE/HIN WN2	23 H5
Harper Fold Rd RAD M26	39 H2
Harper Green Rd FWTH BL4	37 H4
Harper's La BOL BL1	17 H5
Harper St FWTH BL4	37 H3
Harpford Cl BOLE BL2	30 C5
Harpford Dr BOLE BL2	30 C5
Harptree Gv LEIGH WN7	49 F4

Harrier Cl WALK M28 53 H3
Harriet St WALK M28 45 H4
Harrison Crs HOR/BR BL6 13 G4
Harrison Rd CHLY/EC PR7 13 E1
Harrison St HOR/BR BL6 14 D3
LHULT M38 45 E4
WGNE/HIN WN2 40 D5
Harris St BOLS/LL BL3 2 B6
Harrop St BOLS/LL BL3 35 G1
WALK M28 45 F5
Harrowby Fold FWTH BL4 37 G5
Harrowby La FWTH BL4 37 G5
Harrowby Rd BOL BL1 17 F5
BOLS/LL* BL3 35 G2
SWIN M27 55 G4
Harrowby St FWTH BL4 37 F5
Harrow Rd BOL BL1 27 H3
Hartford Rd WHTN BL5 41 H2
Hartington Rd BOL BL1 28 A2
Hartland Cl TYLD M29 51 H3
Hartley St HOR/BR BL6 14 D5
Harts Farm Ms LEIGH WN7 49 H3
Hart St TYLD M29 52 A3
WHTN BL5 40 D1
Hartwell Cl BOLE BL2 19 G5
Harvey St BOL BL1 18 B4
Harwood Crs TOT/BURYW BL8 11 G5
Harwood Gv BOLE * BL2 29 F1
Harwood Meadow BOLE BL2 20 B4
Harwood Rd BOLE BL2 20 D3
Harwood V BOLE BL2 20 A4
Haseley Cl BOLS/LL BL3 30 D5
Hasguard Cl BOL BL1 27 F3
Haskoll St HOR/BR BL6 25 F1
Haslam Hey Cl BOLE * BL2 31 E1
TOT/BURYW BL8 21 H5
Haslam St BOLS/LL BL3 28 B5
Hastings Rd BOL BL1 27 H2
Hatfield Rd BOL BL1 28 A1
Hatford Cl TYLD M29 52 A2
Hathaway Ct LEIGH WN7 50 B5
Hathaway Dr BOL BL1 19 E2
Hatton Av ATH M46 42 D3
Hatton Gv BOL BL1 19 E2
Hatton St CHLY/EC PR7 12 D1
Haven Cl RAD M26 31 F5
Haverhill Gv BOLE BL2 19 F5
Havisham Cl HOR/BR BL6 34 B1
Hawarden St BOL BL1 18 C3
Hawes Av FWTH BL4 36 C5
SWIN* M27 55 H5
Haweswater Av TYLD M29 51 H4
Hawfinch Gv WALK M28 53 H3
Hawker Av BOLS/LL BL3 36 B2
Hawkridge Cl WHTN BL5 41 H2
Hawkshaw La TOT/BURYW BL8 4 D3
Hawkshaw St HOR/BR BL6 14 D5
Hawkshead Dr BOLS/LL BL3 35 G2
Hawksheath Cl EDGW/EG BL7 8 C3
Hawksley St HOR/BR BL6 15 F5
Hawkstone Cl BOLE BL2 20 A4
Haworth St TOT/BURYW BL8 21 G3
Hawthorn Av WALK M28 54 A2
WGNE/HIN WN2 40 C5
Hawthorn Cl TYLD M29 52 B2
Hawthorn Crs TOT/BURYW BL8 11 H5
Hawthorne Av FWTH BL4 37 F5
HOR/BR BL6 25 G1
Hawthorne Dr WALK M28 54 C4
Hawthorne Gv LEIGH * WN7 49 G4
Hawthorne Rd BOLS/LL BL3 35 H1
Hawthorne St BOLS/LL * BL3 27 H5
Hawthorn Rd FWTH BL4 46 D3
WHTN BL5 41 H1
Haydock Dr WALK M28 53 F5
Haydock La EDGW/EG BL7 9 E4
Haydock St BOL BL1 2 E1
Hayes St LEIGH WN7 49 G4
Hayfield Av TYLD M29 52 A5
Hayfield Cl TOT/BURYW BL8 11 H3
Haymill Av LHULT M38 45 E2
Haynes St BOLS/LL BL3 35 H2
Haysbrook Av LHULT M38 44 D4
Hayward Av BOLS/LL BL3 39 E2
Hazel Av LHULT M38 44 C3
RAD M26 38 C5
TOT/BURYW BL8 21 H2
WHTN BL5 41 H1
Hazeldene WHTN BL5 41 F3
Hazelfields WALK M28 54 D4
Hazel Gv FWTH BL4 37 F5
LEIGH WN7 49 G4
RAD M26 39 H5
Hazelhurst Cl BOL BL1 18 C5
Hazelhurst Fold WALK M28 55 E4
Hazelhurst Rd WALK M28 54 D4
Hazelmere Gdns
WGNE/HIN WN2 40 A4
Hazel Mt EDGW/EG BL7 8 C2
Hazel Rd ATH M46 42 C4
Hazelwood Av BOLE BL2 20 A4
Hazelwood Rd BOL BL1 17 H5
Hazlemere FWTH BL4 46 C1
Headingley Wy BOLS/LL BL3 36 B2
Heaplands TOT/BURYW BL8 11 H3
Heap St BOLS/LL BL3 36 C1
Heapy Cl TOT/BURYW BL8 21 H5
Heath Cl BOLS/LL BL3 35 H3
Heather Bank
TOT/BURYW * BL8 11 G5
Heather Cl HOR/BR BL6 14 D3
Heatherfield BOL BL1 18 B2
EDGW/EG BL7 4 A3
Heather Gv LEIGH WN7 49 G4
Heathfield BOLE BL2 20 B3
FWTH BL4 38 A4
Heathfield Dr BOLS/LL BL3 35 H3
TYLD M29 52 B2
Heath Gdns WGNE/HIN WN2 41 E5
Heathlea WGNE/HIN WN2 49 E1
Heathside Gv WALK M28 45 H5
Heaton Av BOL BL1 27 F1
BOLE BL2 20 A2
BOLS/LL BL3 38 C1
FWTH BL4 37 G5
Heaton Court Gdns BOL BL1 27 E3
Heaton Grange Dr BOL * BL1 27 G3
Heaton Mt BOL BL1 27 F1
Heaton Rd BOLS/LL BL3 30 D5
HOR/BR BL6 26 C5
Heatons Gv WHTN BL5 34 A3
Heaton St WGNE/HIN WN2 23 H4
Heaviley Gv HOR/BR BL6 14 C2
Hebble Cl BOLE BL2 19 F2
Hedley St BOL BL1 18 A5
The Heights HOR/BR BL6 25 F1
Helen St FWTH BL4 37 H5
Helias Cl LHULT M38 44 D5
Helmclough Wy WALK M28 53 G3
Helmsdale WALK M28 53 G1
Helmsdale Av BOLS/LL BL3 27 F4
Helsby Gdns BOL BL1 18 D3
Helston Wy TYLD M29 52 A3
Hemley Cl WHTN BL5 41 F2
Hemsworth Rd BOL BL1 2 B1
Henderson Av SWIN M27 55 H2
Hendon Gv LEIGH WN7 49 H3
Hendon St LEIGH WN7 49 H3
Hen Fold Rd TYLD M29 52 A4
Hengist St BOLE BL2 29 G3
Henley Gv BOLS/LL BL3 36 A2
Henley St WGNE/HIN WN2 23 F4
Henniker Rd BOLS/LL BL3 35 G3
Henniker St SWIN M27 55 G5
WALK M28 53 H2
Hennon St BOL BL1 28 B1
Henrietta St BOLS/LL BL3 35 H1
Henry Herman St BOLS/LL BL3 35 G2
Henry Lee St BOLS/LL * BL3 36 A2
Henry St BOLS/LL BL3 3 G6
TYLD M29 51 G2
Henshaw Wk BOL BL1 18 C5
Herbert St BOLS/LL BL3 38 D2
HOR/BR BL6 14 C3
RAD M26 31 H5
WHTN BL5 33 G3
Hereford Dr SWIN M27 55 H5
Hereford Rd BOL BL1 27 H2
WGNE/HIN WN2 40 B2
Hereford St BOL BL1 18 D5
Herevale Gra WALK M28 53 F4
Heron Av FWTH BL4 36 D5
Heron's Wy BOLE BL2 3 G6
Hertford Dr TYLD M29 43 G5
Hesketh Av BOL BL1 18 D2
Hesketh Cl ATH M46 42 C5
Hesketh St ATH M46 42 D4
Heswall Dr TOT/BURYW BL8 21 G2
Hewlett St BOLE * BL2 3 G4
WHTN BL5 40 D1
Hexham Av BOL BL1 27 F1
Hexham Cl ATH M46 43 E4
Heys Av SWIN M27 55 E1
Heys Cl North SWIN M27 55 E1
Hey Willow BOLE BL2 9 G5
Heywood Gdns BOLS/LL BL3 36 C1
Heywood Park Vw BOLS/LL BL3 28 C5
Heywood's Hollow BOL BL1 18 D4
Heywood St BOL BL1 2 E1
BOLS/LL BL3 38 D2
SWIN M27 55 G3
Hibbert St BOL BL1 18 D5
Hibernia St BOLS/LL BL3 28 A5
High Av BOLE * BL2 30 A3
High Bank ATH M46 43 G2
EDGW/EG BL7 8 D5
High Bank La HOR/BR BL6 26 B2
High Bank St BOLE BL2 29 G3
High Beeches BOLS/LL BL3 30 D5
Highbridge Cl BOLE BL2 30 C4
Highbury Cl WHTN BL5 41 F2
Highcrest Gv TYLD M29 52 B2
Higher Ainsworth Rd RAD M26 31 G3
Higher Barn HOR/BR BL6 15 H4
Higher Bridge St BOL BL1 2 E1
Higher Damshead WHTN BL5 33 H5
Higher Darcy St BOLS/LL BL3 29 G5
Higher Dean St RAD M26 39 G2
Higher Drake Meadow
WHTN BL5 41 F3
Higher Dunscar EDGW/EG BL7 8 C3
Higher Highfield Ct
WGNE/HIN (off Haigh Rd) WN2 23 F4
Higher Market St FWTH BL4 38 A5
Higher Ridings EDGW/EG BL7 8 C4
Higher Shady La EDGW/EG BL7 9 G5
Higher Southfield WHTN BL5 41 G1
Higher Swan La BOLS/LL BL3 36 B1
Highfield Av ATH M46 43 E3
BOLE BL2 20 C4
WALK M28 52 C3
Highfield Cl CHLYE PR6 6 A5
Highfield Dr FWTH BL4 45 E1
Highfield Gv WGNE/HIN WN2 23 G5
Highfield Rd BOL BL1 17 H5
CHLYE PR6 6 A5
FWTH BL4 36 C5
HOR/BR BL6 24 A1
LHULT M38 44 D3
Highfield Rd North CHLYE PR6 6 A4
Highfield St FWTH BL4 46 C2
Highgate BOLS/LL BL3 34 C3
Highgate Dr LHULT M38 44 C3
Highgate La LHULT M38 44 C3
Highgrove Cl BOL BL1 18 D4
The Highgrove BOL BL1 26 D1
High Houses
BOL (off Belmont Rd) BL1 18 B1
Highland Rd EDGW/EG BL7 9 F4
HOR/BR BL6 25 G1
Highmeadow RAD M26 39 H4
High Mdw EDGW/EG BL7 9 F4
High Mt BOLE BL2 20 A4
High Rid La HOR/BR BL6 26 B1
High Stile St FWTH BL4 46 A1
High St ATH M46 42 D5
BOLS/LL BL3 36 C1
BOLS/LL BL3 38 D2
HOR/BR BL6 14 D3
TOT/BURYW BL8 21 H4
TYLD M29 51 F2
WALK M28 45 G5
High View St BOL BL1 18 C2
BOLS/LL* BL3 36 A1
Highwood Cl BOLE * BL2 30 B1
Highworth Cl BOLS/LL * BL3 28 C5
Hilary Av ATH M46 42 C3
Hilary Gv FWTH BL4 45 G1
Hilda Av TOT/BURYW BL8 21 H1
Hilda St BOLS/LL BL3 37 E1
LEIGH WN7 49 E5
Hilden St BOLE BL2 3 H5
Hillbank Cl BOL BL1 18 A4
Hill Cot Rd BOL BL1 18 D2
Hill Crs LEIGH WN7 49 E3
Hill Crest ATH M46 43 F3
Hill Crest Av LEIGH WN7 49 E3
Hillcrest Rd TYLD M29 52 B3
Hillfield Dr BOLE BL2 19 F5
WALK M28 53 E4
Hillfield Wk BOLE BL2 29 F1
Hill La BOLE BL2 3 H1
HOR/BR BL6 13 F4
Hillsdale Gv BOLE BL2 20 A4
Hill Side BOL BL1 27 F3
Hillside Av ATH M46 43 E4
EDGW/EG BL7 9 F5
FWTH BL4 45 G1
HOR/BR BL6 15 E3
HOR/BR BL6 24 A1
WALK M28 45 G4
Hillside Cl BOLE BL2 20 A2
BOLS/LL BL3 34 D3
Hillside Crs HOR/BR BL6 15 E3
Hillside St BOLS/LL BL3 28 B5
Hillstone Cl TOT/BURYW BL8 11 H2
Hill St RAD M26 39 H1
TOT/BURYW* BL8 21 H3
Hill Top ATH M46 43 F3
BOLS/LL BL3 38 C1
Hilltop Dr TOT/BURYW BL8 21 G1
Hill Top Rd WALK M28 45 H4
Hillview Rd BOL * BL1 18 C3
Hilly Cft EDGW/EG BL7 8 D4
Hilmarton Cl BOLE BL2 20 A2
Hilton Av HOR/BR BL6 14 C4
Hilton Crs WALK M28 53 F5
Hilton Gv WALK M28 45 F5
Hilton La WALK M28 53 F1
Hilton Pl WGNE/HIN WN2 23 G4
Hilton St BOLE BL2 29 G3
LHULT M38 45 E4
Hinchcombe Cl LHULT * M38 45 E2
Hinchley Wy SWIN M27 55 H1
Hindburn Dr WALK M28 53 E3
Hindles Cl ATH M46 50 A1
Hindley Mill La WGNE/HIN WN2 40 A1
Hindley Rd WHTN BL5 41 F3
Hindsford St ATH M46 51 F2
Hind St BOLE BL2 29 H3
Hinkler Av BOLS/LL BL3 36 C2
Hirst Av WALK M28 45 G3
Hoade St WGNE/HIN WN2 40 A1
Hobart St BOL BL1 18 B5
Hodge Rd WALK M28 53 H1
Hodson Rd SWIN M27 55 G1
Holbeach Cl WGNE/HIN WN2 40 A4
Holbeck Cl HOR/BR BL6 25 F2
Holborn Av LEIGH WN7 49 H3
RAD M26 39 F1
Holbrook Av LHULT M38 45 E2
Holcombe Cl FWTH BL4 46 C2
Holcombe Ct
TOT/BURYW * BL8 11 H2
Holcombe Crs FWTH BL4 46 C2
Holcombe Old Rd
TOT/BURYW BL8 11 H1
Holcombe Rd BOLS/LL BL3 38 B2
TOT/BURYW BL8 11 H1
Holden Av BOL BL1 18 C1
Holden Lea WHTN BL5
Holder Av BOLS/LL BL3
Holdsworth St SWIN M27
Holhouse La TOT/BURYW BL8
Holland St BOL BL1
The Hollies
ATH (off Bolton Old Rd) M46
WGNE/HIN (off Holly Rd) WN2
Hollin Acre WHTN BL5
Hollin Hey Rd BOL BL1
Hollinhurst Dr HOR/BR BL6
Hollins
FWTH (off Plodder La) BL4
Hollins Cl TYLD M29
Hollins Rd WGNE/HIN WN2
Hollins St BOLE BL2
Hollinswood Rd BOLE BL2
WALK M28
Holloway Dr WALK M28
Hollowell La HOR/BR BL6
Hollow Mdw RAD M26
Holly Av WALK M28
Hollybank St RAD M26
Hollycroft Av BOLE BL2
Hollydene
WGNE/HIN
(off St Davids Crs) WN2
Holly Dene Dr HOR/BR BL6
Holly Gv BOL BL1
FWTH BL4
LEIGH WN7
Hollyhurst WALK M28
Holly Mill Crs BOL BL1
Holly Rd SWIN M27
WGNE/HIN WN2
Holly St BOL BL1
TOT/BURYW BL8
Hollywood Rd BOL BL1
Holmbrook TYLD M29
Holmebrook Dr HOR/BR BL6
Holmes Cottages
BOL (off Temple Rd) BL1
Holmes St BOLS/LL BL3
Holmeswood Rd BOLS/LL BL3
Holmfield Gn BOLS/LL BL3
Holthouse Rd TOT/BURYW BL8
Holt St BOLS/LL BL3
LEIGH WN7
SWIN M27
TYLD M29
Holy Harbour St BOL * BL1
Holyhurst Wk BOL * BL1
Holyoake Rd WALK M28
Holyrood Dr SWIN M27
Hondwith Cl BOLE BL2
Honeybourne Cl TYLD M29
Honiton Cl LEIGH WN7
Honiton Dr BOLE BL2
Honiton Gv RAD M26
Hood Cl TYLD M29
Hooton St BOLS/LL BL3
Hope Av BOLE BL2
BOLE BL2
LHULT M38
Hopefield St BOLS/LL BL3
Hope Fold Av ATH M46
Hopefold Dr WALK M28
Hope Hey La LHULT M38
Hope St CHLYE PR6
HOR/BR BL6
LEIGH WN7
LHULT M38
WGNE/HIN WN2
WGNE/HIN WN2
Hope St North HOR/BR BL6
Hopwood Av HOR/BR BL6
Horace St BOL BL1
Horeb St BOLS/LL BL3
Horkers Nook WHTN BL5
Hornby Dr BOLS/LL BL3
Hornby Gv LEIGH WN7
Hornsea Cl TOT/BURYW BL8
Horridge Fold EDGW/EG BL7
Horridge Fold Av WHTN BL5
Horrobin Fold
EDGW/EG (off Horrobin La) BL7
Horrobin La CHLYE PR6
EDGW/EG BL7
Horrocks Fold Av BOL BL1
Horrocks St ATH M46
Horsa St BOLE BL2
Horseshoe La EDGW/EG BL7
Horsfield St BOLS/LL BL3
Horsham Cl WHTN BL5
Horton Av BOL BL1
The Hoskers WHTN BL5
Hospital Rd EDGW/EG BL7
Hotel St BOL BL1
Hough Fold Wy BOLE BL2
Hough La EDGW/EG BL7
TYLD M29
Hough St BOLS/LL BL3
TYLD M29
Houghton St BOLS/LL BL3
LEIGH WN7
Houldsworth St RAD M26
Hove Cl TOT/BURYW BL8
Hove St BOLS/LL BL3
Hove St North BOLS/LL * BL3
Howard Av BOLS/LL BL3

BL4 ....46 B1
.t BOL BL1 ....28 D1
h Av WALK M28 ....55 E4
h Fold
/EG
ackburn Rd) BL7 ....8 B1
h St FWTH BL4 ....45 H1
BL5 ....33 H5
dge Cl WALK M28 ....53 G3
ugh Cl WALK M28 ....54 B1
ugh Dr WALK M28 ....54 B1
ft Cl BOL BL1 ....51 E2
ft St BOLS/LL BL3 ....28 B5
ridge Cl ATH M46 ....50 A2
ft North BOL BL1 ....2 E3
ft South BOL * BL1 ....2 E4
Av BOLE BL2 ....19 F3
Rd BOLS/LL BL3 ....35 H2
den Ct
URYW
klees St BL8.......................11 H5
Av HOR/BR BL6 ....14 C3
BL4 ....18 A5
pus St BOL BL1 ....19 E2
t FWTH BL4 ....37 F3
v LEIGH WN7 ....49 E5
Rd BOLE BL2 ....20 A1
BL4 ....47 E2
WN7 ....49 E5
....................................47 E1
St BOL BL1 ....3 F1
Av WALK M28 ....45 F5
r BOLS/LL BL3 ....35 G2
a BOLS/LL BL3 ....35 G2
· Rd TYLD M29 ....52 A4
Hill Av BOLS/LL BL3 ....35 F3
s Gn TOT/BURYW BL8 ....11 H1
ld Dr TOT/BURYW BL8 ....11 H3
don Wk BOL * BL1 ....18 C5
yde Av BOLE BL2 ....29 F1
ATH M46 ....42 D5
n Rd BOLS/LL BL3 ....36 B3
WHTN BL5.........................43 F1
ld Rd WALK M28 ....53 F3
een Cl RAD M26 ....31 H2
: BOLS/LL BL3....................36 A2
M28 ....45 G2
ood BOL BL1 ....18 B2
ood Ct BOLS/LL BL3 ....37 F1
Av WALK M28......................52 D5
t BOL BL1 ....18 A5
Rd CHLY/EC PR7 ....13 E1
WALK M28 ....53 G1
r WALK M28 ....53 G1
WALK M28 ....53 G1
BOLS/LL * BL3 ....36 A2
t BOLE BL2 ....3 K3
t BOLS/LL * BL3 ....35 G1

I
se Cl WALK M28 ....44 D5
t BOL BL1 ....18 A4
Dr WGNE/HIN WN2 ....32 B2
Dr LEIGH WN7 ....50 D5
OL BL1 ....27 F1
dent St BOLS/LL BL3 ....38 C2
al St WHTN BL5 ....41 H1
y St BOL BL1 ....3 F4
Rd HOR/BR BL6 ....25 G2
St LEIGH WN7 ....49 G3
WALK M28..........................34 A2
ne Gv BOL * BL1 ....17 G5
old WALK M28 ....53 F4
n Cl BOLE BL2.....................19 H3
e St BOL BL1 ....3 F4
l WALK M28 ....55 F2
g Dr BOLE BL2 ....30 C3
l Av BOL BL1 ....27 H2
Cl WHTN BL5 ....41 H2
BOLE BL2 ....19 G5
WTH BL4.............................37 E4
BOL BL1 ....18 C4
BOL BL1 ....18 D4
HOR/BR BL6 ....15 E5
v WALK M28 ....53 E5
: LEIGH WN7 ....49 H5
· BOL BL1 ....18 C5
v LHULT M38 ....45 F4
: RAD M26 ....46 C1
: BOL BL1 ....28 A2
s BOLS/LL BL3 ....28 B5
od St LEIGH WN7 ....49 G3
Ct FWTH BL4 ....37 G3
: St BOLS/LL BL3 ....37 G2
Rd BOL BL1 ....18 C2
WTH BL4.............................37 F5
M38 ....44 D4
OL BL1 ....28 A1
BL5 ....41 H1
OLS/LL BL3 ....36 A1

J
Jackdaw Rd TOT/BURYW BL8....11 H2
Jack's La WHTN BL5 ....40 C1
Jackson St FWTH BL4 ....37 H5
  WALK M28..........................45 G4
Jack St BOLE BL2 ....29 G1
James St ATH M46 ....51 E2
  BOLS/LL BL3......................38 D2
  EDGW/EG BL7 ....9 F4
  FWTH BL4 ....38 B5
  HOR/BR BL6 ....14 B4
  TYLD M29 ....51 F3
  WHTN BL5 ....33 G3
Jauncey St BOLS/LL BL3 .....28 A5
Jedburgh Av BOL BL1 ....27 H2
Jesmond Rd BOL BL1 ....17 H3
Jessie St BOLS/LL BL3 ....28 A5
Jethro St BOLE BL2 ....3 K2
  BOLE BL2 ....19 G3
John Brown St BOL * BL1 ......2 C2
John Cross St BOLS/LL BL3 ..28 A5
Johnson Av WGNE/HIN WN2....48 A2
Johnson Fold Av BOL BL1 ....17 E5
Johnson St ATH M46 ....50 A2
  BOL BL1 ....3 F5
  TYLD M29 ....51 G2
John St BOLS/LL * BL3 ....38 D2
  EDGW/EG BL7 ....9 E5
  FWTH BL4 ....38 A5
  TYLD M29 ....45 G1
  WALK M28...........................45 H4
  WGNE/HIN WN2...................40 D5
Jolly Brows BOLE BL2 ....19 H4
Jones St HOR/BR BL6 ....14 D3
Jonquil Dr LHULT M38 ....52 D1
Joseph St FWTH BL4 ....37 H4
Jubilee Houses
  WALK (off Tynesbank) M28 ....45 G5
Julia St BOL BL1 ....14 D3
Junction Rd BOLS/LL BL3 .....27 F5
Junction Rd West HOR/BR BL6....26 C5
June Av LEIGH WN7 ....49 E5
Juniper Cl BOL BL1 ....28 C1
Juniper Dr WGNE/HIN WN2 ....40 B5
Jury St LEIGH WN7 ....49 G4
Jutland Gv WHTN BL5 ....33 G4

K
Kayfields BOLE BL2 ....20 A3
  BOL BL1 ....3 F2
  BOLS/LL BL3........................38 C2
Kay St ATH M46 ....50 D1
Kearsley Dr BOLS/LL BL3.....37 F2
Kearsley Hall Rd RAD M26 ...47 E1
Kearsley Rd RAD M26 ....39 F5
Kearsley V RAD M26 ....38 D5
Keats Crs RAD M26..............39 G1
Keats Rd TOT/BURYW BL8 ....11 H2
Keats St LEIGH WN7 ....49 F4
Keble Gv LEIGH WN7 ....49 E3
Keighley Cl TOT/BURYW BL8....21 H5
Keighley St BOL BL1 ....18 A5
Keilder Ms BOL BL1 ....27 G2
Kellets Rw
  WALK (off Argyle Av) M28 ......45 H3
Kellett St EDGW/EG BL7 ......18 D1
Kempnough Hall Rd WALK M28....54 A4
Kempston Gdns BOL BL1 ......18 C5
Kempton Av BOLS/LL BL3 .....38 C3
Kendal Gv WALK M28 ....54 B1
Kendal Rd BOL BL1 ....28 A2
  TOT/BURYW BL8 ....11 H2
  WALK M28...........................52 C4
  WGNE/HIN WN2...................40 A3
Kendal Rd West
  TOT/BURYW BL8 ....11 H2
Kendrew Rd BOLS/LL BL3 .....35 G1
Kenilworth Cl RAD M26 ....31 H4
Kenilworth Dr LEIGH WN7 .....51 E4
  WGNE/HIN WN2...................40 B4
Kenilworth Sq BOL BL1 ....27 H1
Kenmay Av BOLS/LL BL3 ......27 F4
Kennedy Dr BOLS/LL BL3 .....39 E2
Kennedy Rd TYLD M29 ....52 B1
Kennet Cl WHTN BL5 ....33 G4
Kenneth Av LEIGH WN7 ....49 F5
Kenneth Gv LEIGH WN7 ....49 F5
Kennet Wy LEIGH WN7 ....49 H4
Kennington Fold BOLS/LL BL3....36 B2
Kensington Av RAD M26 ....39 F1
Kensington Ct
  BOL (off Dawson La) BL1 ....2 B2
Kensington Dr HOR/BR BL6 ...15 E4
  LEIGH WN7 ....51 E4
Kensington St BOL BL1 ....2 C3
Kensworth Cl BOL * BL1 ....28 B1
Kensworth Dr BOL BL1 ....28 B1
Kent Cl WALK M28 ....53 E1
Kent Dr FWTH BL4 ....46 D2
Kent St BOL BL1 ....2 D2
Kentford Rd BOL BL1 ....28 C1
Kentmere Dr TYLD M29.........51 H4
Kentmere Gv FWTH BL4 ....44 D1

Kentmere Rd BOLE BL2.........30 B1
Kenton Cl BOL BL1 ....28 B1
Kent Rd ATH M46 ....42 C4
  TYLD M29 ....51 F1
Kentsford Dr BOLS/LL BL3 ....30 D5
Kent St BOL BL1 ....2 D1
  SWIN M27...........................55 H1
Kenwood Rd BOL BL1 ....17 H4
Kenyon Av BOLS/LL BL3 ....38 A3
Kenyon Rd BOLS/LL BL3 ......30 D5
Kenyon St LEIGH WN7 ....49 F3
Kenyon Ter TYLD M29 ....44 C5
Kenyon Wy LHULT M38 ....44 C5
  TOT/BURYW BL8 ....21 H2
Kerans Dr WHTN BL5 ....33 G2
Kermishaw Nook TYLD M29....51 G5
Kermoor Av BOL BL1 ....18 C1
Kerry Gv BOLE BL2 ....3 K1
Kersal Av LHULT M38 ....45 F4
Kershaw Av BOLS/LL BL3 .....38 C1
Kershaw St BOLE BL2 ....19 G2
  BOLS/LL BL3 ....2 B7
  TYLD M29 ....51 G2
Kestor St BOLE BL2 ....3 H2
Kestrel Av FWTH * BL4 ....44 D1
  LHULT M38 ....45 E3
Kestrel St BOL * BL1 ....18 D2
Keswick Rd WALK M28 ....54 B1
Keswick St BOL BL1 ....18 D5
Kibbles Brow EDGW/EG BL7....9 F4
Kilbride Av BOLE BL2 ....30 B4
Kilburn Clqse LEIGH WN7 .....49 F2
Kilburn Rd RAD M26 ....39 F1
Kildale Cl BOLS/LL BL3 ....35 E1
Kildare Rd SWIN M27 ....55 G4
Kildare St FWTH BL4 ....45 G1
Kildonan Dr BOLS/LL BL3 .....27 F4
Killingworth Ms HOR/BR * BL6....25 F1
Kilmaine Dr BOLS/LL BL3 .....27 E5
Kilmory Dr BOLE BL2 ....30 B4
Kiln Brow EDGW/EG BL7 ....9 G4
Kiln Fld EDGW/EG BL7 ....8 D4
The Kilnhin HOR/BR BL6 ....26 B2
Kilsby Cl FWTH BL4 ....37 F5
  HOR/BR BL6 ....26 C4
Kilworth Dr HOR/BR BL6........26 D4
Kimberley Rd BOL BL1 ....18 C2
Kimble Cl TOT/BURYW BL8 ....11 H2
Kincraig Cl BOLS/LL BL3 ....35 E1
Kingfisher Dr FWTH BL4 ....44 D1
Kingholm Gdns BOL * BL1 .....28 B1
Kingsbridge Av BOL * BL1 .....31 F1
Kingsbury Rd BOL BL1 ....27 F1
Kingscourt Av BOL BL1 ....18 A5
King's Crs TYLD M29 ....51 E3
Kingsdown Dr BOL BL1 ....28 C1
Kingsdown Gdns BOL BL1 .....28 D1
Kingsfield Wy TYLD M29 ....51 H3
Kingsgate BOL * BL1 ....2 D3
Kingsland Rd FWTH BL4 ....36 D4
Kingsley Rd SWIN M27 ....45 G4
  WALK M28...........................45 H4
  WGNE/HIN* WN2.................40 B3
Kingsley St BOL BL1 ....18 B5
  LEIGH WN7 ....49 E4
Kingston Av BOLE BL2 ....29 G1
King St BOL BL1 ....2 D3
  BOLE BL2 ....19 H2
  EDGW/EG BL7 ....8 D4
  FWTH BL4 ....37 H5
  HOR/BR BL6 ....14 C3
  WHTN BL5 ....33 H5
Kingsway FWTH BL4 ....46 B3
  WALK M28...........................53 H3
Kingswear Dr BOL BL1 ....28 A1
Kingthorpe Gdns BOLS/LL * BL3....36 C1
King William St TYLD M29 ....51 F2
Kingwood Av BOL BL1 ....27 F2
Kinloch Dr BOL BL1 ....27 H3
Kinnerly Gv WALK M28 ....53 E2
Kinross Dr BOLS/LL BL3 ....27 E5
Kinsley Dr WALK M28 ....53 G1
Kintyre Dr BOLS/LL BL3 ....27 E5
Kipling Cv LEIGH WN7 ....49 F4
Kirby Av ATH M46 ....42 C3
Kiribati Wy LEIGH WN7 ....49 G5
Kirkby Rd BOL BL1 ....27 H2
Kirkebrok Rd BOLS/LL BL3 ....35 G1
Kirkfell Dr TYLD M29 ....51 H4
Kirkhall La BOL BL1 ....28 A1
  LEIGH WN7 ....49 G4
Kirkham St BOLE BL2 ....29 G1
  LHULT M38 ....45 E3
Kirkhope Dr BOL BL1 ....28 B1
Kirkhope Wk BOL BL1 ....28 B1
Kirklands BOLE BL2 ....19 H5
Kirklees St TOT/BURYW BL8....12 A1
Kirkpatrick St WGNE/HIN WN2....40 D5
Kirkstile Pl WHTN BL5 ....47 G4
Kirkstone Av WALK M28 ....54 B1
Kirkwall Dr BOLE BL2 ....3 K7
Kitchener St BOLS/LL BL3 .....37 F2
Kittiwake Cl TYLD M29 ....51 G4
Kiveton Cl WALK M28 ....53 E1
Knaresborough Rd
  WGNE/HIN WN2...................40 A4
Knight St BOL BL1 ....2 E1
Knightswood BOLS/LL BL3 ....35 F2
Knott La BOL BL1 ....17 F5

Knotts Brow EDGW/EG BL7 .....4 B5
Knowles Edge St BOL BL1 ....18 A5
Knowles St BOL BL1 ....29 E1
Knowsley Av ATH M46 ....42 C4
Knowsley Dr WGNE/HIN WN2....55 F5
Knowsley Gv HOR/BR BL6 .....25 F1
Knowsley Rd BOL BL1 ....17 H5
  BOLE BL2 ....31 E1
Knowsley St BOL BL1 ....2 E3
Knutshaw Crs BOLS/LL BL3....34 D3
Kylemore Av BOLS/LL BL3 ....27 H5

L
Laburnum Av ATH M46 ....43 E5
  LEIGH WN7 ....49 G3
  SWIN M27 ....55 G5
  TOT/BURYW BL8 ....11 H5
Laburnum Gv HOR/BR BL6 ....25 G1
  TYLD M29 ....52 B2
Laburnum Pk BOLE BL2 ....19 F2
Laburnum Rd FWTH BL4 ....37 F5
  WALK M28...........................54 A1
Laburnum St ATH M46 ....43 E5
  BOL BL1 ....2 A2
Ladybridge Av WALK M28 .....53 G3
Lady Bridge La BOL BL1 ....27 F3
Ladyhill Vw WALK M28 ....53 G3
Ladymere Dr WALK M28 ....53 F3
Ladyshore Rd BOLS/LL BL3 ..39 E5
Ladywell Av LHULT M38 ....45 E4
Ladywell Gv LHULT M38 ....45 E4
Lakelands Dr BOLS/LL BL3 ....27 F5
Lakenheath Cl BOL BL1 ....10 D1
Lakenheath Dr BOL BL1 ....18 D1
Lake Side LEIGH WN7 ....49 F5
Lakeside Av BOLS/LL BL3 .....37 E3
  WALK M28...........................45 H3
Lake St BOLS/LL * BL3 ....28 C5
  LEIGH WN7 ....50 A5
Lambeth Cl HOR/BR BL6 ....15 F4
Lambeth St ATH M46 ....42 B5
Lambley Cl LEIGH WN7 ....49 F3
Lambourn Cl BOLS/LL BL3 .....3 C7
Lambton Rd WALK M28 ....55 E4
Lambton St BOLS/LL BL3 .....36 A3
Lancaster Av ATH M46 ....42 D5
  FWTH BL4 ....36 D5
  HOR/BR BL6 ....15 F5
  TYLD M29 ....43 G5
Lancaster Cl BOL BL1 ....3 G4
  CHLYE PR6 ....6 B5
Lancaster Dr BOLS/LL BL3 ....38 D1
Lancaster Pk CHLYE PR6 ....6 A4
Lancaster Rd WGNE/HIN WN2....40 A3
Lancaster St RAD * M26 ....39 G2
Lancaster Wk BOL * BL1 ....18 C5
Lanchester Dr BOLS/LL BL3 ....2 A6
Landedmans WHTN BL5 ....41 H1
Landrace Dr WALK M28 ....53 F5
Lane North BOLS/LL * BL3 .....35 H1
The Lane BOL BL1 ....26 D3
Langdale Dr WALK M28 ....54 B2
Langdale Rd WGNE/HIN WN2....40 A3
Langdale St BOLS/LL BL3 .....36 C2
  FWTH BL4 ....45 G1
Langdon Cl BOL BL1 ....2 B1
Langford Gdns BOLS/LL BL3....36 C1
Langham Cl BOL BL1 ....19 E1
Langholm Dr BOLE BL2 ....30 B4
Langley Dr WALK M28 ....52 C5
Langley Platt La ATH M46 .....50 C3
Langshaw Rd BOLS/LL BL3 ...28 A5
Langshaw Wk BOLS/LL * BL3....28 A5
Langside Dr BOLS/LL BL3 .....35 E1
Langstone Cl HOR/BR BL6 ....14 D4
Langthorne Wk BOLS/LL BL3....2 A6
Langtree Cl WALK M28 ....53 E5
Langworthy Av LHULT M38 ....45 F4
Lansdowne Cl BOLE * BL2 .....29 F1
Lansdowne Rd ATH M46 ....43 F5
  BOLE BL2 ....19 F5
Larch Av SWIN M27 ....55 E5
Larch Gv ATH M46 ....42 C4
  SWIN M27............................54 D1
Larch Rd LEIGH WN7 ....49 G3
Larchwood St BOL BL1 ....18 D5
Larkfield Av LHULT M38 ....44 D3
Larkfield Cl TOT/BURYW BL8....11 G2
Larkfield Gv BOLE BL2 ....3 K1
Lark Hl FWTH BL4 ....45 H1
Larkside Av WALK M28 ....46 A5
Lark St BOL BL1 ....3 F2
  FWTH BL4 ....45 G1
Latham Rd HOR/BR BL6 ....13 G4
Latham St BOL BL1 ....18 D5
Launceston Rd RAD M26 ....31 F5
  WGNE/HIN WN2...................41 E5
Laurel Cl BOL BL1 ....2 E1
Laurel Crs WGNE/HIN WN2 ...40 C5
Laurel Dr LHULT M38 ....45 E4
Laurel Gv LEIGH WN7 ....49 G3
Laurel St BOL BL1 ....28 A3
  TOT/BURYW BL8 ....21 H1
Lauria Ter BOLE BL2 ....31 F1
Lavender Rd FWTH BL4 ....37 E4

Lavender St *RAD* M26 ....39 F2
Lawefield Crs *SWIN* M27 ....47 F3
Lawn Dr *SWIN* M27 ....55 G4
Lawn St *BOL* BL1 ....28 A1
Lawnswood Dr *TYLD* M29 ....52 B2
Lawson Av *LEIGH* WN7 ....49 G2
Lawson Cl *WALK* M28 ....55 E4
Lawson Rd *BOL* BL1 ....18 A5
   HOR/BR BL6 ....15 E3
Lawson St *BOL* BL1 ....18 C3
Laxey Av *ATH* M46 ....51 E1
Laxey Crs *LEIGH* WN7 ....49 E4
Laxford Gv *BOLS/LL* BL3 ....27 E3
Laycock Av *BOLE* BL2 ....19 F4
Layfield Cl *TOT/BURYW* BL8 ....11 F4
Layton Dr *FWTH* BL4 ....46 B2
Lazonby Av *WGNE/HIN* WN2 ....32 B2
Leach St *BOLS/LL* BL3 ....28 C5
   FWTH BL4 ....38 A4
Leaconfield Dr *WALK* M28 ....54 B4
Leacroft Av *BOLE* BL2 ....29 H5
Leafield *TYLD* M29 ....52 A2
Leafield Dr *WALK* M28 ....53 E5
Lea Gate Cl *BOLE* BL2 ....19 H2
Leaside Av *WALK* M28 ....46 A5
Lea Thorn *BOLE* BL2 ....19 H3
Leckenby Cl *WALK* M28 ....54 B4
Lecturers Cl *BOLS/LL* BL3 ....2 E7
Ledbury St *LEIGH* WN7 ....49 H4
Lee Av *BOLS/LL* BL3 ....36 B2
Lee Bank *WHTN* BL5 ....34 A5
Lee Fold *TYLD* M29 ....52 A3
Lee Ga *BOLE* BL2 ....19 H2
Lee Gv *FWTH* BL4 ....36 D5
Leek St *RAD* M26 ....39 G2
Lee La *HOR/BR* BL6 ....14 C3
Lees Rd *CHLYE* PR6 ....6 A3
Lees St *SWIN* M27 ....55 H2
Lee St *ATH* M46 ....50 D5
Leewood *SWIN* M27 ....47 F4
Le Gendre St *BOLE* BL2 ....19 F5
Leicester Av *HOR/BR* BL6 ....14 C4
   WGNE/HIN WN2 ....40 B2
Leicester Rd *TYLD* M29 ....51 G1
Leigh La *TOT/BURYW* BL8 ....11 G5
Leigh Rd *ATH* M46 ....50 A3
   LEIGH WN7 ....49 H4
   WALK M28 ....53 E5
   WGNE/HIN WN2 ....48 D2
   WHTN BL5 ....33 H5
Leigh St *FWTH* BL4 ....37 H5
   TOT/BURYW BL8 ....21 H4
   WGNE/HIN WN2 ....32 B2
   WGNE/HIN WN2 ....48 D2
   WHTN BL5 ....33 G4
Leighton Av *ATH* M46 ....42 B5
   BOL BL1 ....27 H2
Leighton St *ATH* M46 ....42 B5
Leinster Rd *SWIN* M27 ....55 G4
Leinster St *FWTH* BL4 ....37 G5
Le Mans Crs *BOL* BL1 ....2 E4
Lemon St *TYLD* M29 ....51 F3
Lena St *BOL* BL1 ....18 D5
Lenham Gdns *BOLE* BL2 ....30 A4
Lennox Gdns *BOLS/LL* BL3 ....27 F5
Leonard St *BOLS/LL* BL3 ....36 C2
Leslie St *BOLE* BL2 ....29 F1
Lester Rd *LHULT* M38 ....44 C3
Letitia St *HOR/BR* BL6 ....14 C4
Leven Cl *FWTH* BL4 ....46 D3
Levens Dr *BOLE* BL2 ....30 A1
Lever Bridge Pl *BOLS/LL* BL3 ....29 H5
Lever Dr *BOLS/LL* BL3 ....28 C5
Lever Edge La *BOLS/LL* BL3 ....36 A3
Lever Gv *BOLS/LL* BL3 ....3 G7
Lever Hall Rd *BOLE* BL2 ....29 H5
Leverhulme Av *BOLS/LL* BL3 ......37 E2
Lever Park Av *HOR/BR* BL6 ....14 C2
Lever St *BOLS/LL* BL3 ....3 G7
   BOLS/LL BL3 ....38 C1
   RAD M26 ....31 H5
   TYLD M29 ....51 F3
   WHTN BL5 ....33 G2
Levi St *BOL* BL1 ....27 F1
Lewis Cl *CHLY/EC* PR7 ....12 C1
Leybourne St *BOL* BL1 ....18 C5
Ley Crs *TYLD* M29 ....51 H5
Ley Rd *TYLD* M29 ....51 H5
Leyton St *FWTH* BL4 ....36 D4
Library St *WHTN* BL5 ....33 H5
Libra St *BOL* BL1 ....18 B5
Lichfield Av *BOLE* BL2 ....19 F5
   TYLD M29 ....52 A4
Lichfield Cl *FWTH* BL4 ....37 E4
Lichfield Dr *SWIN* M27 ....55 H5
Lichfield Rd *RAD* M26 ....31 F5
Lidgett Cl *WALK* M28 ....45 G3
Lightbounds Rd *BOL* BL1 ....17 F4
Lightbourne Av *SWIN* M27 ....55 H4
Lightburne Av *BOL* BL1 ....27 H3
Lightwood *WALK* M28 ....53 F3
Lightwood Cl *FWTH* BL4 ....38 A4
Lilac Av *LEIGH* WN7 ....49 G5
Lilford Av *ATH* M46 ....50 B1
Lilly St *BOL* BL1 ....2 A1
Lily Av *FWTH* BL4 ....37 F4
Lime Av *LEIGH* WN7 ....49 G5
   SWIN M27 ....55 E5

Limefield Av *FWTH* BL4 ....37 H4
Limefield Cl *BOL* BL1 ....17 C3
Limefield Rd *BOL* BL1 ....17 H3
   RAD M26 ....39 F2
Lime Gv *WALK* M28 ....53 H2
   WGNE/HIN WN2 ....40 B5
Limestale Cl *BOLS/LL* BL3 ....30 D5
Lime St *ATH* M46 ....40 D5
   FWTH BL4 ....38 A5
   TYLD M29 ....51 F2
Linacre Av *BOLS/LL* BL3 ....36 C3
Lincoln Av *BOLS/LL* BL3 ....38 C2
Lincoln Cl *TYLD* M29 ....51 G1
Lincoln Gv *WGNE/HIN* WN2 ....23 H5
Lincoln Gv *BOLE* BL2 ....20 B3
Lincoln Rd *BOL* BL1 ....27 H2
   BOL BL1 ....28 A2
   WGNE/HIN WN2 ....40 A3
Lindale Av *BOL* BL1 ....27 F2
Lindale Cl *WALK* M28 ....52 C4
Lindale Rd *WALK* M28 ....52 C4
Linden Av *ATH* M46 ....50 B1
   BOLS/LL BL3 ....30 C5
   SWIN M27 ....55 F4
Linden Gv *LEIGH* WN7 ....49 G4
Linden Ms *WALK* M28 ....52 D5
Linden Rd *WALK* M28 ....52 D5
   WGNE/HIN WN2 ....40 A1
Linden Wk *BOLE* BL2 ....19 F2
Lindfield Dr *BOL* BL1 ....28 C1
Lindisfarne Pl *BOLE* BL2 ....19 G5
Lindley St *BOLS/LL* * BL3 ....38 D2
   FWTH BL4 ....46 B2
Lindrick Ter *BOLS/LL* BL3 ....28 B5
Lindsay Av *SWIN* M27 ....55 G4
Lindsay St *HOR/BR* BL6 ....25 F1
Lindsay Ter *WGNE/HIN* WN2 ......23 F5
Linfield Cl *BOLE* BL2 ....19 H3
Ling Dr *ATH* M46 ....50 D1
Lingfield Cl *FWTH* BL4 ....45 G1
Lingmell Cl *BOL* BL1 ....27 F2
Lingmoor Dr *TYLD* M29 ....51 H4
Lingmoor Rd *BOL* BL1 ....27 F1
Linkfield Dr *WALK* M28 ....52 D5
Links Dr *HOR/BR* BL6 ....26 B3
Links Rd *BOLE* BL2 ....20 C3
   HOR/BR BL6 ....26 B3
The Linkway *HOR/BR* BL6............25 F2
Linnet's Wood Ms *WALK* M28 ....46 A5
Linslade Gdns *BOLS/LL* BL3 ....2 C7
Linstock Wy *WALK* M28 ....42 A5
Linthorpe Wk *BOLS/LL* BL3 ....35 H1
Lion La *HOR/BR* BL6 ....13 C5
Liscard St *ATH* M46 ....42 B5
Lismore Av *BOLS/LL* BL3 ....27 F5
Lister St *BOLS/LL* BL3 ....35 H2
Litchfield Gv *WALK* M28 ....54 D4
Litherland Rd *BOLS/LL* BL3 ....36 C3
Littlebourne Wk *EDGW/EG* BL7 .19 E1
Little Brow *EDGW/EG* BL7 ....9 E5
Little Factory St *TYLD* M29 ....51 F2
Littlegate *WHTN* BL5 ....41 G3
Little Harwood Lee *BOLE* BL2 ....19 H4
Little Holme Wk *BOLS/LL* BL3 ...36 D1
Little Mdw *EDGW/EG* * BL7 ....8 D5
Little Moor Clough
   EDGW/EG BL7 ....8 C2
Little Moss La *SWIN* M27 ....55 H1
Little Pasture *LEIGH* WN7 ....49 F4
Little Scotland *HOR/BR* BL6 ....13 F5
Little Stones Rd *EDGW/EG* BL7 ...8 C2
Liza St *LEIGH* WN7 ....49 G3
Lloyd Ct
   LEIGH (off Jury St) WN7 ....49 C4
Lobelia Av *FWTH* BL4 ....37 E4
Lock La *HOR/BR* BL6 ....34 C1
Lodge Dr *TYLD* M29 ....51 H5
Lodge Gv *ATH* M46 ....50 C5
Lodge La *ATH* M46 ....50 D2
Lodge Rd *ATH* M46 ....51 E4
Loen Crs *BOL* BL1 ....18 A4
Logan St *BOL* BL1 ....18 C2
Lomax's Buildings *BOL* BL1 ....3 F5
Lomax St *BOL* BL1 ....3 F5
Lombard St *ATH* M46 ....42 B5
Lomond Pl *BOLS/LL* BL3 ....27 E4
London St *BOLS/LL* BL3 ....36 C1
Long Cswy *ATH* M46 ....50 B4
Longcliffe Wk *BOL* * BL1 ....18 D5
Longden St *BOL* BL1 ....28 A2
Longfellow Av *BOLS/LL* BL3 ....35 H2
Longfield Rd *BOLS/LL* BL3 ....35 H3
Longford Av *BOL* BL1 ....18 A5
Longhirst Cl *BOL* BL1 ....17 H4
Longhurst Rd *WGNE/HIN* WN2 ..40 B4
Long La *BOLE* BL2 ....29 H5
   WGNE/HIN WN2 ....40 C3
   WHTN BL5 ....40 C3
Longley Dr *WALK* M28 ....54 D5
Longley St *WALK* M28 ....53 H1
Long Meadow *BOLE* BL2 ....9 G5
Longridge *EDGW/EG* BL7 ....8 C2
Longridge Crs *BOL* BL1 ....17 F5
Longridge Dr *TOT/BURYW* BL8 ..31 H2
Longshaw Av *SWIN* M27 ....55 H2
Longshaw Dr *WALK* M28 ....53 F2
Longshaw Ford Rd *BOL* BL1 ....17 F2
Longsight *BOLE* BL2 ....19 H2

Longsight La *BOLE* BL2 ....19 H3
Longson St *BOL* BL1 ....29 E1
Long St *SWIN* M27 ....55 H4
Longtown Gdns *BOL* * BL1 ....18 C5
Longview Dr *SWIN* M27 ....55 E2
Longwall Av *WALK* M28 ....53 G3
Longworth Av *HOR/BR* BL6 ....13 G4
Longworth Clough
   EDGW/EG BL7 ....8 B2
Longworth La *EDGW/EG* BL7 ....8 B4
Longworth Rd *EDGW/EG* BL7 ......8 A1
   HOR/BR BL6 ....15 E3
Longworth St *BOLE* BL2 ....29 G3
Lonsdale Rd *BOL* BL1 ....28 C4
Lord Av *ATH* * M46 ....51 E2
Lord Gv *ATH* M46 ....51 F2
Lords Fold
   BOL (off New Church Rd) BL1 ..17 F5
Lord's Stile La *EDGW/EG* BL7 ......9 F5
Lord St *ATH* M46 ....51 E2
   BOLS/LL BL3 ....38 D2
   FWTH BL4 ....38 A5
   HOR/BR BL6 ....14 D3
   TYLD M29 ....51 F5
   WHTN BL5 ....33 G4
Lorne St *FWTH* BL4 ....37 G3
Lorton St *WALK* M28 ....52 D5
Lorton Gv *BOLE* BL2 ....30 B2
Lostock Junction La
   HOR/BR BL6 ....26 C4
Lostock La *HOR/BR* BL6 ....25 C4
Lostock Park Dr *HOR/BR* BL6 ....26 A3
Lostock Rd *WHTN* BL5 ....33 E1
Lottery Rw *BOL* BL1 ....3 F4
Loughrigg Cl *TYLD* M29 ....51 H4
Louisa St *BOL* BL1 ....18 B5
   WALK M28 ....45 H4
Louise Gdns *WHTN* BL5 ....41 G2
Louvaine Av *BOL* BL1 ....17 F3
Lovalle St *BOL* BL1 ....28 A1
Lovat Rd *BOLE* BL2 ....30 B3
Lovers' La *ATH* M46 ....49 H1
Lowe Av *ATH* M46 ....51 F2
Lower Bridgeman St
   BOLS/LL BL3 ....3 G6
Lowercroft Rd *TOT/BURYW* BL8 ..21 H5
Lower Darcy St *BOLS/LL* BL3 .....29 G5
Lower Drake Fold *WHTN* BL5 ......41 F3
Lower Goodwin Cl *BOLE* BL2 ......20 A5
Lower Hill Dr *CHLYE* PR6 ....6 A3
Lower House Dr *HOR/BR* BL6 .....26 C3
Lower House Wk *EDGW/EG* BL7 ...9 E4
Lower Landedmans *WHTN* BL5 ..41 H1
Lower Leigh Rd *WHTN* BL5 ....41 H3
Lower Makinson Fold
   HOR/BR * BL6 ....25 F1
Lower Marlands *EDGW/EG* BL7 ...8 D4
Lower Md *EDGW/EG* BL7 ....8 D3
Lower New Rw *WALK* M28 ....53 E2
Lower Rawson St *FWTH* BL4 ......38 A4
Lower Southfield *WHTN* BL5 ......41 G1
Lower St *FWTH* BL4 ....46 B3
Lower Sutherland St *SWIN* M27 .55 G3
Lower Tong *EDGW/EG* BL7 ....8 D5
Lowerwood La *BOLE* BL2 ....29 F1
Lowe St *RAD* M26 ....39 H1
Loweswater Av *TYLD* M29 ....51 G4
Loweswater Rd *FWTH* BL4 ....44 C1
Low Gn *ATH* M46 ....43 F3
Lowick Av *BOLS/LL* BL3 ....37 E2
Lowndes St *BOL* BL1 ....27 H2
Lowry Dr *SWIN* M27 ....55 H2
Lowry Wk *BOL* BL1 ....28 B1
Lowside Av *HOR/BR* BL6 ....26 C4
Lowstern Cl *EDGW/EG* BL7 ....8 C3
Lowther Dr *LEIGH* WN7 ....51 E3
Lowther St *BOLS/LL* BL3 ....37 E3
Loxham St *FWTH* BL4 ....37 H3
Lucas Rd *FWTH* BL4 ....37 E5
Luciol Cl *TYLD* M29 ....52 A2
Lucy St *BOL* BL1 ....27 G1
Ludlow Av *WGNE/HIN* WN2 ....40 C4
Ludlow Dr *LEIGH* WN7 ....50 D4
Lulworth Av *WGNE/HIN* WN2 ......40 C4
Lulworth Rd *BOLS/LL* * BL3 ....35 G2
Lumber La *WALK* M28 ....54 A3
Lumsden St *BOLS/LL* BL3 ....3 G2
Lum St *BOL* BL1 ....3 G2
Lumwood *BOL* BL1 ....17 H4
Lupin Av *FWTH* BL4 ....37 E4
Luton St *BOLS/LL* BL3 ....42 B5
Luton St *BOLS/LL* BL3 ....37 E1
Lydbrook Cl *BOL* BL1 ....2 C5
Lydford Gdns *BOLE* BL2 ....30 B5
Lydgate Av *BOLE* BL2 ....30 A2
Lydiate Cl *BOLS/LL* BL3 ....36 D2
Lymbridge Dr *HOR/BR* BL6 ....13 H5
Lymefield Dr *WALK* M28 ....53 E4
Lymm Cl *WALK* M28 ....45 E5
Lyndale Av *SWIN* M27 ....55 H2
Lyndene Av *WALK* M28 ....54 C3
Lyndon Cl *TOT/BURYW* BL8 ....21 H1
Lynsted Av *BOLS/LL* BL3 ....37 E3
Lynstock Wy *HOR/BR* BL6 ....25 G4
Lynton Av *SWIN* M27 ....55 H1
Lynton Crs *WALK* M28 ....53 H5
Lynton Rd *BOLS/LL* BL3 ....36 A3
   SWIN M27 ....55 H2
   TYLD M29 ....52 B3
   WGNE/HIN WN2 ....40 B2

Lynwood Av *BOLS/LL* BL3 ....
Lynwood Gv *ATH* M46 ....
   BOLE BL2
Lyon Gv *WALK* M28
Lyon Rd *FWTH* BL4
Lyon St *SWIN* M27
Lytton St *BOL* BL1

M

Mabel Av *BOLS/LL* BL3 ....
   WALK M28
Mabel's Brow *FWTH* BL4 ....
Mabel St *BOL* BL1
   WHTN BL5
Macdonald Av *FWTH* BL4 ....
Mackenzie Gv *BOL* BL1 ....
Mackenzie St *BOL* BL1 ....
Madams Wood Rd *WALK* M28 .....
Madeley Gdns *BOL* BL1 ....
Maden St *TYLD* M29
Maesbrook Dr *TYLD* M29 ....
Mafeking Rd *BOLE* * BL2 ....
Maidstone Cl *WGNE/HIN* WN2 ....
Makants Cl *ATH* M46 ....
   TYLD M29
Makinson Av *HOR/BR* BL6 ....
Makinson La *HOR/BR* BL6 ....
Maldon Cl *BOLS/LL* BL3 ....
Maldon Crs *SWIN* M27 ....
Maidwyn Av *BOLS/LL* BL3 ....
Mallard Dr *HOR/BR* BL6 ....
Mallet Crs *BOL* BL1
Mallison St *BOL* BL1
Mallowdale *WALK* M28 ....
Mallowdale Cl *BOL* BL1 ....
Maltby Dr *BOLS/LL* BL3 ....
Malton Av *BOLS/LL* BL3 ....
Malton Cl *LEIGH* WN7 ....
Malton Rd *WALK* M28 ....
Malvern Av *ATH* M46 ....
   BOL BL1
   WGNE/HIN WN2
Malvern Cl *FWTH* BL4 ....
   HOR/BR BL6
Malvern Gv *WALK* M28 ....
Manchester Rd *BOLS/LL* BL3 ......
   FWTH BL4
   HOR/BR BL6
   SWIN M27
   TYLD M29
   WALK M28
   WHTN BL5
Manchester Rd East *WALK* M28...
Manchester Rd West
   LHULT M38
Mancroft Av *BOLS/LL* * BL3 ....
Mancroft Ter *BOLS/LL* BL3 ....
Mandley Cl *BOLS/LL* BL3 ....
Mandon Cl *RAD* M26
Manley Av *SWIN* M27
Manley Cl *LEIGH* WN7 ....
Manley Crs *WHTN* BL5 ....
Manley Ter *BOL* * BL1 ....
Manningham Rd *BOLS/LL* BL3 ....
Manor Av *BOLS/LL* BL3 ....
Manorfield Cl *BOL* BL1 ....
Manor Gate Rd *BOLE* BL2 ....
Manor Gv *WGNE/HIN* WN2 ....
Manorial Dr *LHULT* M38 ....
Manor Rd *HOR/BR* BL6 ....
   SWIN M27
   TYLD M29
   WGNE/HIN WN2
Manor St *BOL* BL1
   FWTH BL4
Mansell Wy *HOR/BR* BL6 ....
Mansfield Gv *BOL* BL1 ....
Maple Av *ATH* M46
   BOL * BL1
   HOR/BR BL6
   WGNE/HIN WN2
Maple Cl *FWTH* BL4
Maplefield Dr *WALK* M28 ....
Maple Gv *WALK* M28
Maple Rd *FWTH* BL4
   SWIN M27
Maple St *BOLE* BL2
   BOLS/LL BL3
Maplewood Gdns *BOL* * BL1 ....
Maplewood House *BOL* BL1 ....
Marcus St *BOL* BL1
Mardale Av *SWIN* M27 ....
Mardale Cl *ATH* M46 ....
   BOLE BL2
Mardale Dr *BOL* BL1
Mardale Rd *SWIN* M27 ....
Maria St *BOL* BL1
Marion St *BOLS/LL* BL3 ....
Market Pl *CHLY/EC* PR7 ....
Market St *ATH* M46
   BOLS/LL BL3
   CHLY/EC PR7
   FWTH BL4
   RAD M26
   TOT/BURYW BL8

M29 .....51 F2
 BL5 .....33 G5
nd Hl BOL BL1 .....27 E2
nd Hill La BOL BL1 .....27 F1
nds Rd HOR/BR BL6 .....15 G2
nd St BOL BL1 .....2 E5
 WALK M28 .....52 D4
rough Gdns FWTH BL4 .....36 D5
rough Rd ATH M46 .....43 E4
rough St BOL BL1 .....2 A2
 Dr WHTN BL5 .....41 G3
ok Ms
ok (off Marlbrook Dr) BL5 .....41 H3
ok Wk BOLS/LL 36 D1
rs BOL BL1 .....17 F5
 CI BOLE BL2 .....30 B1
 Ct CHLY/EC PR7 .....12 D1
 Dr SWIN M27 .....55 G5
od Rd BL BL1 .....17 F5
 nd Gv BOLS/LL BL3 .....35 E1
 Av BOL BL1 .....19 E3
 BOLS/LL BL3 .....36 A2
n Rd BOL BL1 .....2 D3
 n St WALK M28 .....52 D5
 BL5 .....33 G5
n Rd WHTN BL5 .....33 G4
ank WHTN BL5 .....33 G4
rook CI WGNE/HIN WN2 .....40 C2
rook Fold WHTN BL5 .....40 C1
ale Rd BOL BL1 .....27 F2
old La BOL BL1 .....28 A2
a FWTH BL4 .....37 E5
od BOLS/LL BL3 .....38 C1
 M38 .....2 D3
Rw WGNE/HIN WN2 .....40 C4
st HOR/BR BL6 .....14 C3
M28 .....46 B1
 BL5 .....33 G4
EDGW/EG * BL7 .....4 A3
 CI HOR/BR BL6 .....25 H2
St BOLS/LL BL3 .....36 B1
Av BOLS/LL BL3 .....39 E2
 BL4 .....44 D1
ale Gdns BOL BL1 .....18 C5
Gv FWTH BL4 .....46 B1
clough HOR/BR BL6 .....26 C4
 Ct WGNE/HIN WN2 .....40 C2
st ATH * M46 .....42 D5
 Dr ATH M46 .....43 F4
 Av BOLE BL2 .....29 G2
r ATH M46 .....43 E5
od CI RAD M26 .....38 C5
ilton Ct WHTN BL5 .....34 A5
d Av BOLE BL2 .....29 H3
 FWTH BL4 .....46 B2
M29 .....51 G2
East HOR/BR BL6 .....14 D3
West HOR/BR BL6 .....14 C3
y CI BOL BL1 .....8 C5
d Av LEIGH WN7 .....49 F4
26 .....39 G1
d Dr FWTH BL4 .....45 F1
d Rd BOLS/LL BL3 .....38 D1
Gdns BOLS/LL BL3 .....2 C6
a ATH M46 .....51 E1
 St EDGW/EG * BL7 .....4 C4
 BR BL6 .....14 C4
or La HOR/BR BL6 .....15 H3
Fold Rd WALK M28 .....53 F2
St ATH M46 .....42 D5
 BL4 .....38 A5
 CI ATH M46 .....50 D1
 BL4 .....38 A4
ws Av FWTH BL4 .....46 B1
 BOLE BL2 .....19 G2
 Gdns LHULT M38 .....45 G5
ey St BOL BL1 .....2 E4
 St BOL BL1 .....18 C5
 LEIGH WN7 .....49 F5
k BOLS/LL BL3 .....36 B1
ck BOLS/LL BL3 .....28 A5
 HOR/BR BL6 .....15 F4
d RAD M26 .....39 F1
 Dr ATH M46 .....43 F4
 BOLE BL2 .....19 H2
 Av BOLS/LL BL3 .....37 F2
 PR6 .....6 A5
 BL4 .....45 G1
M27 .....55 E5
 .....45 H5
d Houses
off Mount Sion Rd) M26 .....39 G3
 St ATH M46 .....42 C5
 Dr WALK M28 .....54 C3
 st BOLS/LL BL3 .....2 B5
BOLE BL2 .....3 H4
/EG BL7 .....4 A3
 BOLS/LL BL3 .....29 H5
 a St BOL BL1 .....18 A4
 St BOL BL1 .....18 D5
 St BOLS/LL BL3 .....37 E1
nd BOLS/LL BL3 .....36 C3
ne Gv BOL BL1 .....18 D3
vbank Av ATH M46 .....43 E4
vbank Rd BOLS/LL BL3 .....35 H3
vbrook CI HOR/BR BL6 .....34 C2
v CI BOLS/LL BL3 .....38 D3
vcroft RAD M26 .....31 H5

WHTN BL5 .....41 H1
Meadowfield HOR/BR BL6 .....26 B3
Meadowfield Dr WALK M28 .....53 F5
Meadowgate WALK M28 .....54 B3
Meadow La BOLE BL2 .....30 C3
Meadow Pit La WGNE/HIN WN2 .....23 F4
Meadowside Av BOLE BL2 .....29 G2
 WALK M28 .....46 A4
Meadowside Gv WALK M28 .....46 A5
Meadowside Rd WGNE/HIN WN2 .....40 C4
Meadows La BOLE BL2 .....20 B4
The Meadows RAD M26 .....31 G5
Meadow St CHLYE PR6 .....13 E1
The Meadow Wk FWTH BL4 .....37 E5
Meadow Wy HOR/BR BL6 .....24 A1
 TOT/BURYW BL8 .....21 G1
Meads Gv FWTH BL4 .....36 B5
 TYLD M29 .....52 A5
Meadway TYLD M29 .....52 B2
Meadway Rd HOR/BR BL6 .....15 F4
Mealhouse Ct ATH M46 .....42 C5
Mealhouse La ATH M46 .....42 C5
 BOL * BL1 .....2 E3
Meanley Rd TYLD M29 .....51 E4
Meanley St TYLD M29 .....51 E4
Medlock St FWTH BL4 .....37 F5
Medway Dr FWTH BL4 .....46 D3
 HOR/BR BL6 .....15 F4
Medway Rd WALK M28 .....53 F3
Megfield WHTN BL5 .....41 G2
Melbourne CI HOR BR BL6 .....15 E4
Melbourne Gv HOR/BR BL6 .....15 E4
Melbourne Rd BOLS/LL BL3 .....27 H5
Melbury Dr HOR/BR BL6 .....25 H1
Meliden Crs BOL * BL1 .....27 H1
Melling CI
 CHLYE (off Bolton Rd) PR6 .....6 A3
Mellor Dr WALK M28 .....53 C2
Mellor Gv BOL BL1 .....27 H1
Melrose Av BOL BL1 .....27 G1
 LEIGH WN7 .....49 F2
Melrose Gdns RAD M26 .....31 G5
Melrose Rd BOLS/LL BL3 .....38 B2
 RAD M26 .....31 G5
Meltham PI BOLS/LL * BL3 .....36 A1
Melton Ct TYLD M29 .....51 H3
 WALK M28 .....53 C1
Melton St RAD M26 .....39 H1
Melville Rd FWTH BL4 .....46 B2
Melville St BOLS/LL BL3 .....37 E1
Memorial Cottages
 SWIN (off Manchester Rd) M27 .....47 H5
Memorial Rd WALK M28 .....45 H5
Menai Rd BOLS/LL * BL3 .....35 H1
Mendip CI BOLE BL2 .....30 C3
 HOR/BR BL6 .....15 E2
Mendip Dr BOLE BL2 .....30 C4
Mercia Rd BOLS/LL BL3 .....28 A5
Mereclough Av WALK M28 .....54 B2
Meredew Av SWIN M27 .....55 G5
Meredith St BOLS/LL BL3 .....36 D2
Merefold HOR/BR BL6 .....14 B4
Mere Fold WALK M28 .....45 F5
Mere Gdns BOL BL1 .....2 C1
Merehall CI BOL BL1 .....2 C1
Merehall Dr BOL BL1 .....2 C1
Merehall St BOL BL1 .....28 B1
Meremanor WALK M28 .....54 B2
Mereside Gv WALK M28 .....46 A5
Mere Wk BOL BL1 .....2 C1
Meriden CI RAD M26 .....31 H4
Meriden Gv HOR/BR BL6 .....26 C4
Merlewood Dr SWIN M27 .....55 E5
 TYLD M29 .....51 H3
Merlin Gv BOL BL1 .....27 H1
Merrion St FWTH BL4 .....37 G3
Mersey CI WGNE/HIN WN2 .....41 E5
Merton CI BOLS/LL * BL3 .....28 A5
Merton Gv TYLD M29 .....52 A5
Mesne Lea Gv WALK * M28 .....54 A3
Mesne Lea Rd WALK M28 .....54 A3
Metal Box Wy WHTN BL5 .....33 H3
Metcalfe Ct
 LHULT
 (off Manchester Rd West) M38 .....44 D4
Metfield PI BOL BL1 .....28 A2
Methwold St BOLS/LL * BL3 .....36 A1
The Mews BOL BL1 .....27 H2
Mickleton ATH M46 .....43 E4
Middlebrook Dr HOR/BR BL6 .....26 C4
Midford Dr BOL BL1 .....8 C5
Midgley St SWIN M27 .....55 F5
Midland CI LEIGH WN7 .....49 E5
Mile La TOT/BURYW BL8 .....31 H1
Miles St BOL BL1 .....18 B5
Milford Rd BOLE BL2 .....20 B3
 BOLS/LL BL3 .....36 C2
Milk St TYLD M29 .....51 G2
Millbank Gdns BOL * BL1 .....28 A1
Millbeck Gv BOLS/LL BL3 .....36 C1
Millbrook Av ATH M46 .....43 E3
Mill Brow WALK M28 .....54 B5
Mill Cft BOL BL1 .....2 C1
Milldale CI ATH M46 .....42 C5
 BOLE BL2 .....26 B3
Miller's La ATH M46 .....50 D2
Miller St BOL BL1 .....18 C3
 RAD M26 .....31 H4
Millfield Dr WALK M28 .....53 F5

Millfield Rd BOLE BL2 .....30 C3
Millgate EDGW/EG BL7 .....8 B2
Mill Hl
 BOL (off Mill St) BL1 .....3 H2
 LHULT M38 .....44 D2
Mill Hill Caravan Pk BOLE BL2 .....3 H2
Mill Hill St BOL BL1 .....3 H2
Mill La HOR/BR BL6 .....15 F3
 WGNE/HIN WN2 .....32 B2
 WHTN BL5 .....41 G4
Millstone Rd BOL BL1 .....27 F1
Mill St ATH M46 .....51 E2
 BOL BL1 .....3 G3
 CHLYE PR6 .....6 A4
 EDGW/EG BL7 .....8 D4
 FWTH BL4 .....37 G5
 TOT/BURYW BL8 .....11 A4
 WALK M28 .....53 E4
 WHTN BL5 .....33 H5
Milner St RAD M26 .....39 G2
Milnholme BOL BL1 .....17 H4
Milnthorpe Rd BOLE BL2 .....30 A2
Milsom Av BOLS/LL BL3 .....36 A2
Milton Av BOLS/LL * BL3 .....35 H2
 BOLS/LL BL3 .....38 D1
Milton Crs FWTH BL4 .....45 F2
Milton Rd RAD M26 .....39 F1
 SWIN M27 .....55 F2
Milverton CI HOR/BR BL6 .....26 C5
Mimosa Dr SWIN M27 .....55 H1
Minehead Av LEIGH WN7 .....49 F1
Minerva Rd FWTH BL4 .....36 D4
Minnie St BOLS/LL * BL3 .....35 H1
Minorca St BOLS/LL BL3 .....36 C1
Minster CI BOLE BL2 .....19 G5
Minster Gv TYLD M29 .....51 H5
Minster Rd BOLE BL2 .....19 G5
Minstrel CI SWIN M27 .....55 F4
Miriam St BOLS/LL * BL3 .....35 H1
Miry La WHTN BL5 .....41 G3
Mitre St BOL BL1 .....18 C3
Mitton CI TOT/BURYW BL8 .....21 G5
Mobberley Rd BOLE BL2 .....30 B4
Moffat CI BOLE BL2 .....30 B4
Moisant St BOLS/LL BL3 .....36 B2
Mold St BOL BL1 .....18 C3
Molyneux Rd WHTN BL5 .....34 B4
Moncrieffe St BOLS/LL BL3 .....3 F6
Monks La BOLE BL2 .....19 H5
Montague St BOLS/LL * BL3 .....35 H2
Montfort CI WHTN BL5 .....41 H2
Montgomery Wy RAD M26 .....31 E5
Monton St BOLS/LL BL3 .....36 C2
 RAD M26 .....39 H2
Montrose Av BOLE BL2 .....29 G1
Montrose Dr EDGW/EG BL7 .....9 F5
Montserrat Brow HOR/BR BL6 .....16 C4
Montserrat Rd BOL BL1 .....17 E5
Monyash Vw WGNE/HIN WN2 .....40 B5
Moorbottom Rd
 TOT/BURYW BL8 .....5 F3
Moorby Wk BOLS/LL BL3 .....28 C5
Moor CI RAD M26 .....31 G5
Moore's Ct BOL BL1 .....28 A2
Moorfield WALK M28 .....54 B5
Moorfield Cha FWTH BL4 .....45 H1
Moorfield Gv BOL BL1 .....27 H1
Moorfield Gv BOLE BL2 .....29 F5
Moorfield Rd SWIN M27 .....55 E5
Moor Ga BOLE BL2 .....19 H2
Moorgate CI BOLE BL2 .....29 F1
Moorgate Rd RAD M26 .....31 G2
Moorhey Rd LHULT M38 .....44 D2
Moorland Dr HOR/BR BL6 .....15 H4
 LHULT M38 .....45 E2
Moorland Rd BOL BL1 .....17 G5
Moorlands Vw BOLS/LL BL3 .....35 G3
Moor La BOLE BL2 .....2 D4
 BOLS/LL BL3 .....2 D5
 LEIGH WN7 .....49 G5
Moor Platt CI HOR/BR BL6 .....15 H4
Moorside Av BOL BL1 .....17 G5
 BOLE BL2 .....31 F1
 FWTH BL4 .....37 E1
 HOR/BR BL6 .....15 E3
Moorside Rd BOL BL1 .....17 H4
 TOT/BURYW BL8 .....21 F2
Moorside Vw TOT/BURYW BL8 .....21 H1
Moor St SWIN M27 .....55 H4
Moor Wy TOT/BURYW BL8 .....10 D1
Morar Dr BOLE BL2 .....30 D3
Morley Av SWIN M27 .....55 G5
Morley Rd RAD M26 .....39 F1
Morley St ATH M46 .....2 B5
 BOLS/LL BL3 .....2 B5
Mornington Rd ATH M46 .....43 F2
 BOL BL1 .....27 H2
 CHLYE PR6 .....6 B4
 WGNE/HIN WN2 .....40 B3
Morpeth St SWIN M27 .....55 G5
Morris Fold Dr HOR/BR BL6 .....26 C4
Morris Gn BOLS/LL BL3 .....36 A3
Morris Green La BOLS/LL BL3 .....36 A3
Morris Green St BOLS/LL BL3 .....36 A3
Morrison St BOLS/LL BL3 .....36 C2
Morris St BOL BL1 .....3 G3
 TYLD M29 .....51 F2
Mortfield Gdns BOL BL1 .....2 A1
Mortfield La BOL BL1 .....2 A1
Mortlake CI LHULT M38 .....44 D5

Mort La TYLD M29 .....52 C1
Mort St FWTH BL4 .....37 F5
 HOR/BR BL6 .....14 D3
 TYLD M29 .....51 F2
 WGNE/HIN WN2 .....40 C3
Morven Gv BOLE BL2 .....30 B3
Mosedale CI TYLD M29 .....52 A5
Mosley Common Rd WALK M28 .....52 D4
Mosley St RAD M26 .....39 H1
Moss Bank CI BOL BL1 .....18 B3
Moss Bank Gv SWIN M27 .....55 E1
Moss Bank Pk
 BOL (off Moss Bank Wy) BL1 .....17 F4
Moss Bank Rd SWIN M27 .....55 F1
Moss Bank Wy BOL BL1 .....17 G5
Mossbrook Dr LHULT M38 .....44 C2
Moss CI RAD M26 .....31 F5
Moss Colliery Rd SWIN M27 .....47 F5
Mossdale Av BOLE BL2 .....26 D3
Moss Dr HOR/BR BL6 .....15 H4
Mossfield Ct BOL BL1 .....2 C1
Mossfield Rd FWTH BL4 .....37 F5
 SWIN M27 .....55 G1
Moss Fold TYLD M29 .....52 A4
Mossland Gv BOLS/LL BL3 .....34 D3
Moss La BOL BL1 .....17 G4
 FWTH BL4 .....46 D3
 HOR/BR BL6 .....14 B3
 SWIN M27 .....55 F2
 WALK M28 .....46 A4
Moss Lea BOL BL1 .....18 B3
Moss Meadow WHTN BL5 .....33 G3
Moss Rd FWTH BL4 .....46 A1
Moss Shaw Wy RAD M26 .....31 G5
Moss St FWTH BL4 .....38 A4
Moss View Rd BOLE * BL2 .....30 A2
Mottershead Av BOLS/LL BL3 .....38 C1
Mottram St HOR/BR BL6 .....14 D3
Mountain Gv WALK M28 .....45 G4
Mountain St WALK M28 .....45 G4
Mountmorres CI WHTN BL5 .....43 F1
Mount Pleasant BOLS/LL * BL3 .....2 E5
 CHLYE PR6 .....6 A4
Mount Pleasant Rd FWTH BL4 .....36 D5
Mount Pleasant St HOR/BR BL6 .....25 F1
Mount St Joseph's Rd
 BOLS/LL BL3 .....27 H5
Mount Sion Houses
 RAD (off Mount Sion Rd) M26 .....39 F3
Mount Sion Rd RAD M26 .....39 G3
Mount Skip La LHULT M38 .....45 E4
Mount St BOL BL1 .....28 C1
 HOR/BR BL6 .....25 F1
 SWIN M27 .....55 H4
Mowbray St BOL * BL1 .....27 H1
Moyse Av TOT/BURYW BL8 .....21 H2
Muirfield CI BOLS/LL BL3 .....35 F2
Muirfield Dr TYLD M29 .....52 A4
Mule St BOLE BL2 .....3 H2
Mulgrave Rd WALK M28 .....54 C3
Mulgrave St BOLS/LL BL3 .....36 A3
 SWIN M27 .....55 F2
Mulliner St BOL * BL1 .....28 C1
Murray St ATH M46 .....50 B1
Musgrave Gdns BOL BL1 .....28 A2
Musgrave Rd BOL BL1 .....28 A2
Mycroft CI LEIGH WN7 .....49 G5
Myrrh St BOL BL1 .....18 C4
Myrtle Av LEIGH WN7 .....49 G4
Myrtle St BOL * BL1 .....2 B2
 BOL BL1 .....2 D2
Mytham Gdns BOLS/LL BL3 .....38 D3
Mytham Rd BOLS/LL BL3 .....38 D2
Mytton Rd BOL BL1 .....17 H4

N

Nabbs Fold TOT/BURYW BL8 .....11 H1
Nandywell BOLS/LL BL3 .....38 D2
Nantwich Wk BOLS/LL * BL3 .....36 C1
Napier St SWIN M27 .....55 H1
Narborough CI WGNE/HIN WN2 .....40 A4
Nasmyth St HOR/BR BL6 .....15 E4
Naylor St ATH M46 .....42 C5
Near Hey CI RAD M26 .....39 G3
Neasden Gv BOLS/LL BL3 .....28 A5
Neath Fold BOLS/LL BL3 .....36 B2
Nebo St BOLS/LL BL3 .....36 B1
Nebraska St BOL * BL1 .....28 C1
Nel Pan La LEIGH WN7 .....49 E3
Nelson Sq BOL BL1 .....3 H4
Nelson St ATH M46 .....42 B4
 BOLS/LL BL3 .....29 E5
 BOLS/LL* BL3 .....38 D2
 FWTH BL4 .....38 A5
 HOR/BR BL6 .....15 F4
 TYLD M29 .....51 H3
Nene Gv WGNE/HIN WN2 .....40 A4
Nesbit St BOLE BL2 .....19 F4
Neston Av BOL BL1 .....18 D2
Neston Rd TOT/BURYW BL8 .....21 H3
Netherfield Rd BOLS/LL BL3 .....36 C3
Netherfields LEIGH WN7 .....49 F4
Nevada St BOL * BL1 .....28 C1
Nevern CI BOL BL1 .....27 F2
Neville CI BOL BL1 .....28 B2
Nevis Gv BOL BL1 .....18 B2

Nevy Fold Av *HOR/BR* BL6 ....15 H4
Newall Gv *LEIGH* WN7 ....49 H4
Newark Av *RAD* M26 ....31 E5
New Bank St *TYLD* * M29 ....51 G3
New Barn St *BOL* BL1 ....27 H1
Newbridge Gdns *BOLE* BL2 ....20 A3
New Briggs Fold *EDGW/EG* BL7 .....8 C2
Newbrook Rd *ATH* M46 ....43 F2
New Brunswick St *HOR/BR* BL6 ....14 D4
Newbury Rd *BOLS/LL* BL3 ....38 B2
Newbury Wk *BOL* BL1 ....2 C1
Newby Rd *BOLE* BL2 ....30 A1
New Chapel La *HOR/BR* BL6 ....15 G5
New Church Rd *BOL* BL1 ....17 F5
New City Rd *WALK* M28 ....53 G3
New Colliers Rw

BOL (off Colliers Row Rd) BL1 ......17 E2
Newcombe Dr *LHULT* M38 ....44 D2
New Court Dr *EDGW/EG* BL7 ....8 B1
New Drake Gn *WHTN* BL5 ....41 G3
Newearth Rd *WALK* M28 ....53 F3
New Ellesmere Ap *WALK* M28 ....45 G4
New Field Cl *RAD* M26 ....39 G2
Newgate Cottages

WHTN (off Plodder La) BL5 ....35 G4
Newgate Dr *LHULT* M38 ....44 D2
Newhall Av *BOLS/LL* BL3 ....30 D4
New Hall La *BOL* BL1 ....27 G2
New Hall Ms *BOL* BL1 ....26 C1
New Hall Pl *BOL* BL1 ....27 G2
Newhart Gv *WALK* M28 ....53 G1
Newhaven Av *LEIGH* WN7 ....49 H3
New Heys Wy *BOLE* BL2 ....19 H1
New Holder St *BOL* BL1 ....2 C4
Newholme Gdns *LHULT* M38 ....45 G5
Newington Dr *BOL* * BL1 ....28 D1
Newington Wk *BOL* * BL1 ....28 C1
Newland Dr *WHTN* BL5 ....43 H1
Newlands Av *BOLE* BL2 ....30 B1

TYLD M29 ....51 G5
Newlands Dr *HOR/BR* BL6 ....24 A3
New La *BOLE* * BL2 ....29 H1
New Lane Ct *BOLE* * BL2 ....20 A5
Newlea Cl *BOL* BL1 ....18 A5
New Lester Wy *LHULT* M38 ....44 C4
Newmarket Rd *BOLS/LL* BL3 ....38 C3
New Meadow *HOR/BR* BL6 ....26 C5
Newnham St *BOL* BL1 ....18 C4
Newport Rd *BOLS/LL* BL3 ....37 E2
Newport St *BOL* BL1 ....2 E4

FWTH BL4 ....45 H1
Newquay Av *BOLE* BL2 ....31 F1
New Raven Cl *BOLS/LL* * BL3 ....38 C2
New Rd *CHLYE* PR6 ....6 D4

WGNE/HIN WN2 ....23 H4
Newry St *BOL* BL1 ....18 B4
Newsham Cl *BOLS/LL* BL3 ....2 A6
New Springs

BOL (off Smithills Dean Rd) BL1 ...17 H4
Newstead Dr *BOLS/LL* BL3 ....35 G3
New St *BOL* BL1 ....2 D5

HOR/BR BL6 ....13 H5
TOT/BURYW BL8 ....21 H1
New Tempest Rd *HOR/BR* BL6 ......34 C1
New Tong Fld *EDGW/EG* BL7 ....8 D5
Newton St *BOL* BL1 ....18 C5
Newton Ter *BOL* * BL1 ....18 C5
Newton Wk *BOL* BL1 ....18 C5
Newtown Cl *SWIN* M27 ....55 H1
Neyland Cl *BOL* BL1 ....27 F3
Nicholas St *BOLE* BL2 ....3 H2
Nick Hilton's La *CHLYE* PR6 ....6 D1
Nickleton Brow *CHLYE* PR6 ....6 C2
Nicola St *EDGW/EG* BL7 ....8 C4
Nightingale Rd *HOR/BR* BL6 ....13 G4
Nightingale St *CHLYE* PR6 ....6 A4
Nile St *BOLS/LL* BL3 ....2 E7
Nixon Rd *BOLS/LL* BL3 ....36 A2
Nixon Rd South *BOLS/LL* BL3 ....36 A2
Noble St *BOLS/LL* BL3 ....2 C7
Noel St *BOL* BL1 ....2 D3
Nook Flds *BOLE* BL2 ....20 A5
Norbury Gv *BOL* BL1 ....18 D3

SWIN M27 ....55 H2
Norden Cl *BOLS/LL* BL3 ....36 C1
Norfolk Cl *BOLS/LL* BL3 ....28 A5

WGNE/HIN WN2 ....40 C2
Norfolk Dr *FWTH* BL4 ....37 H4
Norfolk Rd *ATH* M46 ....42 C3
Norfolk St *WALK* M28 ....45 H2
Normanby Gv *SWIN* M27 ....55 G2
Normanby Rd *WALK* M28 ....53 G2
Normanby St *BOLS/LL* BL3 ....35 H3

SWIN M27 ....55 G2
Normandale Av *BOL* BL1 ....27 G1
Normandy Crs *RAD* M26 ....39 H2
Norris St *BOLS/LL* BL3 ....2 C7

BOLS/LL BL3 ....38 C2
FWTH BL4 ....45 G1
TYLD * M29 ....51 G3
North Av *FWTH* BL4 ....37 E5

TOT/BURYW BL8 ....11 H2
North Edge *LEIGH* WN7 ....50 B5
Northern Gv *BOL* BL1 ....28 A1
Northfield St *BOLS/LL* BL3 ....28 A5
Northfold Cl *WALK* M28 ....45 G5
Northland Rd *BOL* BL1 ....18 D1
Northlands *RAD* M26 ....31 G5
North La *TYLD* M29 ....51 G5

Northolt Av *LEIGH* WN7 ....49 H3
Northolt Dr *BOLS/LL* BL3 ....36 D1
North Rd *ATH* M46 ....42 B3
North St *ATH* M46 ....43 H5
Northumbria St *BOLS/LL* BL3 ....28 A5
North Wy *BOL* BL1 ....19 F3
Northwell St *LEIGH* WN7 ....49 G3
Northwold Dr *BOL* BL1 ....27 E2
Northwood *BOLE* BL2 ....19 H3
Northwood Crs *BOLS/LL* * BL3 .....28 A5
North Zetland Av *BOLS/LL* BL3 .....35 H3
Norton Rd *WALK* M28 ....52 C4
Norton St *BOL* BL1 ....18 D4
Norway St *BOL* * BL1 ....18 B5
Norwick Cl *BOLS/LL* BL3 ....35 E1
Norwood Av *TYLD* M29 ....51 G5
Norwood Cl *CHLYE* PR6 ....6 A4

WALK M28 ....54 A3
Norwood Dr *SWIN* M27 ....55 E4
Norwood Gv *BOL* * BL1 ....28 A2
Nottingham Dr *BOL* BL1 ....28 C1
Nugent Rd *BOLS/LL* BL3 ....36 C2
Nunnery Rd *BOLS/LL* BL3 ....35 H1
Nuthatch Av *WALK* M28 ....53 H3
Nuttall Av *BOLS/LL* BL3 ....39 E2

HOR/BR BL6 ....14 C4
Nuttall St *ATH* M46 ....43 E5

O

Oak Av *BOLS/LL* BL3 ....38 D2

WGNE/HIN WN2 ....40 C5
Oakbank Dr *BOL* BL1 ....18 B1
Oakbarton *HOR/BR* BL6 ....34 C1
Oak Coppice Av *BOL* BL1 ....27 G3
Oakdale *BOLE* BL2 ....19 H3
Oakdale Dr *TYLD* M29 ....52 A5
Oakdene *SWIN* M27 ....54 D5
Oakenbottom Rd *BOLE* BL2 ....29 H4
Oakenclough Dr *BOL* BL1 ....17 F5
Oakes St *WHTN* BL5 ....46 B1
Oakfield Av *ATH* M46 ....42 C4
Oakfield Cl *HOR/BR* BL6 ....15 H5
Oakfield Crs *WGNE/HIN* WN2 ....23 G5
Oakfield Dr *LHULT* M38 ....44 C3
Oakfield Gv *FWTH* BL4 ....45 G2
Oakford Wk *BOLS/LL* BL3 ....2 B7
Oak Gates *EDGW/EG* BL7 ....8 C3
Oakhill Cl *BOLE* BL2 ....30 C3
Oakhurst Gv *WHTN* BL5 ....41 E1
Oakland Gv *BOL* * BL1 ....17 G5
Oaklands *BOL* BL1 ....27 F3
Oaklands Rd *SWIN* M27 ....55 E5
Oakleigh Av *BOLS/LL* BL3 ....37 E3
Oakley Pk *BOL* BL1 ....18 B2
The Oaklings *WGNE/HIN* WN2 ....40 C5
Oaks Av *BOLE* BL2 ....19 G3
Oaks La *BOL* BL1 ....19 F2
Oak St *ATH* M46 ....50 A2

TYLD M29 ....51 G2
Oak Tree Cl *ATH* M46 ....50 A2
Oakwood Av *SWIN* M27 ....54 D5

WALK M28 ....54 B1
Oakwood Dr *BOL* BL1 ....27 F2

WALK M28 ....54 B1
Oakworth Dr *BOL* BL1 ....18 B2
Oban Av *BOL* * BL1 ....18 C2
Oban St *BOL* * BL1 ....18 B4
Oban Wy *WGNE/HIN* * WN2 ....23 H5
Octagon Ct *BOL* * BL1 ....2 B4
Offerton St *HOR/BR* BL6 ....14 C4
Ogden St *SWIN* M27 ....55 H4
Okehampton Cl *RAD* M26 ....31 E5
Olaf St *BOLE* BL2 ....29 F1
Old Barn Pl *EDGW/EG* BL7 ....9 E4
Old Chapel Ct

CHLYE (off Railway Rd) PR6 ....6 A5
Old Clough La *WALK* M28 ....54 B2
Old Colliers Rw

BOL (off Colliers Row Rd) BL1 ......17 E2
Old Doctors St *TOT/BURYW* BL8 ...11 H5
Old Eagley Ms *BOL* BL1 ....18 D1
Oldfield Cl *WHTN* BL5 ....33 H5
Old Fold Rd *WGNE/HIN* WN2 ....23 H5

WHTN BL5 ....40 D1
Old Gn *BOLE* BL2 ....20 A1
Old Greenwood La *HOR/BR* BL6 ....25 G5
Old Hall Clough *HOR/BR* BL6 ....26 C3
Old Hall La *HOR/BR* BL6 ....26 C3

WALK M28 ....54 A4
WHTN BL5 ....41 G3
Old Hall Mill La *LEIGH* WN7 ....50 A3
Old Hall St *FWTH* BL4 ....46 A1
Old Hall St North *BOL* * BL1 ....2 E3
Oldhams La *BOL* BL1 ....18 B2
Old Kiln La *BOL* BL1 ....16 D5
Old La *HOR/BR* BL6 ....15 H5

LHULT M38 ....44 D2
WHTN BL5 ....33 F5
Old Lord's Crs *HOR/BR* BL6 ....14 D2
Old Manor Pk *ATH* M46 ....50 A1
Old Nans La *BOLE* BL2 ....20 B5
Old Nursery Fold *BOLE* BL2 ....19 H3
Old Oak Cl *BOLS/LL* BL3 ....30 D1
Old Oake Cl *WALK* * M28 ....54 B1
Old Quarry La *EDGW/EG* BL7 ....8 D3
Old Rake *HOR/BR* BL6 ....15 F1

Old Rd *BOL* BL1 ....18 C4
Old School La *CHLY/EC* PR7 ....12 C2
Oldstead Gv *BOLS/LL* BL3 ....35 F1
Old Swan Cl *EDGW/EG* * BL7 ....8 C2
Old Towns Cl *TOT/BURYW* * BL8 ...11 H5
Old Vicarage *WHTN* BL5 ....41 G3
Old Vicarage Gdns *WALK* M28 ....45 H5
Old Vicarage Rd *HOR/BR* BL6 ....15 H4
Old Wells Cl *LHULT* M38 ....45 E2
Old Will's La *HOR/BR* BL6 ....14 D1
Olga St *BOL* BL1 ....18 B5
Oliver St *ATH* M46 ....42 D5
Olive St *BOLS/LL* BL3 ....36 B1
Ollerbrook Ct *BOL* BL1 ....18 D5
Ollerton St *BOL* BL1 ....18 D1

CHLYE PR6 ....6 A4
Openshaw Pl *FWTH* BL4 ....37 F5
Orchard Av *BOL* BL1 ....18 D4

WALK M28 ....53 F4
Orchard Cl *LEIGH* WN7 ....49 H4
Orchard Gdns *BOLE* BL2 ....20 B4
Orchard La *LEIGH* WN7 ....49 H4
The Orchard *WHTN* BL5 ....33 G4
Orchid Av *FWTH* BL4 ....37 F4
Ordsall Av *LHULT* M38 ....45 E4
Organ St *WGNE/HIN* WN2 ....40 D5
Oriel St *BOLS/LL* BL3 ....28 A5
Oriole Cl *WALK* M28 ....53 F4
Oriole Dr *WALK* M28 ....53 F4
Orlando St *BOLS/LL* BL3 ....3 C7
Ormond St *BOLS/LL* BL3 ....29 H5
Ormrod St *BOL* BL1 ....2 D5

BOLE BL2 ....19 C2
FWTH BL4 ....37 G5
Ormside Cl *WGNE/HIN* WN2 ....40 D5
Ormskirk Cl *TOT/BURYW* BL8 ....31 H2
Ormston Av *HOR/BR* BL6 ....14 D2
Ormston Gv *LEIGH* WN7 ....49 H4
Ornatus St *BOL* * BL1 ....18 D2
Orwell Rd *BOL* * BL1 ....17 H5
Osborne Ct *ATH* M46 ....42 C5
Osborne Gv *BOL* BL1 ....28 A1

LEIGH WN7 ....50 D5
Osbourne Cl *FWTH* BL4 ....37 H4
Oscar St *BOL* * BL1 ....18 A5
Oscott Av *LHULT* M38 ....45 E3
Osmund Av *BOLE* BL2 ....29 H3
Osprey Av *WHTN* BL5 ....41 E2
Oswald St *BOLS/LL* BL3 ....36 A1
Oswestry Cl *TOT/BURYW* BL8 ....11 G4
Otterbury Cl *TOT/BURYW* BL8 ......21 H5
Oulton St *BOL* BL1 ....19 E2
Outterside St *CHLY/EC* PR7 ....13 E1
Outwood Av *SWIN* M27 ....47 F4
Outwood Gv *BOL* BL1 ....18 C2
Overdale Dr *BOL* BL1 ....27 G3
Overdene Cl *HOR/BR* BL6 ....26 B4
Overgreen *BOL* BL2 ....20 A4
Owenington Gv *LHULT* M38 ....45 E3
Owlwood Cl *LHULT* M38 ....44 C5
Owlwood Dr *LHULT* M38 ....44 C5
Oxford Cl *FWTH* BL4 ....36 D5
Oxford Rd *ATH* M46 ....42 B3

BOLS/LL BL3 ....38 B2
HOR/BR BL6 ....25 H2
Oxford St *BOL* BL1 ....2 A1

CHLY/EC PR7 ....12 D1
LEIGH WN7 ....49 H4
WGNE/HIN WN2 ....40 B1
Ox Ga *BOLE* BL2 ....19 H2
Ox Hey Cl *HOR/BR* BL6 ....25 G3
Ox Hey La *HOR/BR* BL6 ....25 G3
Oxlea Gv *WHTN* BL5 ....41 G1

P

Packer St *BOL* BL1 ....18 A5
Padbury Wy *BOLE* BL2 ....20 A5
Paddison St *SWIN* M27 ....55 G4
Paddock St *ATH* M46 ....43 E5
The Paddock *WALK* M28 ....54 A4
Paderborn Ct *BOL* BL1 ....2 C6
Pailton Ct *HOR/BR* BL6 ....26 D4
Paiton St *BOL* BL1 ....28 A3
Palace St *BOL* BL1 ....2 E2
Palatine St *BOL* BL1 ....2 E3
Paley St *BOL* BL1 ....3 F3
Palin St *WGNE/HIN* WN2 ....40 D5
Pall Ml

HOR/BR (off Rivington La) BL6 ....7 G5
Palmer Gv *LEIGH* WN7 ....49 G2
Palm St *BOL* BL1 ....18 D4
Pansy Rd *FWTH* BL4 ....37 E5
Panton St *HOR/BR* BL6 ....25 F1
Paper Mill Rd *EDGW/EG* BL7 ....8 D5
Paris St *BOLS/LL* BL3 ....35 H1
Park Av *BOLS/LL* BL3 ....18 C3
Park Bank *ATH* M46 ....43 F2
Park Cottages

BOL (off Smithills Dean Rd) BL1 ...18 A4
Parkdale Rd *BOLE* BL2 ....29 G1
Parkdene Cl *BOLE* BL2 ....19 H3
Park Edge *WHTN* BL5 ....42 A1
Parkfield Av *FWTH* BL4 ....45 G1

TYLD M29 ....51 H5
Parkfield Dr *LEIGH* WN7 ....50 A4

TYLD M29 ....51 H5
Parkfield Dr *TYLD* M29 ....51 H5
Parkfield Rd *BOLS/LL* BL3 ....38 B2
Parkgate *BOL* BL1 ....2 D5
Parkgate Dr *BOL* BL1 ....18 C1
Park Gv *RAD* M26 ....39 H2
Park Hill St *BOL* BL1 ....2 B3
Parkinson St *BOLS/LL* BL3 ....38 A4
Parklands Dr *WGNE/HIN* WN2 ....40 C5
Park La *HOR/BR* BL6 ....14 D5

WGNE/HIN WN2 ....23 H4
Park Meadow *WHTN* BL5 ....41 F2
Park Rd *BOL* BL1 ....2 D4

BOLS/LL BL3 ....37 H3
CHLY/EC PR7 ....12 C2
TOT/BURYW BL8 ....21 H1
WALK M28 ....54 A2
WGNE/HIN WN2 ....23 H5
WHTN BL5 ....41 G3
Parkside *WGNE/HIN* WN2 ....40 C5
Parkside Av *WALK* M28 ....54 A3
Parkside Cl *BOLE* * BL2 ....19 H3
Parks Nook *FWTH* BL4 ....45 G2
Parkstone Cl *TOT/BURYW* BL8 ......21 H4
Park St *ATH* M46 ....43 F2

BOL BL1 ....2 D3
FWTH BL4 ....45 G2
TYLD M29 ....51 G3
Park Vw *FWTH* BL4 ....45 G3
Park View Rd *BOLS/LL* * BL3 ....37 H4
Parkway *LHULT* M38 ....44 D5

WHTN BL5 ....41 F2
Parkway Gv *LHULT* M38 ....44 D5
Parkwood Dr *WHTN* BL5 ....41 E2
Parnham Cl *BOLS/LL* BL3 ....37 E4
Parr Cl *FWTH* BL4 ....37 G5
Parr Fold Av *WALK* M28 ....45 H4
Parrot St *BOLS/LL* BL3 ....3 G5
Parr St *TYLD* M29 ....51 G3
Parsonage Dr *WALK* M28 ....54 A3
Parsonage Rd *RAD* * M26 ....31 G5

WALK M28 ....54 A3
Parsonage Wy *LEIGH* WN7 ....50 A2
Partington Ct *FWTH* BL4 ....37 F5
Partington La *SWIN* M27 ....55 G3
Partington St *BOLS/LL* BL3 ....36 A4

FWTH BL4 ....45 H1
WALK M28 ....45 F5
Part St *WHTN* BL5 ....46 A1
Paton Av *BOLS/LL* BL3 ....38 B3
Patricia Dr *WALK* M28 ....53 F4
Patterdale Rd *BOLE* BL2 ....19 H3
Patterson St *BOLS/LL* BL3 ....3 G5

WHTN BL5 ....40 B1
Paulette St *BOL* BL1 ....18 A5
Paulhan St *BOLS/LL* BL3 ....36 A4
Pauline St *WGNE/HIN* WN2 ....40 A2
Pavilion Wk *RAD* M26 ....31 G5
Peabody St *BOLS/LL* BL3 ....36 B2
Peace St *ATH* M46 ....43 E5

BOLS/LL BL3 ....38 B2
TYLD M29 ....51 G4
Peacock Fold *LEIGH* WN7 ....49 G3
Peak Av *ATH* M46 ....42 C3
Peak St *BOL* BL1 ....3 F3
Pear Tree Gv *TYLD* M29 ....51 H5
Peatfield Av *SWIN* M27 ....55 H1
Pedder St *BOL* BL1 ....2 A3
Peel Cl *ATH* M46 ....43 E5
Peel Dr *LHULT* M38 ....44 C5
Peel Gv *WALK* M28 ....54 B2
Peel Hall Av *TYLD* M29 ....51 H5
Peel La *LHULT* M38 ....44 C5
Peel Park Crs *LHULT* M38 ....44 C5
Peel St *CHLYE* PR6 ....6 A4

FWTH BL4 ....45 G2
WHTN BL5 ....40 B1
Peel Wk *TOT/BURYW* BL8 ....11 H5
Peelwood Av *LHULT* M38 ....45 E3
Peelwood Gv *ATH* M46 ....43 E5
Pegamoid St *BOLE* BL2 ....19 G2
Pelham St *BOLS/LL* BL3 ....36 A4
Pelton Av *SWIN* M27 ....55 H1
Pemberton St *BOL* * BL1 ....18 A5

LHULT M38 ....44 C5
Pembroke Cl *HOR/BR* BL6 ....26 B4

WHTN BL5 ....41 G2
Pembroke Rd *WGNE/HIN* WN2 ....40 A1
Pembroke St *BOL* BL1 ....18 C1
Penarth Rd *BOLS/LL* BL3 ....37 E4
Pendeen Cl *TYLD* M29 ....51 G5
Pendennis Av *HOR/BR* BL6 ....25 H2
Pendennis Cl *RAD* M26 ....31 E5
Pendennis Crs *WGNE/HIN* WN2 .....23 H4
Pendlebury Fold *BOLS/LL* BL3 ....35 F1
Pendlebury La *WGN* WN1 ....22 C5
Pendlebury St *BOL* BL1 ....18 C1
Pendle Ct *BOL* BL1 ....18 C1
Pendle Dr *HOR/BR* BL6 ....25 H2
Pengarth Rd *HOR/BR* BL6 ....25 H2
Pengwern Av *BOLS/LL* BL3 ....37 E4
Penketh Av *TYLD* M29 ....51 H5
Pennine Cl *HOR/BR* BL6 ....25 H2
Pennine Gv *LEIGH* WN7 ....49 H4
Pennine Rd *HOR/BR* BL6 ....25 H2
Pennington Cl *LHULT* M38 ....45 E3

WGNE/HIN WN2 ....40 C5
Pennington La *WGN* WN1 ....22 C5
Pennington Rd *BOLS/LL* BL3 ....35 F1
Pennington St *TOT/BURYW* BL8 ....11 H5

K M28	54	A1
st FWTH BL4	37	G5
/BR BL6	15	E4
yn Cl RAD M26	31	F5
e Fold WALK M28	53	F4
Av BOL BL1	27	G1
St BOL1	54	B1
ord Ct BOLE BL2	20	A1
nd Ter BOL * BL1	28	C1
St BOL * BL1	18	D5
H* BL4	46	A1
St BOLS/LL BL3	36	A2
borough Dr BOL BL1	27	G1
borough Wk BOL BL1	28	C1
ead Cl BOL BL1	28	C1
Martin St HOR/BR BL6	14	D3
sfield Wk BOL BL1	28	C1
St TYLD M29	51	F2
L BL5	40	C1
Cl BOLS/LL BL3	51	G3
St BOLS/LL BL3	35	H1
St Gn WHTN BL5	41	G2
ewfist Spinney WHTN BL5	41	F1
ewfist WHTN BL5	41	G1
Martin St WALK M28	53	F5
ean St BOLE BL2	3	H3
L BL4	37	G4
Av FWTH BL4	45	H1
s St BOL BL1	28	B5
s St LEIGH WN7	49	G3
St WALK M28	28	G4
e St BOLS/LL * BL3	36	A1
ix St BOL1	3	G1
L BL4	45	H1
ing Cl RAD * M26	38	C5
ird Av BOLS/LL BL3	39	E2
y Gdns LEIGH WN7	49	G2
t St FWTH BL4	45	G1
y ATH M46	42	B5
d BOLS/LL BL3	36	B1
ton Rd FWTH BL4	46	B2
M26	31	H5
ton St BOLS/LL BL3	3	D7
Fld EDGW/EG BL7	8	B2
St BOLS/LL BL3	37	E1
t Rd BOL BL1	19	F4
FWTH BL4	37	F5
M27	55	A4
M28	54	A3
W BL5	40	A2
eadow RAD M26	47	E2
BOL BL1	18	D5
M29	51	G2
ood Cl BOL BL1	18	C5
d Cl WHTN BL5	41	F2
d RAD WALK M28	53	G2
le Dr EDGW/EG BL7	8	B2
r Cl HOR/BR BL6	15	E3
r St HOR/BR BL6	15	E3
be Cl BOL BL1	3	J4
La BOLE BL2	20	B4
t St BOLE BL2	3	J4
M26	3	J4
e Av BOL BL1	19	F3
tion Av WALK M28	45	G4
tion Rd EDGW/EG BL7	4	B2
old Rd LEIGH WN7	50	A5
ll Av BOLS/LL BL3	35	G1
a WHTN BL5	42	B2
LEIGH WN7	49	H5
St EDGW/EG BL7	18	D1
Gdns BOL BL1	2	C1
t St TOT/BURYW BL8	21	G5
gton Dr TOT/BURYW BL8	21	G5
St BOLE BL2	3	G3
r La FWTH BL4	36	B5
W BL5	35	G5
fields WHTN BL5	33	G2
s Av BOLS/LL BL3	36	A4
uth Dr FWTH BL4	36	D5
Nook Rd HOR/BR BL6	34	B2
te Dr WGNE/HIN WN2	49	E1
BOLE BL2	29	F1
ater Cl LHULT M38	44	D5
d Cl RAD M26	39	G2
BOL BL1	2	D3
St WHTN BL5	17	G5
Av BOL BL1	18	D3
BL2	19	G1
/BR BL6	25	G1
Gv WGNE/HIN WN2	48	D1
Rd SWIN M27	33	G5
M28	54	F4
plars CHLY/EC PR7	12	D1
St TYLD M29	51	G2
ster Dr BOL BL1	31	E5
d Rd WALK M28	45	G3
d St BOL BL1	18	C5
t BOLE BL2	3	J4
SWIN M27	55	H1
Av BOLE BL2	30	A3
St ATH M46	42	B5
Cl TOT/BURYW BL8	31	H2
n Wy TOT/BURYW BL8	21	H2
St BOLE * BL2	29	G2

Prescot Av ATH M46	43	E4
TYLD M29	52	A2
Prescott St BOLS/LL * BL3	36	A1
LEIGH WN7	49	H5
WALK M28	45	F5
Prestbury Rd BOL BL1	19	E2
Presto Gdns BOLS/LL * BL3	35	H1
Prestolee Rd BOLS/LL BL3	38	C4
RAD M26	39	E4
Preston St BOLS/LL * BL3	37	F1
Presto St BOLS/LL BL3	35	H1
FWTH BL4	38	A4
Prestwich St BOL BL1	18	D5
Prestwood Cl BOL BL1	28	A1
Prestwood Dr BOL BL1	28	B1
Prestwood Rd FWTH BL4	37	G4
Pretoria Rd BOLE BL2	30	A3
Price St FWTH BL4	37	H4
Priestley Rd WALK M28	55	F4
Priestners Wy LEIGH WN7	49	G5
Primrose Av FWTH BL4	37	E4
WALK M28	53	F1
Primrose Bank TOT/BURYW BL8	11	G5
WALK M28	53	F1
Primrose Cl BOLE BL2	20	B1
Primrose St BOL * BL1	18	D3
FWTH BL4	46	A1
Primrose St North TYLD M29	51	G2
Primula St BOL BL1	18	D3
Prince's Av BOLS/LL BL3	38	D1
TYLD M29	51	G5
Princess Av ATH M46	42	C3
FWTH BL4	46	B3
Princess Gv FWTH BL4	37	H5
Princess Rd CHLYE PR6	6	B4
HOR/BR BL6	26	B3
RAD M26	39	G2
Princess St BOL BL1	3	F4
Prince St BOL BL1	2	D1
Princethorpe Cl HOR/BR BL6	26	D4
Printers La BOLE BL2	19	G1
Printshop La ATH M46	51	E2
Priory Av WHTN BL5	41	G2
Priory Cl BOLE BL2	19	G1
Priory Rd SWIN M27	55	G2
Progress St BOL BL1	28	D1
Prospect Av TOT/BURYW BL8	11	H5
Prospect Hl BOLE BL2	20	B3
Prospect Pl FWTH BL4	45	G1
Prospect St BOL BL1	28	D1
TYLD M29	51	F2
Prosser Av ATH M46	50	A1
Providence St BOLS/LL BL3	3	F7
Pryce St BOL BL1	28	B1
Punch La BOLS/LL BL3	34	D3
Punch St BOLS/LL BL3	2	B6
The Pungle WHTN BL5	41	F3
Purbeck Dr HOR/BR BL6	25	H1
Purbeck Wy TYLD M29	51	G4
Purcell Cl BOL * BL1	28	B1
Purple St BOL * BL1	2	F3

Q

Quakerfields WHTN BL5	41	F1
Quakers Fld TOT/BURYW BL8	11	H4
Quarlton Dr TOT/BURYW BL8	10	D1
Quarry Pond Rd WALK M28	44	D3
Quarry Rd FWTH BL4	46	C1
Quebec Pl BOLS/LL BL3	28	A5
Quebec St BOLS/LL BL3	28	B5
Queen Ann Dr WALK M28	53	E4
Queen's Av ATH M46	42	C3
EDGW/EG BL7	9	E5
Queensbrook BOL BL1	2	C1
Queensbury Cl BOL BL1	18	B2
Queens Cl WALK M28	52	D4
Queensgate BOL BL1	27	H2
Queens Pk		
BOL (off Park Rd) BL1	2	A4
Queens Rd BOLS/LL BL3	35	H1
Queen St BOL BL1	2	D4
FWTH BL4	37	H5
HOR/BR BL6	14	C4
LHULT M38	45	F1
WHTN BL5	33	G5
Queensway FWTH BL4	46	B2
WALK M28	53	F3

R

Radbourne Gv BOLS/LL BL3	35	F1
Radcliffe Gv LEIGH WN7	49	H4
Radcliffe Moor Rd BOLS/LL BL3	30	D5
Radcliffe Rd BOLE BL2	3	J3
BOLS/LL BL3	38	C1
Radelan Gv RAD M26	39	F1
Radley Cl BOL BL1	27	G1
Radnor Cl WGNE/HIN WN2	40	C5
Radstock Cl BOL BL1	8	C5
Radway TYLD M29	52	A2
Raglan St BOL BL1	18	B5
Raikes La BOLS/LL BL3	37	F1

Raikes Rd BOLS/LL BL3	29	H5
Raikes Wy BOLS/LL BL3	29	H5
Railway Rd CHLYE PR6	6	A5
Railway St ATH M46	38	B2
FWTH BL4	38	A4
WGNE/HIN WN2	40	A1
Raimond St BOL BL1	18	A4
Rainbow Dr ATH M46	42	D4
Rainford St BOLE BL2	19	G1
Rainham Dr BOL BL1	28	C1
Rainshaw St BOL BL1	18	D3
Rake La SWIN M27	47	H5
Ralph St BOL BL1	18	B5
Ramsay Av FWTH BL4	45	F1
Ramsay St BOL BL1	18	C3
Ramsbottom Rd BOLE BL2	10	B2
HOR/BR BL6	14	D4
Ramsden St BOLS/LL BL3	29	H5
Ramsey Cl ATH M46	51	E1
Ram St LHULT M38	44	D4
Ramwell Gdns BOLS/LL BL3	2	A7
Ramwells Brow EDGW/EG BL7	8	D4
Ramwells Ct		
EDGW/EG		
(off Windy Harbour La) BL7	9	F4
Ramwells Ms		
EDGW/EG		
(off Windy Harbour La) BL7	9	F4
Randal St BOLS/LL BL3	36	A1
Randolph Rd FWTH BL4	46	B1
Randolph St BOLS/LL BL3	28	B2
Rands Clough Dr WALK M28	53	F5
Range St BOLS/LL BL3	36	B1
Ranicar Steet WGNE/HIN WN2	41	E5
Rankine Ter BOLS/LL * BL3	2	B7
Rannoch Rd BOLE BL2	30	B3
Ranworth Cl BOL BL1	19	E1
Raphael St BOL BL1	18	B5
Rasbottom St BOL BL1	2	D3
Ratcliffe Rd WGNE/HIN WN2	23	G4
Ratcliffe St LEIGH WN7	49	H5
TYLD M29	51	H2
Rathybank Cl BOL BL1	17	H5
Raveden Cl BOL BL1	18	A4
Ravenfield Gv BOL BL1	2	B1
Ravenhurst Dr BOL BL1	26	D4
Raven Rd BOLS/LL * BL3	35	G1
Ravenscraig Rd LHULT M38	45	F2
Ravensdale Rd HOR/BR BL6	26	D3
Ravens Holme BOL BL1	27	E3
Ravens Wd BOL BL1	27	E3
Ravenswood Dr BOL BL1	27	E3
WGNE/HIN WN2	40	A2
Rawcliffe Av BOLE BL2	30	B3
Rawlinson St HOR/BR BL6	14	D3
Rawlyn Rd BOL BL1	27	E3
Rawson Av FWTH BL4	38	A4
Rawson Rd BOL BL1	28	A1
Rawson St FWTH BL4	37	H4
Rawsthorne St BOL BL1	18	C5
TYLD M29	52	B3
Rayden Crs WHTN BL5	41	G2
Raymond St SWIN M27	55	H2
The Reach WALK M28	54	A1
Recreation St BOLE BL2	20	B1
BOLS/LL BL3	36	C1
Rectory Gdns WHTN BL5	41	E4
Red Bank Rd RAD M26	31	H5
Redbrook Cl FWTH * BL4	38	A4
Redcar Rd BOL BL1	17	H3
BOLS/LL BL3	38	C2
Redcot		
BOL (off Somerset Rd) BL1	27	H3
Reddish Cl BOLE BL2	20	A1
Redgate Wy FWTH BL4	36	D4
Redhill Gv BOL BL1	28	C1
Redisher Cft TOT/BURYW BL8	11	H1
Redisher La TOT/BURYW BL8	11	G1
Red La BOLE BL2	29	H1
Redpol Av LEIGH WN7	50	B5
Redpoll Cl WALK M28	53	F4
Red Rock La RAD M26	47	F2
Redshank Gv LEIGH WN7	50	B5
Redshaw Av BOLE BL2	19	F1
Redstart Gv WALK M28	53	E4
Redstock Cl WHTN BL5	34	A4
Red St ATH M46	43	E5
Redwater Cl WALK M28	53	E5
Red Waters LEIGH WN7	50	A5
Redwing Rd TOT/BURYW BL8	11	H2
Redwood BOL BL1	40	A1
Reedham Cl BOL BL1	28	A2
Reedley Dr WALK M28	53	G3
Reedmace Cl WALK M28	54	A2
Reeves St LEIGH WN7	49	H5
Regaby Gv WGNE/HIN WN2	40	C3
Regan St BOL BL1	18	B4
Regent Av LHULT M38	45	E3
Regent Dr HOR/BR BL6	26	B3
LEIGH WN7	50	A5
Regent Rd HOR/BR BL6	26	B4
Regent St ATH M46	51	E1
Regent Wk FWTH * BL4	37	H5
Regina Crs LEIGH WN7	51	E5
Reginald St BOLS/LL * BL3	35	G3
SWIN M27	55	G3
Renfrew Dr BOLS/LL BL3	35	F2
Renfrew Rd WGNE/HIN WN2	23	H5
Renton Rd BOLS/LL BL3	35	H2

Reservoir St WGNE/HIN WN2	32	B2
Restormel Av HOR/BR BL6	23	H5
Reynolds Cl WHTN BL5	43	F2
Reynolds Dr WHTN BL5	43	F1
Rhine Cl TOT/BURYW BL8	11	H5
Rhode St TOT/BURYW BL8	21	H1
Rhosleigh Av BOL BL1	18	C3
Ribble Av BOLE BL2	30	A3
Ribble Dr FWTH BL4	46	B3
WALK M28	52	D5
Ribblesdale Rd BOLS/LL BL3	36	B5
Ribbleton Cl TOT/BURYW BL8	31	H1
Ribchester Gv BOLE BL2	30	A1
Richard Gwyn Cl WHTN BL5	41	F2
Richard St RAD M26	39	H2
Richelieu St BOLS/LL BL3	37	E1
Richmond Cl TOT/BURYW BL8	21	H1
Richmond Dr LEIGH WN7	51	E4
WALK M28	55	E3
Richmond Gdns BOLS/LL BL3	37	F2
Richmond Gv FWTH * BL4	37	E4
WALK M28	50	D5
Richmond Rd WALK M28	52	C4
WGNE/HIN WN2	40	C5
Richmond St BOL * BL1	18	D1
Ridgemont Cl HOR/BR BL6	15	H4
Ridgeway BOL * BL1	2	E3
Ridgmont Dr HOR/BR BL6	15	H4
WALK M28	52	D5
Ridgway HOR/BR BL6	13	G5
Riding Cl TYLD M29	52	B4
Riding Ga BOLE BL2	20	A1
Riding Gate Ms BOLE BL2	20	A1
Ridyard St LHULT M38	45	E4
Riefield BOL BL1	17	H4
Rigby Av HOR/BR * BL6	13	G5
Rigby Ct BOLS/LL BL3	36	D1
Rigby Gv LHULT M38	44	C4
Rigby La BOLE BL2	19	G1
Rigbys Houses		
CHLY/EC (off The Common) PR7	12	C1
Rigby St BOLS/LL BL3	36	D1
WGNE/HIN WN2	40	A2
Riley Ct BOL BL1	28	D1
Riley La WGNE/HIN WN2	23	F3
Riley St ATH M46	50	A2
Ringley Gv BOL BL1	18	C2
Ringley Mdw RAD M26	47	E1
Ringley Old Brow RAD M26	47	E1
Ringley Rd RAD M26	38	D5
Ringley Rd West RAD M26	39	F5
Ringlow Av SWIN M27	55	E4
Ringlow Park Rd SWIN M27	55	E4
Ringway Av LEIGH WN7	49	H3
Ripley Dr LEIGH WN7	49	H3
Ripley St BOL BL1	19	F3
Ripon Av BOL BL1	27	F1
Ripon Cl BOLS/LL BL3	38	B2
Ripon Dr BOL BL1	27	F1
Rishton Av BOLS/LL BL3	36	D3
Rishton La BOLS/LL BL3	36	D1
The Riverbank RAD M26	38	C5
Riverside BOL BL1	18	D5
Riverside Dr RAD M26	38	D5
Riversleigh Cl BOL BL1	17	F4
Riversmeade BOLE BL2	9	G5
LEIGH WN7	50	A5
River St BOLE BL2	3	G4
Riverview Wk BOL BL1	2	A5
Rivington Av CHLYE PR6	6	A5
Rivington Dr WGNE/HIN WN2	48	B2
Rivington La CHLYE PR6	6	D5
HOR/BR BL6	7	F3
Rivington St ATH M46	50	A1
HOR/BR BL6	13	H5
Rix St BOL BL1	18	C5
Rixton Dr TYLD M29	51	H3
Roading Brook Rd BOLE BL2	20	C4
Robertshaw St LEIGH WN7	49	G4
Robert St ATH * M46	51	E1
BOLE* BL2	20	A2
Robinson St HOR/BR BL6	14	D3
Rochester Av BOLE BL2	30	A1
WALK M28	53	G3
Rock Av BOL BL1	18	A5
Rock Fold		
EDGW/EG (off Cox Green Rd) BL7	8	D3
Rockhaven Av HOR/BR BL6	15	E3
Rock St HOR/BR BL6	14	D4
Rock Ter EDGW/EG BL7	8	D3
Rodgers Cl WHTN BL5	41	G2
Rodgers Wy WHTN BL5	41	G2
Rodmell Cl EDGW/EG BL7	8	D5
Rodney St ATH * M46	50	C1
Roebuck St WGNE/HIN WN2	41	H5
Roe Gn WALK M28	54	C3
Roe Green Av WALK M28	54	C3
Rogerstead BOLS/LL BL3	28	A4
Roland St BOLS/LL BL3	28	A5
Roman St RAD M26	39	G2
Romer St BOLE BL2	29	G3
Romford Av LEIGH WN7	49	H5
Romford Pl WGNE/HIN WN2	40	A3
Romiley Crs BOLE BL2	29	H2
Romiley Dr BOLE BL2	29	H2
Romney Rd BOL BL1	17	E5
Romsley Dr BOLS/LL BL3	36	A2
Roocroft Cl BOL BL1	28	B1
Roocroft Sq HOR/BR BL6	13	G5
Roosevelt Rd FWTH BL4	46	B1

Rosamond St *BOLS/LL* BL3 ....**36** A1
Roscoe Ct *WHTN* BL5 ....**41** H1
Roscoe Lowe Brow *CHLYE* PR6 ......**6** D5
Roscow Av *BOLE* BL2 ....**30** A2
Roscow Rd *FWTH* BL4 ....**46** C2
Rose Acre *WALK* M28 ....**53** F4
Rosebank *HOR/BR* BL6 ....**26** C3
Rosebank Cl *BOLE* BL2.............**31** E1
Roseberry St *BOLS/LL* BL3 ....**36** A1
Rosebery St *WHTN* BL5.............**33** H5
Rosedale Av *ATH* M46 ....**42** C5
BOL BL1 ....**18** C2
Rose Gv *FWTH* BL4 ....**46** B1
Rose Hl *BOLS/LL* BL3 ....**3** H7
Rose Hill Cl *EDGW/EG* BL7 ....**9** E5
Rose Hill Dr *EDGW/EG* BL7 ....**9** E5
Rosehill Rd *SWIN* M27 ....**55** H1
Rose Lea *BOLE* BL2.............**20** A3
Rosemary La *WHTN* BL5 ....**43** H2
Roseneath Gv *BOLS/LL* BL3 ....**36** B2
Roseneath Rd *BOLS/LL* BL3 ....**36** B2
Rosewood *WHTN* BL5 ....**41** G2
Rossall Cl *BOLE* BL2 ....**29** C2
Rossall St *BOLE* BL2 ....**29** G2
Ross Dr *SWIN* M27 ....**47** G4
Rossini St *BOL* BL1 ....**18** A4
Rostherne Gdns *BOLS/LL* BL3.......**35** H1
Rothay St *BOLE* BL2 ....**30** B1
Rothbury Cl *TOT/BURYW* BL8.......**21** H5
Rothbury Ct *BOLS/LL* BL3 ....**35** H2
Rotherhead Cl *HOR/BR* BL6 ......**14** B5
Rothesay Rd *BOLS/LL* * BL3 ......**35** H2
Rothwell Crs *LHULT* M38.............**44** C2
Rothwell La *LHULT* M38.............**44** C3
Rothwell Rd *CHLYE* PR6 ....**6** B5
Rothwell St *BOLS/LL* BL3 ....**2** C7
WALK M28.............**46** B5
Roughlee Av *SWIN* M27 ....**55** F4
Round Hill Wy *BOL* BL1 ....**3** F1
Roundthorn La *WHTN* BL5 ....**41** G1
The Rowans *BOL* BL1 ....**27** E3
Rowena St *BOLS/LL* BL3 ....**37** G3
Rowe St *TYLD* * M29 ....**51** H3
Rowland St *ATH* M46 ....**42** D5
Rowsley Av *BOL* BL1 ....**27** G1
Rowton St *BOLE* BL2 ....**19** F4
Roxalina St *BOLS/LL* BL3 ....**36** C1
Roxby Cl *WALK* M28 ....**45** F5
Royal Court Dr *BOL* BL1 ....**2** B3
Royal Dr *LEIGH* WN7 ....**50** D5
Royds St *TOT/BURYW* BL8.......**11** H5
Royland Av *BOLS/LL* BL3 ....**37** E2
Royle St *WALK* M28 ....**53** H1
Roynton Rd *HOR/BR* BL6 ....**14** D1
Royston Av *BOLE* BL2 ....**3** K1
Royston Cl *TOT/BURYW* BL8.......**11** H3
Roy St *BOLS/LL* BL3 ....**35** H1
Ruabon Crs *WGNE/HIN* WN2 ......**40** B4
Ruby St *BOL* BL1 ....**18** D4
Rudford Gdns *BOLS/LL* * BL3 ......**36** D1
Rudolph St *BOLS/LL* BL3 ....**36** D2
Rufford Dr *BOLS/LL* BL3 ....**36** B3
Rufford Gv *BOLS/LL* BL3 ....**36** B3
Ruins La *BOLE* BL2 ....**20** A3
Rumworth Rd *HOR/BR* BL6 ......**26** C4
Rumworth St *BOLS/LL* BL3 ....**36** B1
Runnymede Ct *BOLS/LL* BL3 ....**2** A7
Rupert St *BOLS/LL* BL3 ....**36** D1
Rush Acre Cl *RAD* M26 ....**39** G2
Rushey Fld *EDGW/EG* BL7 ....**8** D4
Rushey Fold La *BOL* BL1 ....**18** B5
Rusheylea Cl *BOL* BL1 ....**18** A5
Rushford Gv *BOL* BL1 ....**18** D3
Rushlake Dr *BOL* BL1 ....**28** C1
Rushton Av *LEIGH* WN7 ....**49** F3
Rushton Rd *BOL* BL1 ....**27** H1
Rushton St *WALK* M28 ....**53** H1
Ruskin Av *FWTH* BL4 ....**46** B1
Rusland Dr *BOLE* BL2 ....**20** A5
Russell Cl *BOL* BL1 ....**28** A2
Russell Ct *FWTH* * BL4 ....**38** A5
LHULT M38 ....**45** G5
Russell St *ATH* M46 ....**42** C5
FWTH BL4 ....**45** H1
LHULT M38 ....**45** C5
WGNE/HIN WN2 ....**49** E1
Rutherford Dr *WHTN* BL5 ....**43** F1
Rutherglen Dr *BOLS/LL* BL3 ....**27** E4
Ruth St *BOL* BL1 ....**2** C2
Rutland Av *ATH* M46 ....**43** F3
SWIN M27 ....**55** H1
Rutland Cl *BOLS/LL* BL3 ....**38** D1
Rutland Gv *BOL* BL1 ....**28** A1
FWTH * BL4 ....**45** G1
Rutland Rd *TYLD* M29 ....**51** F1
WALK M28 ....**53** G2
WGNE/HIN WN2 ....**40** B2
Rutland St *BOLS/LL* BL3 ....**36** B1
SWIN M27 ....**55** G2
Rydal Av *WGNE/HIN* WN2 ......**40** A3
Rydal Cl *HOR/BR* BL6 ....**13** G4
Rydal Ct
BOL (off Kingsbury Av) BL1 ......**27** F1
Rydal Crs *SWIN* M27 ....**55** H5
WALK M28.............**54** A2
Rydal Gv *FWTH* BL4 ....**44** D5
Rydal Rd *BOL* BL1 ....**27** G1

BOLS/LL BL3 ....**38** C2
Ryder St *BOL* BL1 ....**18** A5
Ryde St *BOLS/LL* * BL3 ....**35** C1
Rydley St *BOL* * BL3 ....**3** J5
Ryeburn Dr *BOLE* BL2 ....**19** F2
Ryecroft Av *TOT/BURYW* BL8......**21** H1
Ryecroft Dr *WHTN* BL5 ....**33** F2
Ryefield St *BOL* BL1 ....**29** E1
Rye Hl *WHTN* * BL5 ....**33** H5
Ryelands *WHTN* BL5.............**33** H5
Ryelands Ct
WHTN (off Ryelands) BL5 ....**33** H5
Ryley Av *BOLS/LL* BL3 ....**27** H5
Ryley St *BOLS/LL* * BL3 ....**2** A6

S

Sabden Rd *BOL* BL1 ....**17** E5
Sackville St *BOLE* * BL2 ....**29** G3
Saddleback Cl *WALK* M28 ....**53** F5
Saddle St *BOLE* BL2 ....**19** F5
Sadler St *BOLS/LL* BL3 ....**37** E1
St Andrews Ct *BOL* * BL1 ....**2** E4
St Andrews Rd *HOR/BR* BL6 ......**26** A3
RAD M26.............**31** H4
St Andrew's Vw *RAD* M26.............**31** H4
St Anne's Av *ATH* M46 ....**51** E2
St Annes Meadow
TOT/BURYW BL8 ....**11** H5
St Annes Rd *HOR/BR* BL6 ....**15** E3
St Ann's St *SWIN* M27 ....**55** G3
St Ann St *BOL* * BL1 ....**28** C1
St Aubin's Rd *BOLE* BL2.............**3** J6
St Augustine St *BOL* BL1 ....**18** B5
St Austell Av *TYLD* M29 ....**52** A3
St Austell Dr *TOT/BURYW* BL8 ......**11** H2
St Bartholomews St *BOLS/LL* BL3...**37** E1
St Bede's Av *BOLS/LL* BL3 ....**35** H3
St Bees Rd *BOLE* BL2 ....**19** C5
St Brides Cl *HOR/BR* BL6 ....**14** C3
St Clair Rd *TOT/BURYW* * BL8 ......**11** H1
St Clare Ter
HOR/BR
(off Chorley New Rd) BL6 ....**25** H2
St David's Crs *WGNE/HIN* WN2 ......**23** F5
St Dominics Ms *BOLS/LL* BL3 ....**36** A2
St Edmund St *BOL* BL1 ....**2** D3
St Elizabeth's Rd
WGNE/HIN WN2 ....**23** F5
St Ethelbert's Av *BOLS/LL* BL3 ......**27** H5
St George's Av *WHTN* BL5 ....**41** G2
St George's Ct *BOL* * BL1 ....**3** F2
TYLD M29 ....**51** F3
St George's Crs *WALK* M28 ....**53** H1
St George's Pl *ATH* * M46 ....**42** B4
St George's Rd *BOL* BL1 ....**2** B2
St Georges Sq *BOL* BL1 ....**3** F2
St George's St *BOL* BL1 ....**3** F2
TYLD M29 ....**51** F3
St Germain St *FWTH* BL4 ....**37** G5
St Gregorys Cl *FWTH* BL4 ....**37** G5
St Helena Rd *BOL* BL1 ....**2** C3
St Helens Rd *BOLS/LL* BL3 ....**35** C3
St Heliers St *BOLS/LL* BL3 ....**36** B1
St James Av *BOLE* BL2 ....**30** A2
St James Crs *WGNE/HIN* WN2 ......**48** B3
St James St *FWTH* BL4 ....**45** F1
WHTN BL5 ....**41** H3
St John's Av *WHTN* BL5 ....**33** F2
St John's Rd *HOR/BR* BL6 ....**14** D5
WALK M28.............**52** C4
WGNE/HIN WN2 ....**23** F5
St John's St *FWTH* BL4 ....**38** A5
St John St *ATH* M46 ....**42** D5
HOR/BR BL6.............**14** D3
RAD M26.............**45** G4
St Johns Wd *HOR/BR* BL6 ....**34** B1
St Joseph St *BOL* BL1 ....**18** B5
St Katherines Dr *HOR/BR* BL6 ......**13** C4
St Kilda Av *FWTH* BL4.............**46** B2
St Leonard's Av *HOR/BR* BL6 ......**25** H1
St Margaret's Cl *BOL* * BL1 ....**27** H2
St Margaret's Rd *BOL* BL1.............**27** H2
St Mark's Crs *WALK* M28 ....**53** H2
St Mark's St *BOLS/LL* BL3 ....**28** D5
St Mark's Vw *BOLS/LL* * BL3 ....**28** D5
St Marks Wk *BOLS/LL* BL3 ....**36** C1
St Mary's Av *BOLS/LL* BL3 ....**27** G5
St Mary's Cl *ATH* M46 ....**43** E5
WGNE/HIN * WN2 ....**23** F5
St Mary's Rd *WALK* M28.............**45** G4
WGNE/HIN WN2 ....**23** F4
St Matthews Gra *BOL* * BL1 ....**28** C1
St Matthews Wk *BOL* * BL1 ....**28** C1
St Mawes Ct *RAD* * M26 ....**31** E5
St Michael's La *ATH* M46.............**50** A2
BOLS/LL BL3 ....**37** F5
St Michaels Ct *TOT/BURYW* BL8 ......**31** H2
St Osmund's Dr *BOLE* BL2.............**30** A3
St Osmund's Gv *BOLE* BL2.............**30** A3
St Paul's Cl *CHLYE* PR6.............**6** A4
St Pauls Rd *WALK* * M28 ....**54** A1
St Peter's Av *BOL* BL1 ....**17** G5
St Peter's Rd *SWIN* M27 ....**55** G4
St Peter's Ter *FWTH* BL4 ....**45** H1
St Peter's Wy *BOL* BL1 ....**3** F2
BOLE BL2 ....**3** H6

BOLS/LL BL3 ....**37** F1
St Philip's Av *BOLS/LL* BL3 ....**36** B1
St Stephen's Cl *BOLE* BL2 ....**29** G5
St Thomas St *BOL* * BL1.............**18** B5
St Williams Av *BOLS/LL* BL3 ....**36** C2
Salcombe Av *BOLE* BL2 ....**31** F1
Salcombe Gv *BOLE* BL2 ....**30** B4
Sale La *TYLD* M29 ....**52** B2
Salford Rd *WHTN* BL5 ....**40** A2
Salisbury Rd *HOR/BR* BL6 ....**25** G1
RAD M26.............**31** C5
SWIN M27 ....**55** G4
Salisbury St *BOLS/LL* BL3 ....**2** B5
Salisbury Ter *BOLS/LL* BL3 ....**39** E2
Salisbury Wy *TYLD* M29.............**51** H3
Salop St *BOLE* BL2 ....**3** C5
Saltergate *BOLS/LL* BL3 ....**35** F1
Salters Ct *ATH* M46 ....**42** D5
Salterton Dr *BOLS/LL* BL3 ....**35** F3
Saltram Cl *BOLS/LL* BL3 ....**31** E5
Saltwood Gv *BOL* BL1 ....**28** D1
Samuel St *ATH* M46 ....**51** F2
Sandalwood *WHTN* BL5 ....**41** F2
Sand Banks *BOL* BL1 ....**18** B2
Sanderling Cl *WHTN* BL5 ....**41** F2
Sanderson Cl *WALK* M28 ....**54** D3
Sandfield Dr *HOR/BR* BL6 ....**26** C4
Sandford Cl *BOLE* BL2 ....**20** A4
Sandgate Cl *LEIGH* WN7 ....**49** H5
Sandham St *BOLS/LL* BL3 ....**36** D1
Sandhill Cl *BOLS/LL* BL3 ....**36** D1
Sand Hole Rd *FWTH* BL4 ....**46** C2
Sandhurst Cl *BOLE* BL2 ....**30** A4
Sandhurst Dr *BOLE* BL2 ....**30** A4
Sandiway Cl *WHTN* BL5 ....**33** C5
Sandon St *BOLS/LL* BL3 ....**36** B1
Sandown Crs *BOLS/LL* BL3 ....**38** C3
Sandown Rd *BOLE* BL2 ....**20** A4
Sandpiper Cl *FWTH* BL4 ....**44** D1
Sandray Cl *BOLS/LL* BL3 ....**27** F5
Sandridge Cl *FWTH* BL4 ....**44** D1
Sandringham Cl *CHLY/EC* PR7 ......**12** C1
Sandringham Dr *LEIGH* WN7 ......**51** E4
Sandringham Rd *HOR/BR* BL6 ......**15** F5
WALK M28.............**53** E5
WGNE/HIN WN2 ....**40** A4
Sandwich St *WALK* M28.............**53** H1
Sandwick Crs *BOLS/LL* BL3 ....**28** B5
Sandwood Av *BOLS/LL* BL3 ....**27** E5
Sandyacre *WHTN* BL5 ....**43** C2
Sandybrook Cl *TOT/BURYW* BL8......**21** H1
Sandygate Cl *SWIN* M27 ....**55** G4
Sandy Gv *SWIN* M27 ....**55** H3
Sandyhills *BOLS/LL* BL3 ....**36** C1
Sandy La *WGNE/HIN* WN2 ......**40** B2
Sandy Pk *WGNE/HIN* WN2 ......**40** C2
Sandy Wy *WGNE/HIN* WN2 ......**40** B2
Sapling Rd *BOLS/LL* BL3 ....**36** A3
Sarah St *WGNE/HIN* WN2 ....**48** D1
Saunton Av *BOLE* BL2 ....**20** B5
Savick Av *BOLE* BL2 ....**30** A3
Saville Rd *RAD* M26 ....**31** H3
Saville St *BOLE* BL2.............**3** G4
Saviours Ter
BOLS/LL (off BankField St) BL3....**28** A5
Saw St *BOL* BL1 ....**18** C5
Saxby Av *EDGW/EG* BL7 ....**8** D4
Saxon St *RAD* M26 ....**39** H2
Scant Rw
HOR/BR (off Chorley Old Rd) BL6 ...**16** C4
Scardale Av *BOL* BL1 ....**27** G1
Scargill Rd *BOLS/LL* BL3 ....**35** G1
Scarthwood Cl *BOLE* BL2 ....**20** A2
Scawfell Av *BOLE* BL2 ....**19** F5
Schofield La *ATH* M46 ....**41** H5
Scholes Bank *HOR/BR* BL6 ......**14** C5
Scholey St *BOLE* BL2 ....**29** E5
School Brow *WALK* M28 ....**54** B5
School Hl *BOL* BL1 ....**2** D1
School La *WGNE/HIN* WN2 ......**22** C2
School St *ATH* M46 ....**50** B1
BOLS/LL BL3 ....**38** D2
EDGW/EG BL7 ....**8** D5
HOR/BR BL6.............**15** E4
LEIGH WN7 ....**49** G3
RAD M26.............**39** H2
TYLD M29 ....**51** F3
WHTN BL5 ....**33** G5
Scobell St *TOT/BURYW* BL8.......**21** H2
Scorton Av *BOLE* BL2 ....**30** B3
Scorton St *BOL* * BL1 ....**28** A2
Scot La *WGNE/HIN* WN2 ......**23** H4
Scott Av *WGNE/HIN* WN2 ......**40** A3
Scott St *RAD* M26 ....**47** F1
WHTN BL5.............**33** G3
Scout Rd *BOL* BL1 ....**17** G1
Scowcroft La *BOLE* BL2 ....**29** F5
Seaford Rd *BOLE* BL2 ....**20** A1
Seaforth Av *ATH* M46 ....**42** C5
Seaforth Rd *BOL* BL1 ....**18** C2
Seathwaite Cl *TYLD* M29 ....**51** G4
Seathwaite Rd *FWTH* BL4 ....**44** D1
Seaton Rd *BOL* BL1 ....**18** A5
Second Av *ATH* M46 ....**42** D4
BOL BL1 ....**17** H5
Second St *BOL* BL1 ....**17** F3
Section St *BOL* BL1.............**2** E5
Seddon Cl *ATH* M46 ....**42** C5

Seddon Gdns *RAD* M26 ....
Seddon La *RAD* M26.............
Seddon St *BOLS/LL* * BL3 ....
LHULT M38 ....
WHTN BL5 ....
Sedgefield Dr *BOL* BL1 ....
Sedgefield Rd *RAD* M26 ....
Sedgemoor V *BOLE* BL2 ....
Sedgley Dr *WHTN* BL5 ....
Sedgwick Cl *ATH* M46 ....
Seedley Av *LHULT* M38 ....
Seed St *BOL* BL1 ....
Sefton Av *ATH* M46 ....
Sefton Dr *SWIN* M27 ....
WALK M28.............
Sefton La *HOR/BR* BL6 ....
Sefton Rd *BOL* BL1 ....
SWIN M27 ....
Selbourne Cl *WHTN* BL5 ....
Selbourne St *LEIGH* WN7 ....
Selkirk St *BOL* BL1 ....
Selwyn St *BOLE* * BL2 ....
LEIGH WN7 ....
Sennicar La *WGN* WN1 ....
Settle Cl *TOT/BURYW* BL8 ....
Settle St *BOLS/LL* BL3 ....
BOLS/LL BL3 ....
Seven Oaks *LEIGH* WN7 ....
Sevenoaks Dr *BOLS/LL* BL3 ....
Severn Dr *WGNE/HIN* WN2 ....
Severn Wy *FWTH* BL4 ....
Seymour Dr *BOLE* BL2 ....
Seymour Gv *FWTH* * BL4 ....
Seymour Rd *BOL* BL1 ....
Seymour St *BOLE* BL2 ....
Shackleton Gv *BOL* BL1 ....
Shadwell Gv *LEIGH* WN7 ....
Shady La *BOLE* BL2 ....
Shaftesbury Av *HOR/BR* BL6 ....
Shaftesbury Rd *SWIN* M27 ....
Shakerley La *TYLD* M29 ....
Shakerley Rd *TYLD* M29 ....
Shakespeare Av *RAD* M26 ....
Shakespeare Rd *SWIN* M27 ....
Shalbourne Rd *WALK* M28 ....
Shalfleet Ct *BOLE* BL2 ....
Shanklin Wk *BOLS/LL* BL3 ....
Shap Dr *WALK* M28.............
Sharman St *BOLS/LL* BL3.............
Sharnford Cl *BOLE* BL2 ....
Sharples Av *BOL* BL1 ....
Sharples Dr *TOT/BURYW* BL8 ....
Sharples Hall Dr *BOL* BL1 ....
Sharples Hall Fold *BOL* BL1 ....
Sharples Hall Ms *BOL* BL1 ....
Sharples Pk *BOL* BL1 ....
Sharp St *WALK* M28 ....
Shaving La *WALK* M28 ....
Shawbrook Av *WALK* M28 ....
Shawbury Cl *HOR/BR* BL6 ....
Shawes Dr *CHLYE* PR6 ....
Shaw Rd *HOR/BR* BL6 ....
Shaw St *BOLS/LL* BL3.............
FWTH * BL4 ....
Shearwater Av *TYLD* M29 ....
Shearwater Dr *WALK* M28 ....
WHTN BL5.............
The Sheddings *BOLS/LL* * BL3 ....
Sheep Gate Dr *TOT/BURYW* BL8 ....
Sheep House La *HOR/BR* BL6.......
Shelbourne Av *BOL* BL1 ....
Shelley Rd *LHULT* * M38 ....
SWIN M27 ....
Shelley St *LEIGH* WN7 ....
Shelley Wk *BOL* BL1 ....
Shepherd Cross St *BOL* BL1 ....
Shepherds Cl *HOR/BR* BL6 ....
TOT/BURYW BL8
Shepherd's Dr *HOR/BR* BL6 ....
Shepherd St *TOT/BURYW* BL8 ....
Shepley Av *BOLS/LL* BL3 ....
Shepton Cl *BOL* BL1 ....
Sherborne Av *WGNE/HIN* WN2 ...
Sherbourne Cl *RAD* M26 ....
Sherbourne Rd *BOL* BL1 ....
Sheriffs Dr *TYLD* M29.............
Sheriff St *BOLE* BL2 ....
Sheringham Dr *SWIN* M27 ....
Sheringham Pl *BOLS/LL* BL3.............
Sherwood Av *RAD* M26 ....
TYLD M29 ....
Sherwood Cl *TOT/BURYW* BL8 ....
Sherwood St *BOL* BL1 ....
Shield Dr *WALK* M28 ....
Shiel St *WALK* M28 ....
Shiffnall St *BOLE* BL2 ....
Shillingford Rd *FWTH* BL4.............
Shillingstone Cl *BOLE* BL2 ....
Shillingten Cl *LHULT* M38 ....
Shilton Gdns *BOLS/LL* BL3.............
Shipgate *BOL* * BL1 ....
Shipham Cl *LEIGH* WN7 ....
Shipton St *BOL* BL1 ....
Shireburn Av *BOLE* BL2 ....
Shires Cl *WGNE/HIN* WN2 ....
Shorefield Mt *EDGW/EG* BL7 ......
Shoreswood *BOL* BL1 ....
Shorland St *SWIN* M27 ....
Shorrocks St *TOT/BURYW* BL8.......
Shortland Pl *WGNE/HIN* WN2 ......

ury Cl WGNE/HIN WN2 ... 40 B2
ury Rd BOL BL1 ... 27 H2
ton Rd ATH M46 ... 43 F3
St BOLS/LL BL3 ... 36 A1
illock Rd
'HIN WN2 ... 48 B4
t TYLD M29 ... 51 F2
HIN WN2 ... 40 A2
l BOLS/LL BL3 ... 29 H5
: BOLS/LL BL3 ... 3 F7
St HOR/BR BL6 ... 15 E5
r Wy BOLE BL2 ... 30 A1
v WALK M28 ... 53 H2
HTN * BL5 ... 33 G4
e Rd BOL BL1 ... 28 A3
L4 ... 37 E4
HIN WN2 ... 40 B3
Gv BOL BL1 ... 18 D3
l La BOL BL1 ... 3 F4
l St BOL BL1 ... 3 F4
? BL6 ... 14 D3
St HOR/BR * BL6 ... 13 H5
ry Cl TOT/BURYW BL8 ... 21 H5
Gv WALK M28 ... 53 E5
Rd WALK M28 ... 53 E5
Gv BOLS/LL BL3 ... 36 C2
Rd SWIN M27 ... 55 F1
Av BOLE BL2 ... 30 A3
? BL6 ... 15 E2
Gv WHTN BL5 ... 34 B5
St RAD M26 ... 39 F1
AD M26 ... 39 H3
Gv WALK M28 ... 53 G3
BOL BL1 ... 27 H3
t BOL BL1 ... 28 C1
v BOLE BL2 ... 30 B2
Av BOLS/LL BL3 ... 36 D3
v WGNE/HIN WN2 ... 40 C4
l TOT/BURYW BL8 ... 21 H5
t BOLE BL2 ... 29 G3
row FWTH BL4 ... 47 E3
old WGNE/HIN WN2 ... 48 D2
d La FWTH BL4 ... 36 B4
BOLE BL2 ... 10 A5
BL5 ... 33 H3
CHLYE PR6 ... 6 B2
BOLS/LL BL3 ... 38 C2
Av BOLE BL2 ... 30 B4
Dr TOT/BURYW BL8 ... 21 G4
HOR/BR BL6 ... 15 E3
d BOLS/LL BL3 ... 28 C5
BOL BL1 ... 3 G1
ook WHTN BL5 ... 33 G4
BOL BL1 ... 2 D1
Cl BOL BL1 ... 18 D5
e Cl BOLE BL2 ... 30 C1
BOLS/LL BL3 ... 35 H2
ge Cl WALK M28 ... 53 G3
ok La LEIGH WN7 ... 41 G5
St HOR/BR * BL6 ... 15 E5
Av BOLS/LL BL3 ... 37 E2
t La BOLS/LL BL3 ... 35 H3
w HOR/BR BL6 ... 13 G5
d La WALK M28 ... 45 E5
Croft Rd BOL BL1 ... 17 G4
Dean Rd BOL BL1 ... 17 G2
Dr BOL BL1 ... 17 F5
EDGW/EG BL7 ... 8 D4
WGNE/HIN WN2 ... 48 C3
d BOLS/LL BL3 ... 37 H2
ATH * M46 ... 42 C5
28 ... 45 H5
HIN WN2 ... 23 G5
od Av WGNE/HIN WN2 ... 40 B2
t EDGW/EG BL7 ... 8 D4
BOLS/LL BL3 ... 35 G1
t RAD M26 ... 39 H2
RAD M26 ... 31 H4
OLS/LL BL3 ... 28 D5
St BOL BL1 ... 2 C2
Dr HOR/BR BL6 ... 15 E2
Rd BOLS/LL BL3 ... 29 H5
l WHTN BL5 ... 34 A3
Vy BOLS/LL BL3 ... 34 D3
OL BL1 ... 27 H1
WGNE/HIN WN2 ... 40 A4
OL BL1 ... 2 E5
BOLS/LL BL3 ... 29 G5
BOLS/LL BL3 ... 36 B2
7 ... 47 G4
e Av BOL BL1 ... 27 G2
Dr EDGW/EG BL7 ... 8 D4
Wk BOLS/LL * BL3 ... 28 C5
Av TYLD M29 ... 43 F5
Rd ATH M46 ... 42 B4
... 27 H2
Rd BOLE BL2 ... 30 B5
e Sq BOL BL1 ... 18 A4
e St BOL BL1 ... 18 A4
r BOLS/LL BL3 ... 35 G3
FWTH BL4 ... 46 B2
ok Gv BOLS/LL BL3 ... 36 D2
rt LEIGH WN7 ... 50 B5
n Dr WALK M28 ... 52 D5
BOLE BL2 ... 20 A4
St BOLS/LL BL3 ... 36 A2
St WALK M28 ... 45 H3
Dr WHTN BL5 ... 41 G1
St BOLS/LL BL3 ... 37 F1
e BOLE BL2 ... 20 A3

South Gv WALK M28 ... 53 G1
Southgrove Av BOL BL1 ... 18 C1
Southleigh Dr BOLE BL2 ... 30 C4
South Meade SWIN M27 ... 55 G5
Southmoor Wk BOLS/LL * BL3 ... 28 C5
Southover WHTN BL5 ... 41 G2
South Royd St TOT/BURYW BL8 ... 11 H5
South St ATH M46 ... 51 E2
BOLS/LL BL3 ... 36 C2
South Vw ATH M46 ... 42 C5
South View St BOLE BL2 ... 29 G3
Southwell Cl BOL BL1 ... 2 C1
Southwood Cl BOLS/LL BL3 ... 36 D2
Sovereign Fold Rd LEIGH WN7 ... 49 G2
Sowerby Cl TOT/BURYW BL8 ... 21 H5
Spa Crs LHULT M38 ... 45 E2
Spa Gv LHULT M38 ... 45 E2
Spa La LHULT M38 ... 45 E2
Spa Rd ATH M46 ... 42 C3
BOL BL1 ... 2 B5
BOLS/LL BL3 ... 2 A5
Sparta Av WALK M28 ... 53 G1
Spencer Av BOLS/LL BL3 ... 39 E2
Spenleach La TOT/BURYW BL8 ... 5 E5
Spenser Av RAD M26 ... 39 G1
Spindlepoint Dr WALK M28 ... 53 G3
Spindle Wk WHTN BL5 ... 33 H3
Spiningdale LHULT M38 ... 44 B2
Spinners Ms BOL BL1 ... 2 D1
Spinney Nook BOLE BL2 ... 19 H5
The Spinney EDGW/EG BL7 ... 9 G2
SWIN (off Chatsworth Rd) M27 ... 55 E5
Spinningfields BOL * BL1 ... 2 A1
Spinning Meadow BOL BL1 ... 2 B1
Spinning Mdw BOL BL1 ... 2 A1
Sportside Av WALK M28 ... 46 A4
Sportside Cl WALK M28 ... 45 H4
Sportside Gv WALK M28 ... 45 H4
Springburn Cl WALK M28 ... 53 E5
Spring Cl TOT/BURYW BL8 ... 21 G1
Spring Clough Av WALK M28 ... 54 B1
Spring Clough Dr WALK M28 ... 54 B1
Springfield RAD M26 ... 47 E2
Springfield Gdns FWTH BL4 ... 46 C2
Springfield Rd ATH M46 ... 43 E4
BOL BL1 ... 8 C5
CHLYE PR6 ... 6 A4
FWTH BL4 ... 37 E4
FWTH BL4 ... 46 B2
HOR/BR BL6 ... 25 F1
Springfield St BOLS/LL BL3 ... 37 E1
Spring Gdns BOLE BL2 ... 20 B3
HOR/BR BL6 ... 14 D3
Springlawns
BOL (off Markland Hl) BL1 ... 27 F2
Springside Av WALK M28 ... 46 A5
Springside Cl WALK * M28 ... 46 A5
Springside Gv WALK M28 ... 46 A5
Spring St BOLS/LL BL3 ... 28 D5
FWTH BL4 ... 37 H4
HOR/BR BL6 ... 14 D3
TOT/BURYW BL8 ... 11 H5
Spring Vale Dr TOT/BURYW BL8 ... 11 G5
Spring Vale St TOT/BURYW BL8 ... 21 G1
Springwater Cl BOLE BL2 ... 20 A4
Squires La TYLD M29 ... 51 E3
Squirrel La HOR/BR BL6 ... 14 C3
Stafford Rd SWIN M27 ... 55 H3
WALK M28 ... 53 G2
Stainforth Cl TOT/BURYW BL8 ... 21 H4
Stainsbury St BOLS/LL BL3 ... 36 A1
Stainton Cl RAD M26 ... 39 G1
Stainton Rd RAD M26 ... 31 G5
Stamford St ATH M46 ... 43 E4
Stanbourne Dr BOL BL1 ... 18 D3
Stancliffe Gv WGNE/HIN WN2 ... 23 G4
Standfield Dr WALK M28 ... 53 E4
Standish St TYLD M29 ... 51 G3
Stanford Cl RAD * M26 ... 47 E1
Stanhope St LEIGH WN7 ... 49 F5
Stanier Pl HOR/BR BL6 ... 15 E5
Stanley Cl WHTN BL5 ... 42 A1
Stanley Dr LEIGH WN7 ... 49 F3
Stanley Gv HOR/BR BL6 ... 25 F1
Stanley La WGNE/HIN WN2 ... 23 G3
Stanley Ms BOLE BL2 ... 29 H3
Stanley Park Wk BOLE BL2 ... 29 G2
Stanley Rd BOL BL1 ... 27 H1
FWTH BL4 ... 36 C5
RAD M26 ... 31 G4
WALK M28 ... 53 H1
WGNE/HIN WN2 ... 23 G4
Stanley St ATH M46 ... 50 C1
Stanley St South BOLS/LL BL3 ... 2 C5
Stanmoor Dr WGNE/HIN WN2 ... 23 G5
Stanmore Dr BOLS/LL BL3 ... 28 A5
Stanrose Cl EDGW/EG BL7 ... 8 C3
Stansfield Cl BOLE BL2 ... 29 G3
Stansfield Rd BOLE BL2 ... 3 J2
Stanway Av BOLS/LL BL3 ... 2 B6
Stanway Cl BOLS/LL * BL3 ... 2 B6
Stanwell Rd SWIN M27 ... 55 G4
Stanworth Av BOLE BL2 ... 30 A3
Stapleford Cl WHTN BL5 ... 43 G2
Staplehurst Cl WGNE/HIN WN2 ... 49 E1
Stapleton Av BOL BL1 ... 27 E2
Starbeck Cl TOT/BURYW BL8 ... 21 H5
Starcliffe St BOLS/LL BL3 ... 37 H3
Starkie Rd BOLE BL2 ... 3 K3
Starkie St WALK M28 ... 54 C3

Star La HOR/BR BL6 ... 14 B4
Starling Dr FWTH BL4 ... 44 D1
Starling Rd RAD M26 ... 31 G2
TOT/BURYW BL8 ... 31 G1
Starmount Cl BOLE BL2 ... 30 C4
Station Rd CHLY/EC PR7 ... 12 D1
FWTH BL4 ... 46 B1
HOR/BR BL6 ... 24 A1
SWIN M27 ... 55 H2
TOT/BURYW BL8 ... 11 H3
Station St BOLS/LL * BL3 ... 3 F6
Staton Av BOLE BL2 ... 29 G2
Staveley Av BOL BL1 ... 18 C1
Steele Gdns BOLE BL2 ... 29 H5
Stephenson St HOR/BR BL6 ... 14 D5
Stephens St BOLE BL2 ... 29 H2
Sterndale Rd WALK M28 ... 52 D5
Sterratt St BOL BL1 ... 2 A4
Stetchworth Dr WALK M28 ... 53 F4
Stevenson Rd SWIN M27 ... 55 G3
Stevenson St WALK M28 ... 45 F5
Stewart Av FWTH BL4 ... 45 F1
Stewart St BOL BL1 ... 28 C1
Steynton Cl BOL BL1 ... 27 F2
Stirling Rd BOL BL1 ... 18 C2
WGNE/HIN WN2 ... 40 B4
Stitch-mi-Lane BOLE BL2 ... 20 A5
Stockdale Gv BOLE BL2 ... 30 B1
Stockley Av BOLE BL2 ... 20 A5
Stocks Cottages
HOR/BR (off Gingham Brow) BL6 ... 15 F3
Stocksfield Dr LHULT M38 ... 44 D3
Stocks Park Dr HOR/BR BL6 ... 15 E4
Stockton Rd FWTH BL4 ... 37 G3
Stockton St SWIN M27 ... 55 G4
Stoneacre HOR/BR BL6 ... 25 H2
Stoneacre Ct SWIN M27 ... 55 H4
Stonebridge Cl HOR/BR BL6 ... 26 C4
Stonechat Cl WALK M28 ... 53 F3
Stoneclough Rd FWTH BL4 ... 46 B1
Stonedelph Cl BOLE BL2 ... 31 F1
Stonefield TYLD M29 ... 52 A2
Stonegate Fold CHLYE PR6 ... 6 B3
Stonehaven BOLS/LL BL3 ... 35 F2
Stone Hill Rd FWTH BL4 ... 45 H2
Stonehouse EDGW/EG BL7 ... 9 F5
Stoneleigh Dr RAD M26 ... 46 D1
Stonemead Cl BOLS/LL BL3 ... 36 D1
Stonesteads Dr EDGW/EG BL7 ... 9 E4
Stonesteads Wy EDGW/EG BL7 ... 9 E4
Stone St BOLE BL2 ... 29 F1
Stoney Bank RAD M26 ... 47 E1
Stoneycroft Av HOR/BR BL6 ... 15 F3
Stoneycroft Cl HOR/BR BL6 ... 15 F2
Stoney La CHLY/EC PR7 ... 12 C3
Stoneyside Av WALK M28 ... 46 A4
Stoneyside Gv WALK M28 ... 46 A5
Stonyhurst Av BOL BL1 ... 18 C2
Stopes Rd BOLS/LL BL3 ... 39 E1
Store St HOR/BR BL6 ... 15 E3
Stott La BOLE BL2 ... 29 F1
Stott Rd SWIN M27 ... 55 F5
Stourbridge Av LHULT M38 ... 45 E2
Stour Rd TYLD M29 ... 51 H3
Stowell Ct BOL BL1 ... 28 C1
Stowell St BOL BL1 ... 28 C1
The Straits TYLD M29 ... 52 A5
The Strand HOR/BR BL6 ... 15 F4
Strangford St RAD M26 ... 39 F1
Stranton Dr WALK M28 ... 55 E3
Stratford Av BOL BL1 ... 27 H1
Stratford Cl FWTH BL4 ... 36 D4
Strathmore Rd BOLE BL2 ... 30 A1
Stratton Rd SWIN M27 ... 55 H2
Strawberry Hill Rd BOLE BL2 ... 3 J7
The Stray BOL BL1 ... 19 F3
Streetgate LHULT M38 ... 45 E3
Street Kirklees TOT/BURYW BL8 ... 11 H5
Street La RAD M26 ... 31 G2
Stretton Rd BOLS/LL BL3 ... 35 H1
Stuart Av WGNE/HIN WN2 ... 40 D5
Studley Ct TYLD M29 ... 51 E3
Sudbury Dr HOR/BR BL6 ... 26 C4
Sudren St TOT/BURYW * BL8 ... 21 H4
Suffolk Cl BOLS/LL BL3 ... 30 D5
Sulby St RAD M26 ... 38 D5
Summerfield Dr TYLD M29 ... 51 H3
Summerfield Rd BOLS/LL BL3 ... 37 F1
WALK M28 ... 54 C4
Summer St HOR/BR BL6 ... 14 D3
Sumner Av BOLE BL2 ... 31 F1
Sumner St ATH M46 ... 42 C5
WGNE/HIN WN2 ... 23 H5
Sunadale Cl BOLS/LL BL3 ... 27 H5
Sundridge Cl BOLS/LL BL3 ... 35 G2
Sunleigh Rd WGNE/HIN WN2 ... 40 A2
Sunlight Rd BOL BL1 ... 28 A3
Sunningdale Av RAD M26 ... 31 F5
Sunningdale Gv LEIGH WN7 ... 50 D4
Sunningdale Wk BOLS/LL * BL3 ... 28 A5
Sunning Hill St BOLS/LL BL3 ... 36 B1
Sunny Bank RAD M26 ... 38 C5
Sunnybank Rd BOL BL1 ... 18 A5
TYLD M29 ... 51 H5
Sunny Bower St
TOT/BURYW BL8 ... 21 G1
Sunny Garth WHTN BL5 ... 33 G5
Sunnymead Av BOL BL1 ... 18 D3
Sunnyside Rd BOL BL1 ... 18 A5
Surrey Cl BOLS/LL BL3 ... 38 D1

Sussex Cl WGNE/HIN WN2 ... 40 C3
Sutcliffe St BOL BL1 ... 18 C5
Sutherland Gv FWTH BL4 ... 37 G5
Sutherland Rd BOL BL1 ... 27 G2
Sutherland St FWTH BL4 ... 37 G5
SWIN M27 ... 55 G2
Sutton La CHLYE PR6 ... 6 A3
Sutton Rd BOLS/LL BL3 ... 35 F1
Swan La BOLS/LL BL3 ... 36 B1
WGNE/HIN WN2 ... 40 D4
Swan Rd TOT/BURYW BL8 ... 11 H2
Sweetloves Gv BOL BL1 ... 18 C2
Sweetloves La BOL BL1 ... 18 C2
Swinside Rd BOLE BL2 ... 30 B2
Swinton St BOLE BL2 ... 30 A3
Swithemby St HOR/BR BL6 ... 14 C3
Sycamore Av RAD M26 ... 39 H5
TYLD M29 ... 52 B2
WGNE/HIN WN2 ... 40 B5
Sycamore Rd ATH M46 ... 43 E5
TOT/BURYW BL8 ... 21 H2
The Sycamores RAD M26 ... 46 D2
Syderstone Cl WGNE/HIN WN2 ... 40 A4
Sydney St SWIN M27 ... 55 F3

T

Tabley Rd BOLS/LL BL3 ... 35 H1
Tackler Cl SWIN M27 ... 55 H4
Tadmor Cl LHULT M38 ... 44 D4
Talbenny Cl BOL BL1 ... 27 F2
Talbot Ct BOL BL1 ... 18 D3
Tamar Cl FWTH BL4 ... 46 D3
Tamarin Cl SWIN M27 ... 55 E2
Tamer Gv LEIGH WN7 ... 49 E3
Tanfield Dr RAD M26 ... 46 D1
Tanhouse Av TYLD M29 ... 52 B4
Tanworth Wk BOL * BL1 ... 18 C5
Tarbet Dr BOLE BL2 ... 30 B4
Tarleton Av ATH M46 ... 42 B3
Tarleton Pl BOLS/LL BL3 ... 35 G2
Tarnbrook Dr WGNE/HIN WN2 ... 23 F5
Tarn Gv WALK M28 ... 54 B2
Tarvin Wk BOL BL1 ... 18 C5
Tattersall Av BOL BL1 ... 17 E5
Taunton Av LEIGH WN7 ... 49 F1
Taunton Cl BOL * BL1 ... 28 A1
Taunton Dr FWTH BL4 ... 36 D4
Tavistock Rd BOL BL1 ... 2 A5
WGNE/HIN WN2 ... 40 C4
Tavistock St ATH M46 ... 42 B5
Taylor Gv WGNE/HIN WN2 ... 41 E5
Taylor Rd WGNE/HIN WN2 ... 41 E5
Taylor's La BOLE BL2 ... 30 D3
Taylor St BOL * BL1 ... 3 F5
HOR/BR BL6 ... 14 D4
LEIGH WN7 ... 49 F3
Tayton Cl TYLD M29 ... 52 A2
Taywood Rd BOLS/LL BL3 ... 34 D3
Teak Dr FWTH BL4 ... 47 F4
Teal St BOLS/LL BL3 ... 36 D1
Telford Crs LEIGH WN7 ... 49 F3
Telford St ATH M46 ... 50 A1
HOR/BR BL6 ... 15 E5
Tellers Cl ATH M46 ... 42 D5
Temperance St BOLS/LL BL3 ... 2 C7
Tempest Cha HOR/BR BL6 ... 34 B1
Tempest Ct
HOR/BR (off Lock La) BL6 ... 34 C1
Tempest Rd HOR/BR BL6 ... 26 C5
Tempest St BOLS/LL BL3 ... 35 H1
Templecombe Dr BOL BL1 ... 18 B1
Temple Dr BOL BL1 ... 18 A4
Temple Rd BOL BL1 ... 18 A4
Templeton Cl WHTN BL5 ... 33 G5
Tenby Av BOL BL1 ... 27 G1
Tennis St BOL BL1 ... 18 B5
Tennyson Av LEIGH WN7 ... 49 E3
RAD M26 ... 39 G1
Tennyson Rd FWTH BL4 ... 45 F2
SWIN M27 ... 55 F3
Tennyson St BOL BL1 ... 28 B1
Tensing Av ATH M46 ... 42 C3
Tern Av FWTH BL4 ... 36 D5
Ternhill Ct FWTH BL4 ... 37 G5
Tetbury Dr BOLE BL2 ... 30 B2
Thaxted Pl BOL BL1 ... 28 A2
Thelwall Av BOLE BL2 ... 29 H2
Thetford Cl WGNE/HIN WN2 ... 40 A4
Thicketford Brow BOLE BL2 ... 29 H1
Thicketford Cl BOLE BL2 ... 19 G5
Thicketford Rd BOLE BL2 ... 29 F1
Third Av BOL BL1 ... 27 H3
BOLS/LL BL3 ... 38 B1
Third St BOL BL1 ... 17 F3
Thirlmere Av HOR/BR BL6 ... 15 E5
TYLD M29 ... 51 G4
Thirlmere Cl CHLYE PR6 ... 6 B4
Thirlmere Dr LHULT M38 ... 45 E3
Thirlmere Gv FWTH BL4 ... 36 C5
Thirlmere Rd HOR/BR BL6 ... 13 G4
WGNE/HIN WN2 ... 40 A3
WHTN BL5 ... 43 F1
Thirlspot Cl BOL BL1 ... 18 C1
Thirsk Rd BOLS/LL BL3 ... 38 C3
Thistleton Rd BOLS/LL BL3 ... 35 F2
Thomas Dr BOLS/LL BL3 ... 28 B5

Thomas Holden St BOL BL1 ....2 B2
Thomas More CI FWTH BL4 ....46 B2
Thomasson CI BOL BL1 ....28 C1
Thomas St ATH M46 ....42 D5
  BOLS/LL BL3 ....28 B5
  FWTH BL4 ....38 A5
  WGNE/HIN WN2 ....40 D5
  WHTN* BL5 ....33 G2
Thompson Av BOLE BL2 ....31 F1
Thompson Rd BOL BL1 ....27 H1
Thompson St BOLS/LL BL3 ....28 D5
  HOR/BR BL6 ....14 C4
Thoresby CI BOLS/LL BL3 ....31 E5
Thornbank BOLS/LL BL3 ....28 A4
Thornbeck Dr BOL BL1 ....27 F1
Thornbeck Rd BOL BL1 ....27 F1
Thorncliffe Rd BOL BL1 ....18 C2
Thorne St FWTH BL4 ....37 G4
Thorneyholme CI HOR/BR BL6 ....26 C4
Thornfield Crs LHULT M38 ....44 D3
Thornfield Dr SWIN M27 ....55 G4
Thornfield Gv LHULT M38 ....44 D3
Thornfield Rd TOT/BURYW BL8 ....11 F5
Thornham Dr BOL BL1 ....18 D1
Thornhill Dr WALK M28 ....54 A3
Thorn Lea ATH M46 ....51 E1
Thornlea Av SWIN M27 ....55 F5
Thorn Lea CI BOL BL1 ....27 F3
Thornley Av BOL BL1 ....18 A5
Thornley Ms
  BOL (off Thornley Av) BL1 ....18 A5
Thornmere CI SWIN M27 ....55 E1
Thorn Rd SWIN M27 ....55 G5
Thorns Av BOL BL1 ....18 B4
Thorns CI BOL BL1 ....18 B4
Thorns Rd BOL BL1 ....18 B4
Thorn St BOL BL1 ....18 D5
Thornton Av BOL BL1 ....27 F1
Thornton CI BOLS/LL BL3 ....39 E2
  FWTH BL4 ....45 F1
  WALK M28 ....52 C4
Thornton Rd WALK M28 ....52 C4
Thornton St BOLE BL2 ....3 H3
Thornway WALK M28 ....53 E4
Thorn Well WHTN BL5 ....41 G1
Thornydyke Av BOL BL1 ....18 C2
Thorpe Av SWIN M27 ....55 G2
Thorpe St BOL BL1 ....18 B5
  WALK M28 ....45 H4
Thorsby CI EDGW/EG BL7 ....8 D4
Threlkeld Rd BOL BL1 ....8 B5
Thrush Av FWTH BL4 ....45 F1
Thurlestone Av BOLE BL2 ....31 F1
Thurnham St BOLS/LL BL3 ....36 A2
Thursford Gv HOR/BR BL6 ....23 H1
Thurstane St BOL BL1 ....18 A5
Thynne St BOLS/LL BL3 ....3 F6
  FWTH BL4 ....37 G4
Tig Fold Rd FWTH BL4 ....36 C5
Tildsley St BOLS/LL BL3 ....36 A1
Timberbottom BOLE BL2 ....19 G3
Timsbury CI BOLE BL2 ....31 E2
Tindle St WALK M28 ....46 B5
Tinkersfield LEIGH WN7 ....49 F4
Tinsley Gv BOLE BL2 ....3 K1
Tin St BOLS/LL BL3 ....2 D7
Tintagel CI RAD M26 ....31 E5
Tintagel Rd WGNE/HIN WN2 ....40 C4
Tintern Av BOLE BL2 ....19 F5
  TYLD M29 ....52 A4
Tipton CI RAD M26 ....31 F5
Tithe Barn Crs BOL BL1 ....19 F3
Tithe Barn St BOL BL1 ....19 F3
Tiverton Av LEIGH WN7 ....49 F1
Tiverton CI RAD M26 ....31 F5
  TYLD M29 ....52 A4
Tiverton Wk BOL* BL1 ....28 A2
Toddington La WGNE/HIN WN2 ....23 F2
Tomlinson St HOR/BR BL6 ....14 A4
Tomlin Sq BOLE BL2 ....29 G3
Tonge Bridge Wy BOLE BL2 ....3 J2
Tonge Moor Rd BOLE BL2 ....29 F1
Tonge Old Rd BOLE BL2 ....29 G1
Tonge Park Av BOLE BL2 ....29 G1
Tongfields EDGW/EG BL7 ....8 D4
Tong Head Av BOL BL1 ....19 F5
Tong Rd BOLS/LL BL3 ....38 C1
Tong St FWTH BL4 ....46 D3
Top o' th Brow
  BOLE (off Riding Ga) BL2 ....20 A1
Top o' th' La BOLS/LL* BL3 ....29 H5
Toppings Gn EDGW/EG BL7 ....9 E5
Topping St BOL BL1 ....28 C1
Topp St FWTH BL4 ....46 A1
Topp Wy BOL BL1 ....2 D2
Tor Av TOT/BURYW BL8 ....11 H3
Torkington St SWIN M27 ....55 H2
Toronto St BOLE BL2 ....30 A2
Torra Barn CI EDGW/EG BL7 ....8 C2
Torridon Rd BOLE BL2 ....30 B3
Torrington Av BOL BL1 ....18 C5
Torrisdale CI BOLS/LL BL3 ....27 H4
Torside Wy SWIN M27 ....55 H1
Torver Dr BOLE BL2 ....30 B2
Tottington Av BOLE BL2 ....20 A2
  TOT/BURYW BL8 ....10 B2
Tower Buildings
  HOR/BR
  (off Chorley Old Rd) BL6 ....16 A4

Tower Ct
  TOT/BURYW
  (off Shepherd St) BL8 ....11 H4
Tower Gv LEIGH WN7 ....50 C5
Towers Av BOLS/LL BL3 ....35 G1
Towncroft La BOL BL1 ....27 E2
Townsend Rd SWIN M27 ....55 H2
Townsfield Rd WHTN BL5 ....41 G1
Toxhead CI HOR/BR BL6 ....14 C4
Trafford Dr LHULT M38 ....45 F3
Trafford St FWTH BL4 ....38 A4
Trafford St FWTH BL4 ....37 H4
Travers St HOR/BR BL6 ....25 F1
Trawden Av BOL BL1 ....18 A5
Tredgold St HOR/BR BL6 ....15 E5
Treen Rd TYLD M29 ....52 A3
Tree Tops BOLE BL2 ....19 G1
Tregaron Gv WGNE/HIN WN2 ....40 C5
Trencherbone RAD M26 ....31 G5
Trent Dr WALK M28 ....53 F1
  WGNE/HIN WN2 ....41 E5
Trentham Av FWTH BL4 ....37 G4
Trentham CI FWTH BL4 ....37 G4
Trentham St FWTH BL4 ....37 G4
  SWIN* M27 ....55 E5
Trent Wy FWTH BL4 ....46 C3
Trevarrick CI HOR/BR BL6 ....15 G5
Trevor Rd SWIN M27 ....55 G5
Trillo Av BOLE BL2 ....3 K6
Trinity Crs WALK M28 ....54 A1
Trinity St BOLS/LL BL3 ....2 D6
Troon CI BOLS/LL BL3 ....35 F2
Troutbeck CI TOT/BURYW BL8 ....10 D2
Troutbeck Dr TYLD M29 ....51 G4
Truro CI TYLD M29 ....52 A3
Tucker's Hill Brow
  WGNE/HIN WN2 ....23 F1
Tudor Av BOL BL1 ....27 H3
  FWTH BL4 ....45 F1
Tudor St BOLS/LL* BL3 ....36 A1
Tulip Av FWTH BL4 ....37 E4
Turf St RAD M26 ....39 H2
Turks Rd RAD M26 ....31 F5
Turk St BOL BL1 ....28 A2
Turnberry BOLS/LL BL3 ....35 F2
Turnberry CI TYLD M29 ....52 A3
Turncroft Wy WALK M28 ....52 D4
Turner Av WGNE/HIN WN2 ....48 A2
Turner Bridge Rd BOLE BL2 ....29 G2
Turnerford CI EDGW/EG BL7 ....8 C3
Turner St BOL BL1 ....3 H1
  WHTN BL5 ....41 G3
Turnstone CI LEIGH WN7 ....50 A5
Turnstone Rd BOLE BL2 ....3 G6
Turton Hts BOLE BL2 ....19 F1
Turton Rd BOLE BL2 ....19 G1
  TOT/BURYW BL8 ....10 C2
Turton St BOL BL1 ....3 F1
Twisse Rd BOLE BL2 ....30 B2
Two Brooks La TOT/BURYW BL8 ....10 D2
Tybyrne CI WALK M28 ....52 C4
Tyldesley Old Rd ATH M46 ....50 D1
Tyldesley Pas ATH M46 ....51 F2
Tyldesley Rd ATH M46 ....50 D1
Tyne Ct WALK M28 ....45 G5
Tynesbank WALK M28 ....53 C1
Tynesbank Cottages
  WALK (off Tynesbank) M28 ....45 G5

U

Uganda St BOLS/LL BL3 ....36 A1
Ulleswater CI BOLS/LL BL3 ....38 B2
Ulleswater St BOL BL1 ....18 D5
Ullswater Dr FWTH BL4 ....44 C1
Ullswater Rd FWTH M29 ....51 G4
Umberton Rd WHTN BL5 ....43 F1
Union Buildings BOL* BL1 ....3 F5
Union Ct
  BOL (off Union Rd) BL1 ....19 E5
Union Rd BOL BL1 ....19 E5
Union St BOL BL1 ....3 F2
  EDGW/EG BL7 ....8 B2
  SWIN M27 ....55 G3
  TYLD M29 ....51 F2
Unsworth Av TYLD M29 ....51 H3
Unsworth St LEIGH WN7 ....49 G4
  RAD M26 ....39 H1
Upland Dr LHULT M38 ....44 D2
Upper George St TYLD M29 ....51 E2
Upper Lees Dr WHTN BL5 ....34 A4
Upper Md EDGW/EG BL7 ....8 D3
Upton La TYLD M29 ....52 A3
Upton Rd ATH M46 ....43 E4
Upton Wy TOT/BURYW BL8 ....21 H2
Uttley St BOL BL1 ....18 B5

V

Valdene CI FWTH BL4 ....45 H1
Valdene Dr FWTH BL4 ....45 H1
  WALK M28 ....53 H3
Vale Av HOR/BR BL6 ....14 C4
  RAD M26 ....47 E1

Vale Coppice HOR/BR BL6 ....14 C4
Valentines Rd ATH M46 ....50 A2
Vale St BOL BL2 ....30 C3
Valletts La BOL BL1 ....28 A1
Valley Ml
  EDGW/EG (off Cottonfields) BL7 ....8 D4
The Valley ATH M46 ....43 E5
Valpy Av BOLE BL2 ....19 F4
Vantomme St BOL BL1 ....18 C3
Varley Rd BOLS/LL BL3 ....35 G1
Vauze Av HOR/BR BL6 ....23 H1
Vauze House CI HOR/BR BL6 ....13 H5
Vendale Av SWIN M27 ....55 F5
Venice St BOLS/LL BL3 ....36 A1
Ventnor St BOL BL1 ....18 D4
Verbena Av FWTH BL4 ....37 E4
Verdure Av BOL BL1 ....27 E2
Vermont St BOL BL1 ....2 A1
Verne Av SWIN M27 ....55 G3
Vernham Wk BOLS/LL BL3 ....36 C1
Vernon St BOL BL1 ....2 C2
  FWTH BL4 ....38 A5
Vernon Wk BOL BL1 ....2 D1
Vicarage CI CHLYE PR6 ....6 A4
Vicarage Rd HOR/BR BL6 ....13 H5
  SWIN M27 ....55 G3
  WALK M28 ....45 H5
Vicarage Rd West HOR/BR BL6 ....13 G5
Vicarage St BOLS/LL BL3 ....2 B7
Vicker CI SWIN M27 ....55 H1
Vickerman St BOL BL1 ....18 B5
Vickers Rw FWTH BL4 ....37 F5
Vickers St BOLS/LL* BL3 ....2 B7
Victoria Av WGNE/HIN WN2 ....48 A2
Victoria CI WALK* M28 ....53 E5
  WGNE/HIN WN2 ....23 F4
Victoria Ct FWTH BL4 ....37 G3
Victoria Gv BOL BL1 ....28 A1
Victoria La SWIN M27 ....55 F3
Victoria Rd BOL BL1 ....26 D3
  FWTH BL4 ....46 C2
  HOR/BR BL6 ....15 E4
Victoria Sq BOL* BL1 ....2 E4
Victoria St FWTH BL4 ....37 H4
  HOR/BR BL6 ....14 H5
  LEIGH WN7 ....49 G5
  TOT/BURYW BL8 ....11 G5
  WALK M28 ....53 E5
  WHTN BL5 ....33 H5
Victoria Ter WGNE/HIN WN2 ....48 B3
Victoria Wy LEIGH WN7 ....49 G4
Victory Rd BOLS/LL BL3 ....38 C1
Victory St BOL* BL1 ....28 A2
View St BOLS/LL BL3 ....28 B5
Vigo Av BOLS/LL BL3 ....35 H2
Viking St BOLS/LL BL3 ....37 E1
Vincent St BOL BL1 ....2 A5
Violet Av FWTH BL4 ....37 E4
Virginia St BOLS/LL* BL3 ....35 H1

W

Waddington CI TOT/BURYW BL8 ....21 G5
Waddington Rd BOL BL1 ....27 G5
Wade Bank WHTN BL5 ....33 H5
Wadebridge Dr TOT/BURYW BL8 ....21 H5
Wade St BOLS/LL BL3 ....36 D2
Wadsley St BOL BL1 ....2 C1
Waggoners Ct SWIN M27 ....55 H4
Waggon Rd BOLE BL2 ....29 H2
Wagner St BOL BL1 ....18 B4
Wagtail CI WALK M28 ....53 H3
Wainscot CI TYLD M29 ....51 H4
Wakefield Dr SWIN M27 ....47 F4
Waldeck St BOL BL1 ....18 D4
Walden CI WGNE/HIN WN2 ....40 B4
Waldon CI BOLS/LL BL3 ....35 H1
Walkdene Dr WALK M28 ....45 F5
Walkden Market Pl
  WALK (off High St) M28 ....45 H5
Walkden Rd WALK M28 ....53 H2
Walkdens Av ATH M46 ....50 A1
Walker CI FWTH BL4 ....46 C2
Walker Fold Rd BOL BL1 ....16 D2
Walkers Ct FWTH BL4 ....37 H5
Walker St BOL BL1 ....2 B5
  WHTN BL5 ....33 H5
The Walk ATH M46 ....42 D5
The Walkway BOLS/LL BL3 ....27 F5
Wallbrook Crs LHULT M38 ....45 E2
The Walled Gdn SWIN M27 ....55 F5
Walley St BOL BL1 ....18 C4
Wallsuches HOR/BR BL6 ....15 H3
Wallwork Rd TYLD M29 ....52 B5
Walmer Rd WGNE/HIN WN2 ....40 C3
Walmley Gv BOLS/LL BL3 ....36 A2
Walnut CI SWIN M27 ....47 F4
Walnut Gv LEIGH WN7 ....49 H3
Walnut St BOLE BL2 ....18 D4
Walshaw Brook CI
  TOT/BURYW BL8 ....21 H3
Walshaw Dr SWIN M27 ....55 H4
Walshaw La TOT/BURYW BL8 ....21 H3
Walshaw Rd TOT/BURYW BL8 ....21 H3

Walsh St HOR/BR BL6 ....C1
Walter St WALK M28 ....C1
Walton CI BOLS/LL BL3 ....C1
Walton PI FWTH BL4 ....C1
Walton St ATH* M46 ....C1
  CHLY/EC PR7 ....C1
Wanborough CI ATH* WN7 ....C1
Wapping St BOL BL1 ....C1
Warbeck CI WGNE/HIN WN2 ....C1
Warburton PI ATH M46 ....C1
Warburton St BOL BL1 ....C1
Wardend CI LHULT* M38 ....C1
Wardens Bank WHTN BL5 ....C1
Wardle CI RAD M26 ....C1
Wardle St BOLE BL2 ....C1
Wardley Av WALK M28 ....C1
Wardley Hall La WALK M28 ....C1
Wardley Hall Rd WALK M28 ....C1
Wardley Rd TYLD M29 ....C1
Wardley Sq TYLD M29 ....C1
Wardley St SWIN M27 ....C1
Wardlow St BOLS/LL BL3 ....C1
Wardour St ATH M46 ....C1
Wareing St TYLD M29 ....C1
Wareing Wy BOLS/LL BL3 ....C1
The Warke WALK M28 ....C1
Warlow Dr LEIGH WN7 ....C1
Warren CI ATH M46 ....C1
Warren Rd WALK M28 ....C1
Warton CI TOT/BURYW BL8 ....C1
Warwick Av WALK* M28 ....C1
Warwick Dr WGNE/HIN WN2 ....C1
Warwick Gdns BOLS/LL BL3 ....C1
Warwick Rd ATH M46 ....C1
  RAD M26
  TYLD M29
  WALK M28
  WGNE/HIN* WN2
Warwick St BOL BL1 ....C1
  CHLY/EC PR7
  SWIN M27
Wasdale Av BOLE BL2 ....C1
Washacre WHTN BL5 ....C1
Washacre CI WHTN BL5 ....C1
Washbrook Av WALK M28 ....C1
Washburn CI WHTN BL5 ....C1
Washington St BOLS/LL BL3 ....C1
Washwood CI LHULT* M38 ....C1
Waterford CI CHLYE PR6 ....C1
Watergate Dr WHTN BL5 ....C1
Watergate La WHTN BL5 ....C1
Water La FWTH BL4 ....C1
Water Lane St RAD M26 ....C1
Waterloo St BOL BL1 ....C1
Watermans CI HOR/BR BL6 ....C1
Watermillock Gdns BOL BL1 ....C1
Water's Edge FWTH BL4 ....C1
Waterslea Dr BOL BL1 ....C1
Watersmead CI BOL BL1 ....C1
Watersmead St BOL BL1 ....C1
Waters Meeting Rd BOL BL1 ....C1
Water's Nook Rd WHTN BL5 ....C1
Water St ATH M46 ....C1
  BOL BL1
  CHLY/EC PR7
  EDGW/EG BL7
Watling St TOT/BURYW BL8 ....C1
  TOT/BURYW BL8
Watson Rd FWTH BL4 ....C1
Watson St SWIN M27 ....C1
Watton CI SWIN M27 ....C1
Watts St HOR/BR BL6 ....C1
Waverley Av FWTH BL4 ....C1
Waverley Gv LEIGH* WN7 ....C1
Waverley Rd BOL BL1 ....C1
  WALK M28
Wavertree Av ATH M46 ....C1
Wayfarers Wy SWIN M27 ....C1
Wayfaring WHTN BL5 ....C1
Wayside Gv WALK M28 ....C1
Wealdstone Gv BOL* BL1 ....C1
Wearish La WHTN BL5 ....C1
Weaste Av LHULT M38 ....C1
Weaver Av WALK M28 ....C1
Weavers Ct BOLS/LL BL3 ....C1
Weavers Gn FWTH BL4 ....C1
Webb St HOR/BR BL6 ....C1
Weber Dr BOLS/LL BL3 ....C1
Webster St BOLS/LL BL3 ....C1
Weeton Av BOLE BL2 ....C1
Welbeck Rd BOL BL1 ....C1
  WALK M28
Weldon Av BOLS/LL BL3 ....C1
Wellbank St TOT/BURYW BL8 ....
Wellfield Rd BOLS/LL BL3 ....C1
  WGNE/HIN WN2
Welling St BOLE BL2 ....C1
Wellington Dr TYLD M29 ....C1
Wellington Rd ATH M46 ....C1
  SWIN M27
Wellington St BOLS/LL BL3 ....C1
  FWTH BL4
  WHTN BL5
Wellington Wk BOLS/LL BL3 ....C1
Wells CI TYLD M29 ....C1
Wellstock La LHULT M38 ....C1
Well St BOL BL1 ....C1
  BOLE BL2
  TYLD M29
Wemsley Gv BOLE BL2 ....C1

er Dr *BOLS/LL* BL3 ....27 E5	Whitbeam Gv *WGNE/HIN* WN2....48 A1
Cl *HOR/BR* BL6 ....15 E1	Whitburn Cl *BOLS/LL* BL3 ....35 E1
st *SWIN* M27 ....55 F3	Whitby Cl *TOT/BURYW* BL8.........21 H5
dge Rd *BOL* BL1 ....2 B2	Whitchurch Gdns *BOL* BL1 ....18 C5
rth Av *FWTH* BL4 ....45 C1	Whiteacres *SWIN* M27 ....55 E4
rth Cl *RAD* M26 ....39 F1	Whitebeam Wk *WHTN* BL5 ....33 H3
l *WHTN* BL5 ....33 G3	White Birk Cl *TOT/BURYW* BL8....11 H2
	Whitecroft Dr *TOT/BURYW* BL8 ....21 H5
off Mountain St) M28 ....45 H4	Whitecroft Rd *BOL* BL1 ....27 G1
or *WALK* M28 ....54 B3	Whitegate *BOLS/LL* BL3 ....34 C3
ls	Whitegate Dr *BOL* BL1 ....18 D2
off Castle St) BL2 ....3 J4	Whitehall La *BOL* BL1 ....18 B1
st *ATH* * M46 ....43 E5	*HOR/BR* BL6 ....13 H4
L BL3 ....28 C5	Whitehead Crs *RAD* M26 ....46 D1
Gv BL7 ....9 E4	Whitehead St *WALK* M28 ....45 H4
BL4 ....46 A1	White Horse Cl *HOR/BR* BL6.........15 E2
28 ....55 H3	White Horse Gdns
JRYW BL8 ....11 C5	*SWIN* (off Worsley Rd) M27 ....55 E5
BL5 ....33 C3	White Horse Gv *WHTN* BL5............34 A3
FWTH BL4 ....37 F5	White Lady Cl *WALK* M28 ....44 D5
28 ....45 C5	Whiteland Av *BOLS/LL* BL3 ....27 H5
k Rd *HOR/BR* BL6 ....26 D4	Whiteoak Vw *BOLS/LL* BL3 ....29 H5
ATH M46 ....51 E2	Whites Cft *SWIN* M27....................55 H3
rne Av *BOLS/LL* BL3 ....37 E2	Whitestone Cl *HOR/BR* BL6 ....26 D4
BL4 ....47 F3	Whiting Gv *BOLS/LL* BL3 ....27 F2
WN7 ....49 C4	Whitland Av *BOL* BL1....................27 F2
ok Cl *BOLE* BL2 ....3 G6	Whitley St *BOLS/LL* BL3 ....37 H3
ok Ct	Whitsters Hollow *BOL* BL1 ....17 H4
off Grosvenor St) BL2 ....3 G6	Whitsundale *WHTN* BL5 ....33 H3
ok St *SWIN* M27 ....55 C4	Whittle Dr *WALK* M28 ....45 F5
ok St *BOLE* BL2 ....3 H6	Whittle Gv *BOL* BL1 ....27 H1
y Cl *WHTN* BL5 ....34 A4	*WALK* M28 ....46 A5
Gv *BOLE* BL2 ....3 K2	Whittle Hl *EDGW/EG* BL7...............8 C1
e Rd *BOL* BL1 ....18 D1	Whittle St *SWIN* M27.....................55 G4
ATH M46 ....51 E2	*WALK* M28 ....46 A5
e Cl *BOLE* BL2 ....20 A2	Whitworth St *HOR/BR* BL6 ....15 E5
rt Rd *BOLS/LL* BL3........................36 B2	Whoolden St *FWTH* BL4................37 G4
st *FWTH* BL4 ....37 F5	Whowell Fold *BOL* BL1 ....18 A4
ale Cl *TYLD* M29 ....51 H3	Whowell St *BOLS/LL* * BL3 ....2 C6
ale Dr *BOLS/LL* BL3 ....27 G5	Wichbrook Rd *WALK* M28.............44 D5
an Ct *BOLS/LL* BL3 ....2 A7	The Wicheries *LHULT* M38............44 C5
d Rd *BOLS/LL* BL3........................35 H5	Wicket Gv *SWIN* M27 ....47 G4
e Av *BOL* BL1 ....28 A3	Wickliffe St *BOL* * BL1 ....2 D2
JRYW BL8 ....11 H2	Widcombe Dr *BOLS/LL* BL3 ....30 B5
e Dr *SWIN* M27 ....55 H5	Wigan Rd *ATH* M46.......................49 H1
29 ....52 A5	*BOLS/LL* BL3 ....36 A1
WHTN BL5 ....41 C2	*LEIGH* WN7 ....49 E4
e Av *BOL* * BL1 ....18 C1	*WHTN* BL5 ....40 C1
Gv *WGNE/HIN* WN2....................40 D4	Wilbraham Rd *WALK* M28 ....45 H5
Av *BOL* BL1...................................27 G1	Wilbraham St *WHTN* BL5..............33 C5
BL4 ....45 C2	Wilby Av *BOLS/LL* BL3 ....30 C5
n La *LEIGH* WN7 ....49 F1	Wildbrook Cl *LHULT* M38 ....44 C5
sh Cl *BOL* BL1 ....28 C1	Wildbrook Gv *LHULT* M38.............44 C5
ale *BOLS/LL* BL3 ....36 C3	Wildbrook Rd *LHULT* M38 ....44 C5
28 ....55 C5	Wilderswood Av *HOR/BR* BL6 ....15 E3
ade Rd *WALK* M28 ....45 G3	Wilderswood Ct *HOR/BR* BL6.........15 F3
ster Av *FWTH* BL4........................37 G5	Wildman La *FWTH* BL4 ....36 D5
26 ....39 F1	Wilfred Rd *WALK* M28 ....53 H1
ster Dr *LEIGH* WN7 ....51 E5	Wilfred St *EDGW/EG* * BL7.............9 E5
ster Rd *BOL* BL1 ....18 C2	Wilfrid St *SWIN* M27 ....55 H3
28 ....53 H1	Wilkinson Av *BOLS/LL* BL3 ....38 C1
ster St *FWTH* BL4 ....37 G5	Wilkinson Rd *BOL* BL1 ....18 B2
27 ....52 F2	Willand Cl *BOLE* BL2 ....30 C4
land Rd *TYLD* M29.......................51 G1	Willand Dr *BOLS/LL* BL3 ....30 C5
v *SWIN* M27 ....47 H4	Williamson Av *RAD* M26 ....31 H4
t *ATH* M46 ....43 E4	Williams St *BOLS/LL* BL3 ....38 D2
r L BL3 ....46 B4	William St *HOR/BR* BL6 ....14 C4
e St *SWIN* M27 ....55 G2	*WGNE/HIN* WN2............................40 A3
LEIGH WN7 ....50 A4	Willis St *BOLS/LL* BL3 ....36 A1
BOL BL1 ....28 A3	Willow Av *TYLD* M29 ....51 G5
L4 ....38 A4	Willowbank Av *BOLE* BL2................3 K6
HIN WN2 ....40 D5	Willow Cl *BOLS/LL* BL3 ....35 H1
	CHLYE PR6 ....6 B4
R (off Wildderswood) BL6........15 F2	Willow Crs *LEIGH* WN7 ....49 G3
EDGW/EG BL7................................8 B2	Willowcroft Av *WGNE/HIN* WN2...32 B2
BOL BL1 ....19 F4	Willowdene Cl *EDGW/EG* BL7.........8 D4
M38 ....45 E3	Willow Dr *WGNE/HIN* WN2 ....40 B5
Gv *LEIGH* WN7 ....49 G3	Willowmoss Cl *WALK* M28.............54 A2
St *LEIGH* WN7 ....49 G3	Willows La *BOLS/LL* BL3 ....36 A1
ale *WALK* M28 ....53 E1	The Willows *BOLS/LL* BL3 ....30 C5
od Cl *FWTH* BL4 ....37 H5	*WALK* M46 ....42 C4
l *BOL* BL1 ....28 A2	*WALK* M28....................................55 E4
th Cl *BOL* BL1 ....2 B1	Wilmcote Cl *HOR/BR* BL6 ....26 D4
Cl *WGNE/HIN* WN2 ....41 E5	Wilmot St *BOL* BL1 ....18 A4
Dr *BOLS/LL* BL3 ....36 C2	Wilmslow Av *BOL* BL1 ....18 C2
ne Gv *BOLE* BL2 ....19 F3	Wilson Fold Av *HOR/BR* BL6.........25 H1
e Cl *BOLE* BL2 ....30 C4	Wilson St *BOL* * BL1 ....2 E5
th Dr *WGNE/HIN* WN2 ....40 C4	*FWTH* BL4 ....38 A5
th St *BOL* BL1 ....18 D3	*HOR/BR* BL6 ....14 C3
e Dr *BOL* BL1 ....18 D3	*RAD* M26 ....39 H1
Av *BOL* BL1 ....17 F4	Wilton Rd *BOL* BL1........................18 C2
Dr *TOT/BURYW* BL8.....................21 H5	Wilton St *BOL* BL1 ....18 A4
Gv *LEIGH* WN7 ....49 F2	Wimberry Hill Rd *WHTN* BL5.........33 F2
Gv *WHTN* BL5 ....33 H3	Wimborne Cl *HOR/BR* BL6 ....25 H1
La *LHULT* M38 ....44 B4	Wincanton Dr *BOL* BL1 ....8 B5
d St *BOLE* BL2 ....3 K7	Winchester Av *TYLD* M29...............52 A4
e Rd *SWIN* M27 ....55 F1	Winchester Rd *RAD* M26...............31 F5
e Cl *BOLS/LL* BL3 ....18 C5	Winchester Wy *BOLE* BL2..............29 H1
l Rd *TYLD* M29 ....52 A4	Windale *WALK* M28 ....45 F5
FWTH BL4 ....36 C5	Windermere Av *ATH* M46..............42 D3
est *HOR/BR* BL6 ....26 C3	*BOLS/LL* BL3 ....38 C1
e Dr *HOR/BR* BL6 ....26 C3	Windermere Dr *CHLYE* PR6 ....6 B3
Dr *BOLE* BL2 ....29 C4	

Windermere Rd *FWTH* BL4 ....44 C1	BOL BL1 ....3 F4
WGNE/HIN WN2............................40 A3	*HOR/BR* BL6 ....15 E4
Windermere St *BOL* BL1 ....18 D4	TYLD M29 ....39 G5
Winder St *BOL* BL1 ....2 E1	TYLD M29 ....51 H5
Windlehurst Dr *WALK* M28 ....53 F4	*WGNE/HIN* WN2 ....40 C5
Windley St *BOLE* BL2.......................3 H1	*WHTN* BL5 ....35 F1
Windmill Cl *WALK* M28 ....45 G3	Wood Ter *BOLE* BL2 ....31 F1
Windmill Rd *WALK* M28 ....45 G3	Woodvale Av *ATH* M46 ....42 B3
Windover Cl *BOLS/LL* BL3 ....43 G1	*BOLS/LL* BL3 ....36 B3
Windover St *BOLS/LL* BL3 ....35 G1	*WALK* M28 ....32 B2
Windrush Dr *WHTN* BL5 ....33 H4	Woodvale Dr *BOLS/LL* BL3 ....36 B3
Windsor Av *BOLS/LL* BL3 ....38 C2	Woodvale Gdns *BOLS/LL* BL3 ....36 B3
CHLY/EC PR7 ....12 C1	Woodvale Gv *BOLS/LL* BL3 ....36 B3
LHULT M38 ....45 F3	Woodwards Rd *WHTN* BL5 ....41 G2
TYLD M29 ....51 G5	Woolston Dr *TYLD* M29.................52 A3
Windsor Crs *WGNE/HIN* WN2.......23 H5	Worcester Av *WGNE/HIN* WN2......40 B2
Windsor Dr *HOR/BR* BL6 ....15 C5	Worcester Rd *WALK* M28 ....38 B2
Windsor Gv *BOL* BL1 ....28 A1	*SWIN* M27 ....55 F1
RAD M26 ....46 D1	Worcester St *BOL* * BL1 ....28 C1
WGNE/HIN WN2............................40 D5	Wordsworth Av *ATH* M46..............42 D3
Windsor Rd *EDGW/EG* BL7..............9 E5	*FWTH* BL4 ....45 F1
LEIGH WN7 ....51 E5	*LEIGH* WN7 ....49 F4
Windsor St *ATH* M46.....................51 E1	*RAD* M26 ....39 G1
Windy Harbour La *EDGW/EG* BL7....9 F4	Wordsworth Rd *LHULT* M38 ....35 E3
Windyhill Dr *BOLS/LL* BL3 ....35 G2	*SWIN* M27 ....55 H3
Wingate Rd *LHULT* M38................45 F4	Wordsworth St *BOL* * BL1..............18 B5
Wingates Gv *WHTN* BL5 ....3 H1	Worsbrough Av *WALK* M28 ....53 G3
Wingates La *WHTN* BL5 ....33 G1	Worsel St *BOLS/LL* BL3 ....36 A1
Wingates Rd *WGN* WN1 ....22 A5	Worsley Av *WALK* M28 ....53 G3
Wingates Sq *WHTN* BL5 ....33 G2	Worsley Brow *WALK* M28 ....54 A5
Winifred Rd *FWTH* BL4 ....45 F1	Worsley Ct *WALK* M28 ....45 H3
Winmarleigh Cl *TOT/BURYW* BL8 ..31 H1	Worsley Gv *WALK* M28 ....53 E1
Winsford Gv *BOLS/LL* BL3 ....27 F5	Worsley La *BOLS/LL* * BL3 ....35 G1
Winslade Ms *FWTH* BL4 ....37 H4	*FWTH* BL4 ....45 H2
Winslow Rd *BOLS/LL* BL3 ....34 C3	Worsley Rd North *WALK* M28 ....28 C5
Winsmoor Dr *WGNE/HIN* WN2 .....40 A4	Worsley St *BOLS/LL* * BL3 ....28 C5
Winster Cl *BOLE* BL2 ....30 B1	*SWIN* M27 ....55 H1
Winster Dr *BOLE* BL2 ....30 A1	*TOT/BURYW* BL8...........................11 G5
Winston Av *BOLS/LL* BL3 ....39 E2	Worston Av *BOL* BL1 ....17 F5
Winston Cl *RAD* M26 ....31 G5	Worthing Gv *ATH* M46 ....42 B5
Winterburn Av *BOL* BL1 ....19 F1	Worthington St *BOLS/LL* BL3.........36 F1
Winterfield Dr *BOLS/LL* BL3 ....35 G2	Wrath Cl *BOLE* BL2 ....19 F1
Winter Hey La *HOR/BR* BL6 ....14 D4	Wraxhall Crs *LEIGH* WN7...............49 F4
Winter St *BOL* BL1 ....18 B4	Wrenbury Dr *EDGW/EG* BL7 ....18 D1
Winterton Cl *WHTN* BL5 ....34 A4	Wren Cl *FWTH* BL4 ....36 D5
Winton Gn *HOR/BR* BL6................26 H2	Wrenswood Dr *WALK* M28 ....53 G3
Winton Gv *BOLS/LL* BL3 ....35 E1	Wrigglesworth Cl *TOT/BURYW* BL8 ..21 H4
Winward St *BOLS/LL* * BL3 ....35 G1	Wright St *HOR/BR* BL6 ....14 D3
WHTN BL5 ....33 G4	*RAD* M26 ....39 H2
Wisbeck Rd *BOLE* BL2 ....29 G2	Wright St West *HOR/BR* * BL6 ....14 D3
Withington Dr *TYLD* M29..............52 A4	Wrington Cl *LEIGH* WN7 ....49 F3
Withins Cl *BOLE* BL2 ....30 A2	Wroe St *SWIN* M27 ....47 H5
Withins Dr *BOLE* BL2.....................30 A2	Wroe Ter
Withins Gv *BOLE* BL2 ....30 A2	*SWIN* (off Wyndham Av) M27 .....47 H5
Withins La *BOLE* BL2 ....30 A1	Wycombe Dr *TYLD* M29 ....51 H4
Woburn Av *BOLE* BL2 ....19 G4	Wykeham Ms *BOL* BL1 ....27 G3
LEIGH WN7 ....49 F2	Wyndham Av *BOLS/LL* BL3 ....35 G3
Woking Back Gdns *BOL* BL1 ....28 C1	Wynne Av *SWIN* M27....................55 H1
Woking Ter *BOL* * BL1 ....28 C1	Wynne St *BOL* BL1 ....45 E4
Wolfenden St *BOL* BL1 ....18 C5	*LHULT* M38 ....45 E4
Wolfenden Ter *BOL* * BL1 ....18 C5	*TYLD* M29 ....51 F2
Wolford Dr *TYLD* M29...................52 A2	Wyre Dr *WALK* M28 ....53 F4
Wolver Cl *LHULT* * M38 ....45 F2	Wyresdale Rd *BOL* BL1 ....28 A2
Woodbank *BOLE* BL2 ....19 H5	Wythall Av *LHULT* M38.................45 F2
Woodbine Rd *BOLS/LL* BL3 ....18 B3	Wythburn Av *BOL* BL1 ....28 A2
Woodburn Dr *BOL* BL1 ....1 H4	Wyville Dr *SWIN* M27 ....55 G5
Wood Cottage Cl *WALK* M28.........53 E1	
Wooddagger Cl *WGNE/HIN* WN2...40 B3	
Wood Edge Cl *BOLS/LL* * BL3 ....37 G2	
Woodfield Dr *WALK* M28 ....53 F5	**Y**
Woodfield Gv *FWTH* BL4 ....45 G2	
Woodfield St *BOLS/LL* BL3 ....37 E3	
Wood Fold *BOLE* BL2 ....19 G1	Yarn Cft *TYLD* M29 ....51 H3
Woodford Dr *SWIN* M27 ....55 G1	Yarrow Gv *HOR/BR* BL6.................14 D3
Woodford Gv *BOLS/LL* BL3 ....36 A1	Yarrow Pl *BOL* BL1 ....28 B1
Woodford St *WGNE/HIN* WN2 ....40 A2	Yates Dr *WALK* M28 ....45 E5
Woodgarth Dr *SWIN* M27 ....55 G5	Yates St *BOLE* BL2 ....3 H1
Woodgate St *BOLS/LL* BL3 ....37 E2	*LEIGH* WN7 ....49 G4
Woodhall Cl *BOLE* BL2 ....19 G4	Yealand Gv *WGNE/HIN* WN2.........40 C3
Woodham Wk *BOLS/LL* BL3 ....2 A7	Yellow Brook Cl *WGNE/HIN* WN2 ..23 G4
Wood Hey Cl *RAD* M26..................39 F2	Yellow Lodge Dr *WHTN* BL5..........34 B4
Woodhouse St *ATH* M46 ....50 D1	Yewbarrow Cl *TYLD* M29...............51 H4
Woodland Av *BOLS/LL* BL3 ....37 F3	Yew Cl *BOLS/LL* BL3 ....35 H1
WGNE/HIN WN2............................40 A4	Yewdale Av *BOLE* BL2 ....20 B5
Woodland Gv *EDGW/EG* BL7 ....8 B2	Yewdale Gdns *BOLE* BL2 ....20 B5
Woodland Rd *TYLD* M29................51 H1	Yewtree Av *ATH* M46 ....42 C4
Woodlands Av *SWIN* M27 ....55 E5	Yew Tree Dr *HOR/BR* BL6 ....26 B4
Woodlands Cl *WALK* M28 ....54 A4	Yew Tree La *BOL* BL1 ....19 E2
Woodlands Dr *ATH* M46 ....43 F3	York Av *BOLS/LL* BL3 ....38 C2
Woodlands Rd *WALK* M28 ....54 A4	*SWIN* M27 ....55 F1
The Woodlands *HOR/BR* BL6 ....26 C4	*TYLD* M29 ....51 F1
Woodland Vw *EDGW/EG* BL7 ....9 F4	York Pl *CHLYE* PR6 ....6 A4
Woodlea *WALK* M28 ....54 A4	York Rd *WGNE/HIN* WN2 ....40 B3
Woodpecker Pl *WALK* * M28 ....53 H3	York St *ATH* M46 ....42 D5
Woodridge Dr *BOLE* BL2 ....29 F1	*FWTH* BL4 ....38 A5
Woodshaw Gv *WALK* M28 ....53 G3	Young St *FWTH* BL4 ....45 H1
Woodside Av *WALK* M28 ....54 B4	
Woods Lea *BOL* BL1 ....27 F3	
Woodsley Rd *BOL* BL1 ....17 F5	
Woodsmoor Rd *SWIN* M27 ....55 H4	**Z**
Woodstock Dr *BOL* BL1 ....27 G1	
TOT/BURYW BL8...........................11 F5	
WALK M28.....................................54 C5	Zetland Av *BOLS/LL* BL3 ....35 H3
Wood St *ATH* M46 ....42 B4	Zulu St *BOLE* BL2 ....3 K3

Adlington Cricket Club
CHLY/EC PR7 .... 13 E1
Adlington Medical Centre
CHLYE PR6 .... 6 B4
Ainsworth CE Primary School
BOLE BL2 .... 31 E1
Albert Street Business Park
HOR/BR BL6 .... 14 D2
All Saints CE Junior School
FWTH BL4 .... 37 H4
All Saints CE Primary School
WCNE/HIN WN2 .... 40 A3
Ash Field Primary School
WALK M28 .... 54 A2
Aspull Clinic
WCNE/HIN WN2 .... 23 G5
Astley Bridge Cricket Club
BOL BL1 .... 18 B3
Astley St Stephens CE
Primary School
TYLD M29 .... 51 H5
Atherton Industrial Centre
ATH M46 .... 42 D4
Atherton Public Baths
ATH M46 .... 42 C5
Avondale Health Centre
BOL BL1 .... 28 A1
Bag Lane Industrial Estate
ATH M46 .... 42 C4
Beaumont County
Primary School
HOR/BR BL6 .... 27 E5
Beaumont Hospital
HOR/BR BL6 .... 26 B2
Bee Fold Medical Centre
ATH M46 .... 50 B1
Bee Hive Industrial Estate
HOR/BR BL6 .... 25 H2
Beehive Works
BOL BL1 .... 3 G1
Bickershaw CE School
WCNE/HIN WN2 .... 48 C3
Birtenshaw School
BOL BL1 .... 19 F1
Bishop Bridgeman CE
Primary School
BOLS/LL BL3 .... 36 C1
Blackrod Church School
HOR/BR BL6 .... 13 G5
Blackrod CP School
HOR/BR BL6 .... 24 A2
Blackrod Galleries
HOR/BR BL6 .... 13 H5
Blackshaw CP School
BOLE BL2 .... 30 C4
Blind School
BOLE BL2 .... 3 J4
Bolton Business Centre
BOLE BL2 .... 3 G5
Bolton Cricket Club
BOLS/LL BL3 .... 37 F3
Bolton Excel Leisure Centre
BOLE BL2 .... 3 G6
Bolton Gates Retail Park
BOL BL1 .... 3 F1
Bolton Golf Club
HOR/BR BL6 .... 26 A2
Bolton Health Authority
BOL BL1 .... 2 A2
Bolton Institute
BOLE BL2 .... 3 H5
Bolton Institute
BOLE BL2 .... 3 J5
Bolton Institute
BOLS/LL BL3 .... 2 C6
Bolton Little Theatre
WHTN BL5 .... 2 C4
Bolton Metropolitan College
BOLE BL2 .... 3 J5
Bolton Metropolitan College
BOLE BL2 .... 3 G6
Bolton Old Links Golf Club
BOL BL1 .... 16 D4
Bolton Open Golf Club
BOLE BL2 .... 19 H4
Bolton Parish Church
C of E Primary School
BOLE BL2 .... 3 J3
Bolton Road Industrial Estate
ATH M46 .... 42 D5
Bolton Road Industrial Estate
WHTN BL5 .... 33 H4
Bolton RUFC
BOL BL1 .... 2 A1
Bolton Running Track
HOR/BR BL6 .... 25 E3
Bolton School
BOL BL1 .... 27 H3
Bolton Sports Arena
HOR/BR BL6 .... 25 E3
Bolton Trophy & Sports Centre
BOLE BL2 .... 3 K3

Bolton Wanderers FC
(Reebok Stadium)
HOR/BR BL6 .... 25 F3
Bolton Wyresdale AFC
BOLE BL2 .... 30 C4
Boothstown Holy Family RC
Junior & Infant School
WALK M28 .... 52 B4
Boothstown Methodist School
WALK M28 .... 52 D5
Boundary Industrial Estate
BOLE BL2 .... 30 C3
Bowness CP School
BOLS/LL BL3 .... 38 B2
Brackley Municipal Golf Club
LHULT M38 .... 44 C2
Bradley Fold Trading Estate
BOLS/LL BL3 .... 31 E4
Bradshaw Cricket Club
BOLE BL2 .... 19 G2
Brandwood County
Infant School
BOLS/LL BL3 .... 36 A1
Breightmet CP School
BOLE BL2 .... 30 B1
Breightmet FC
BOLE BL2 .... 30 B3
Breightmet Golf Club
BOLE BL2 .... 30 C1
Breightmet Industrial Estate
BOLE BL2 .... 30 B3
Bridgebank Industrial Estate
HOR/BR BL6 .... 14 D4
Bridgewater Primary School
LHULT M38 .... 45 F4
Bridgewater School
WALK M28 .... 54 C5
Britannia Business Park
BOLE BL2 .... 19 F5
Broadoak County
Primary School
SWIN M27 .... 55 B5
Brookside Works
TYLD M29 .... 51 F2
Brownlow Business Centre
BOL BL1 .... 28 B1
Brownlow Fold CP School
BOL BL1 .... 28 B1
Burnden Industrial Estate
BOLS/LL BL3 .... 37 F1
Bury Industrial Estate
BOLE BL2 .... 30 B2
Cambrian Business Park
BOLS/LL BL3 .... 28 B5
Cams Lane Primary School
RAD M26 .... 39 H2
Cannon Street Health Centre
BOLS/LL BL3 .... 2 B7
Canon Slade School
BOLE BL2 .... 19 F3
Carlton Industrial Centre
BOLE BL2 .... 3 G5
Castle Hill CE School
WCNE/HIN WN2 .... 40 B4
Central Industrial Estate
BOLS/LL BL3 .... 28 D5
Century Mill Industrial Estate
FWTH BL4 .... 37 F5
Chalfont Street CP School
BOL BL1 .... 18 D5
Chanters Industrial Estate
ATH M46 .... 43 F1
Chanters Industrial Estate
ATH M46 .... 51 E1
Chequerbent Works
WHTN BL5 .... 34 C4
Cherry Tree School
FWTH BL4 .... 36 C5
Chorley Golf Club
CHLYE PR6 .... 6 A2
Chorley New Road CP School
HOR/BR BL6 .... 15 F5
Chow Bent School
ATH M46 .... 42 D5
Christs Church CE School
BOLE BL2 .... 20 B5
Christ the King School
WALK M28 .... 54 A1
Church Road CP School
BOL BL1 .... 17 H5
Clarendon Street CP School
BOLS/LL BL3 .... 28 C5
Cleggs Lane Industrial Site
LHULT M38 .... 45 F2
Clevelands Preparatory School
BOLE BL2 .... 27 G3
Clifton Cricket Club
SWIN M27 .... 47 G4
Clifton Primary School
SWIN M27 .... 47 H5
Cobden Mill Industrial Estate
FWTH BL4 .... 37 G4
Collier Brook Industrial Estate
ATH M46 .... 42 C4

Comtech Business Park
WHTN BL5 .... 33 G2
Constellation Trading Estate
RAD M26 .... 31 H4
County Primary School
BOL BL1 .... 19 F4
County Primary School
RAD M26 .... 38 D5
Craft Shops
BOL BL1 .... 2 E2
Crompton Fold CP School
BOLE BL2 .... 30 A3
Crompton Place Shopping
Centre
BOL BL1 .... 2 E4
Daisy Hill CE School
WHTN BL5 .... 41 H3
Deakins Business Park
EDGW/EG BL7 .... 8 B2
Deane CE School
BOLS/LL BL3 .... 35 F1
Deane Comprehensive School
BOLS/LL BL3 .... 35 F1
Deane & Derby Cricket Club
BOLE BL2 .... 36 B2
Deane Golf Club
BOLS/LL BL3 .... 27 G5
Deane Leisure Centre
BOLS/LL BL3 .... 35 F1
The Deans CP School
SWIN M27 .... 55 G3
Deans Road Industrial Estate
SWIN M27 .... 55 F3
Derby Shopping Centre
BOL BL1 .... 2 A7
Devonshire Road CP School
BOL BL1 .... 27 H2
Dodd Lane Industrial Estate
WHTN BL5 .... 32 D1
Douglas Valley Business Park
WGN WN1 .... 22 A5
Dukesgate Primary School
LHULT M38 .... 45 E3
Dunscar Golf Club
EDGW/EG BL7 .... 8 B4
Dunscar Industrial Estate
EDGW/EG BL7 .... 8 C5
Eagley County Infant School
EDGW/EG BL7 .... 9 E4
Eatock CP School
WHTN BL5 .... 41 G2
Edge Fold Industrial Estate
FWTH BL4 .... 36 A4
Edgworth Cricket Club
EDGW/EG BL7 .... 4 A3
Egerton CP School
EDGW/EG BL7 .... 8 B1
Egerton Cricket Club
EDGW/EG BL7 .... 8 B1
Egerton & Dunscar
Health Centre
EDGW/EG BL7 .... 8 D5
Ellenbrook Primary School
WALK M28 .... 53 F3
Ellesmere Bowling &
Tennis Club
WALK M28 .... 54 A3
Ellesmere Golf Club
WALK M28 .... 54 B2
Ellesmere Retail Park
WALK M28 .... 45 G5
Ellesmere Shopping Centre
LHULT M38 .... 45 G5
Europa Trading Estate
RAD M26 .... 46 D1
Express Trading Estate
FWTH BL4 .... 45 H2
Fall Birch Hospital Lodge
HOR/BR BL6 .... 26 A1
Farnworth Leisure Centre
FWTH BL4 .... 37 H5
Farnworth Little Theatre
FWTH BL4 .... 37 H5
Farnworth Park
Industrial Estate
FWTH BL4 .... 37 H4
Farnworth Social Circle
Cricket Club
FWTH BL4 .... 45 G1
Firsdale Industrial Estate
LEIGH WN7 .... 49 E5
Firwood Industrial Estate
BOLE BL2 .... 19 G5
Firwood School
BOLE BL2 .... 19 G5
Fishbrook Industrial Estate
FWTH BL4 .... 46 B1
Fourgates County School
WHTN BL5 .... 33 E1
Fowler Industrial Estate
HOR/BR BL6 .... 15 E5
Fred Longworth High School
TYLD M29 .... 51 E2

Garrett Hall School
TYLD M29 ....
Gaskell Street CP School
BOL BL1 ....
The Gates Shopping Centre
BOL BL1 ....
George Tomlinson School
FWTH BL4 ....
Gilnow CP School
BOL BL1 ....
Gilnow Mill Industrial Estate
BOL BL1 ....
Globe Works
BOLE BL2 ....
Granada Superbowl
WALK M28 ....
Grasmere Street Health Centre
LEIGH WN7 ....
Great Lever & Farnworth
Golf Club
FWTH BL4 ....
Greenbank Industrial Estate
WCNE/HIN WN2 ....
Green Fold School
FWTH BL4 ....
Greenhall School
ATH M46 ....
Greenhill CP School
TOT/BURYW BL8 ....
Greenmount CP School
TOT/BURYW BL8 ....
Greenmount Cricket Club
TOT/BURYW BL8 ....
Greenpine Industrial Park
HOR/BR BL6 ....
Green Vale Works
WHTN BL5 ....
Grimeford Industrial Estate
CHLY PR6 ....
Haigh Hall Country Park
WCNE/HIN WN2 ....
Haigh Hall Golf Club
WCNE/HIN WN2 ....
Halliwell Industrial Estate
BOL BL1 ....
Harcourt Industrial Centre
WALK M28 ....
Hare Krishna Temple
BOL BL1 ....
Harper Green Comprehensive
School & Leisure Centre
FWTH BL4 ....
Hart Common Golf Club
WHTN BL5 ....
Harwood Golf Club (Bolton)
BOLE BL2 ....
Harwood Health Centre
BOLE BL2 ....
Harwood Meadows CP School
BOLE BL2 ....
Haslam Park CP School
BOLS/LL BL3 ....
Hayward Leisure Centre
BOLS/LL BL3 ....
Hayward School & Bolton
South 6th Form College
BOLS/LL BL3 ....
The Health & Leisure Centre
EDGW/EG BL7 ....
Heathfield CP School
BOLS/LL BL3 ....
Heathside Primary School
WALK M28 ....
Heaton Cricket Club
BOL BL1 ....
Heaton Medical Centre
BOL BL1 ....
Hesketh Fletcher CE
High School
ATH M46 ....
Highfield CP School
FWTH BL4 ....
High Lawn CP School
BOL BL1 ....
Hilton Lane CP School
WALK M28 ....
Hindley Green CE School
WCNE/HIN WN2 ....
Hindley Leisure Centre
WCNE/HIN WN2 ....
Hollins CP School
WCNE/HIN WN2 ....
Holly Bank Industrial Estate
RAD M26 ....
Holly Mount School
TOT/BURYW BL8 ....
Hollywood Bowl
HOR/BR BL6 ....
Holy Infant RC Primary School
BOL BL1 ....
Horwich Business Park
HOR/BR BL6 ....
Horwich Leisure Centre
HOR/BR BL6 ....

Parish CE School
3R BL6 .... 15 E3
dge Sports Centre
46 .... 50 B2
ospital
LL BL3 .... 35 G1
indley
: & Junior School
M28 .... 53 G2
Fold CP School
.... 17 F4
astham
ry School
M28 .... 53 F1
Country Park
BL2 .... 9 H3
Cricket Club
BL4 .... 46 C2
Leisure Centre
BL4 .... 46 A2
West CP School
BL4 .... 46 A1
Business Park
LL BL3 .... 2 D7
Business Centre
LL BL3 .... 2 B7
k Christian School
WN7 .... 50 A3
ge CP School
LL BL3 .... 27 F5
WN7 .... 49 G5
her Fold
y School
WN7 .... 50 D4
ohns CE
School
WN7 .... 49 H5
ge Lane CP School
LL BL3 .... 36 C3
ne Park
ics Stadium
BL2 .... 29 H4
w Industrial Estate
BL4 .... 46 A2
ton
unity School
M38 .... 45 E4
ton Cricket Club
M38 .... 44 C3
er
rehensive School
LL BL3 .... 38 A2
er Cricket Club
LL BL3 .... 38 D1
atre
M29 .... 51 F3
t CP School
BL2 .... 20 A3
lege
LL BL3 .... 3 G6
et CP School
3R BL6 .... 14 D3
CP School
3R BL6 .... 26 C4
ndustrial Estate
3R BL6 .... 25 G3
ft CP School
URYW BL8 .... 21 G5
d Industrial Estate
BL4 .... 46 A3
sque
1 .... 18 B5
y Health Centre
1 .... 18 C1
olf Club
BL4 .... 46 D4
ace Shopping Centre
1 .... 2 E3
Hill CP School
1 .... 27 F2
CP School
LL BL3 .... 38 D1
ter Works
1 .... 28 D1
osque
LL BL3 .... 36 D1
ealth Centre
BL2 .... 30 B1
a CP School
M28 .... 54 A2
itan College
1 .... 18 C5
t Industrial Estate
1 .... 3 G3
orks
BL2 .... 3 H3
e CP School
BL2 .... 3 K1
High School
M27 .... 55 F4
Primary School
M27 .... 55 F4

Mornington High School
WGNE/HIN WN2 .... 40 B3
Morris Green Business Park
BOLS/LL BL3 .... 36 A1
Moss CP School
BOLE BL2 .... 30 B4
Mossfield Primary School
SWIN M27 .... 55 H2
Mount St Joseph RC School
BOLS/LL BL3 .... 35 H1
Mount St Josephs School
FWTH BL4 .... 36 D3
Mytham CP School
BOLS/LL BL3 .... 38 D2
Newlands Medical Centre
BOL BL1 .... 27 G3
Newspaper Offices
BOL BL1 .... 3 F3
Newton West Park CP School
LEIGH WN7 .... 49 E3
Noorul Islam Mosque
BOL BL1 .... 28 D1
Nortex Business Centre
BOL BL1 .... 28 A2
North Bolton Sixth
Form College
BOL BL1 .... 17 H3
North Walkden Primary School
WALK M28 .... 45 G3
Oakhill Trading Estate
WALK M28 .... 45 G2
The Oaks CP School
BOL BL1 .... 18 D1
Octagon Theatre
BOL BL1 .... 2 E4
Old Haigh School
WGNE/HIN WN2 .... 22 C3
Oldhams Lane CP School
BOL BL1 .... 18 A2
Our Lady of Lourdes RC
Junior & Infant School
FWTH BL4 .... 37 E5
Our Ladys RC Primary School
WGNE/HIN WN2 .... 23 F5
Our Lady & the
Lancashire Martyrs School
WALK M28 .... 45 E5
Oxford Grove CP School
BOL BL1 .... 28 A1
Paragon Business Park
HOR/BR BL6 .... 25 F2
The Parochial CE
Primary School
WHTN BL5 .... 33 G5
Parsonage Retail Park
LEIGH WN7 .... 49 G5
Pearlbrook Industrial Estate
HOR/BR BL6 .... 14 D4
Peel Hall Primary School
LHULT M38 .... 44 D5
Pendlebury Recreation Centre
SWIN M27 .... 55 G2
Pikes Lane Infant School
BOLS/LL BL3 .... 2 A6
Pike View Medical Centre
HOR/BR BL6 .... 14 D3
Pilot Industrial Estate
BOLS/LL BL3 .... 37 F1
Plodder Lane CP School
FWTH BL4 .... 37 F4
Prestwich Industrial Estate
ATH M46 .... 42 B4
The Quadrangle
Business Centre
WGNE/HIN WN2 .... 40 D4
Queen Street CP Infant School
FWTH BL4 .... 37 H5
Radcliffe Ainsworth CE School
BOLE BL2 .... 31 E1
Radcliffe Borough AFC
RAD M26 .... 39 G1
Radcliffe CP School
RAD M26 .... 39 G1
Radcliffe Cricket Club
RAD M26 .... 39 G1
Radcliffe High School
RAD M26 .... 39 H1
Raikes Lane Industrial Estate
BOLS/LL BL3 .... 37 F1
Ravenside Retail Park
BOLS/LL BL3 .... 3 F6
Red Lane CP School
BOLE BL2 .... 30 B1
Reebok Museum
HOR/BR BL6 .... 25 F2
Regent Park Golf Course
HOR/BR BL6 .... 26 B3
Rivington & Blackrod
High School
HOR/BR BL6 .... 14 D1
Rivington Primary School
HOR/BR BL6 .... 7 F3
Roe Green Cricket Club
WALK M28 .... 54 B3

Royal Bolton Hospital
FWTH BL4 .... 36 D4
Sacred Heart RC Infant School
ATH M46 .... 51 E2
Sacred Heart RC Primary School
WHTN BL5 .... 33 H4
Sacred Heart RC Primary School
WGNE/HIN WN2 .... 40 D5
St Ambrose Barlow RC
High School
SWIN M27 .... 55 H4
St Andrew Primary School
WALK M28 .... 53 E5
St Andrews CE Primary School
WHTN BL5 .... 35 G5
St Andrews CE School
RAD M26 .... 31 H4
St Andrews Methodist School
WALK M28 .... 45 F5
St Andrews RC Primary School
BOLE BL2 .... 30 A2
St Bedes CE Primary School
BOLS/LL BL3 .... 36 A3
St Bernards RC School
BOLS/LL BL3 .... 27 E5
St Brendans RC School
BOLE BL2 .... 30 A2
St Catherines CE Primary School
HOR/BR BL6 .... 14 D4
St Charles RC Primary School
SWIN M27 .... 55 F3
St Columbas RC School
BOLE BL2 .... 19 F3
St Davids CE Primary School
WGNE/HIN WN2 .... 23 E3
St Gabriels RC Primary School
LEIGH WN7 .... 51 E4
St Georges Central CE School
TYLD M29 .... 51 H2
St Georges CP School
WHTN BL5 .... 41 F1
St Georges Infant School
ATH M46 .... 42 B4
St Georges Junior School
ATH M46 .... 42 B4
St Georges RC High School
WALK M28 .... 53 G1
St Gregorys RC CP School
FWTH BL4 .... 38 A5
St James CE School
FWTH BL4 .... 37 F5
St Johns CE Primary School
WGNE/HIN WN2 .... 40 D5
St Johns CE School
FWTH BL4 .... 38 A5
St Johns Mosley Common CE
Primary School
WALK M28 .... 52 D4
St Josephs RC Primary School
BOL BL1 .... 18 A5
St Josephs RC Primary School
CHLYE PR6 .... 6 B5
St Josephs RC Secondary School
HOR/BR BL6 .... 25 G1
St Josephs School
LHULT M38 .... 45 E3
St Marks CE Primary School
WALK M28 .... 54 B4
St Marys CE Hawkshaw
Primary School
TOT/BURYW BL8 .... 11 E2
St Mary's RC Primary School
HOR/BR BL6 .... 15 F5
St Marys School
SWIN M27 .... 55 H3
St Mathews CE Aided
Primary School
BOLS/LL BL3 .... 38 C2
St Mathews CE School
BOL BL1 .... 28 C1
St Maxentius CE School
BOLE BL2 .... 19 H2
St Michaels CE Primary School
BOLS/LL BL3 .... 37 G2
St Osmunds RC School
BOLE BL2 .... 29 H3
St Pauls CE Primary School
BOL BL1 .... 18 D4
St Pauls CE School
CHLYE PR6 .... 6 A4
St Pauls CE School
WALK M28 .... 54 A1
St Pauls Junior School
LHULT M38 .... 44 D3
St Peter & Pauls RC School
BOLS/LL BL3 .... 2 D7
St Peters CE School
FWTH BL4 .... 45 H1
St Peters School CE
Primary School
SWIN M27 .... 55 G3

St Peters Smithills Dean CE
Primary School
BOL BL1 .... 17 H3
St Philips CE Primary School
ATH M46 .... 43 E5
St Richards RC School
ATH M46 .... 42 C4
St Saviour Ringley CE
Primary School
RAD M26 .... 47 E1
St Simon & St. Judes CE
Primary School
BOLS/LL BL3 .... 36 D2
St Stephen & All Martyrs School
BOLE BL2 .... 29 G4
St Stephens (Kearsley Moor)
CE Primary School
FWTH BL4 .... 46 C2
St Teresa Junior School
BOLS/LL BL3 .... 38 C2
St Thomas CE Primary School
WHTN BL5 .... 34 B4
St Thomas CE School
BOL BL1 .... 18 B5
St Thomas of Canterbury RC
Primary School
BOL BL1 .... 27 G2
St Williams RC School
BOLS/LL BL3 .... 36 C2
Salford College
SWIN M27 .... 55 E1
Salford College
WALK M28 .... 53 H2
Scot Lane End CE School
HOR/BR BL6 .... 24 A3
Scot Lane Industrial Estate
HOR/BR BL6 .... 24 A4
Seven Brooks Medical Centre
ATH M46 .... 42 D5
Shackerley CE Primary School
TYLD M29 .... 51 G1
Sharples CP School
BOL BL1 .... 19 E2
Shepherd Cross
Industrial Estate
BOL BL1 .... 18 A5
Smithills Hall Museum
BOL BL1 .... 17 H3
Soho Ironworks
BOLS/LL BL3 .... 2 E6
Southside Industrial Park
ATH M46 .... 42 B3
Spa Road Industrial Estate
BOL BL1 .... 2 B4
Spindle Point CP School
FWTH BL4 .... 47 E3
Stirling Industrial Estate
HOR/BR BL6 .... 15 E5
Stocks Park Special School
HOR/BR BL6 .... 15 E4
Stone Hill Industrial Estate
FWTH BL4 .... 45 G1
Stopes Works
BOLS/LL BL3 .... 39 E1
Sughar Mosque
FWTH BL4 .... 37 G3
Sunning Hill CP School
BOLS/LL BL3 .... 36 B1
Sunset Business Centre
FWTH BL4 .... 47 E3
Swaminarayan Temple
BOLS/LL BL3 .... 2 B6
Swinton High School
SWIN M27 .... 55 E1
Swinton Leisure Centre
SWIN M27 .... 55 H3
Tanfield School
WGNE/HIN WN2 .... 40 B3
Thomason Memorial
Special School
BOL BL1 .... 27 H2
Thornleigh Salesian College
BOL BL1 .... 18 B3
Tonge Bridge Industrial Estate
BOLE BL2 .... 3 J2
Tonge Cricket Club
BOLE BL2 .... 19 F4
Tonge Moor County School
BOLE BL2 .... 29 H4
Tonge Moor Health Centre
BOLE BL2 .... 29 G1
Top o' th' Brow CP School
BOLE BL2 .... 19 H5
Tottington CP School
TOT/BURYW BL8 .... 21 H2
Tottington Health Centre
TOT/BURYW BL8 .... 11 G5
Tottington High School
TOT/BURYW BL8 .... 21 H1
Tower Works
BOLE BL2 .... 3 H2
Towngate Business Centre
LHULT M38 .... 44 C3

Town Hall & Albert Halls
  BOL BL1 .... **2** E4
Trinity Retail Park
  BOLE BL2 .... **3** H6
Turton Eagley County
  Junior School
  EDGW/EG BL7 .... **9** F4
Turton Edgworth CE School
  EDGW/EG BL7 .... **4** A4
Turton Golf Club
  EDGW/EG BL7 .... **9** E2
Turton Harwood Hardy Mill
  County Primary School
  BOLE BL2 .... **20** B3
Turton High School
  EDGW/EG BL7 .... **9** F5
Turton Leisure Centre
  EDGW/EG BL7 .... **9** E2
Turton Tower
  EDGW/EG BL7 .... **9** G1
Twelve Apostles Mixed &
  Infants School
  LEIGH WN7 .... **49** F3
Tyldesley Highfield School
  WALK M28 .... **52** D4
Tyldesley Swimming Pool
  TYLD M29 .... **51** F2
Undershore Works
  BOLE BL2 .... **29** H2

Vale Works
  WHTN BL5 .... **41** G4
Victoria Industrial Estate
  LEIGH WN7 .... **49** G5
Victoria Works
  BOLE BL2 .... **29** H4
Victory Trading Estate
  BOLS/LL BL3 .... **29** E5
Wadsworth Industrial Park
  BOLS/LL BL3 .... **36** C1
Walkden Cricket Club
  WALK M28 .... **45** H5
Walkden High School
  WALK M28 .... **54** A1
Walshaw CE School
  TOT/BURYW BL8............ **21** H3
Walshaw Sports Club
  TOT/BURYW BL8............ **21** H2
Wardley CE School
  SWIN M27 .... **55** F1
Wardley Industrial Estate
  WALK M28 .... **55** E2
Washacre County
  Primary School
  WHTN BL5 .... **41** H1
Waterloo Industrial Park
  BOL BL1 .... **3** G1
The Water Place
  BOL BL1 .... **2** E5

Waterside Industrial Park
  BOLS/LL BL3 .... **37** G2
Wesley Methodist
  Primary School
  RAD M26 .... **31** H5
West End Trading Estate
  SWIN M27 .... **55** H2
Westhoughton Clinic
  WHTN BL5 .... **33** G4
Westhoughton County
  Secondary School
  WHTN BL5 .... **33** H4
Westhoughton Cricket Club
  WHTN BL5 .... **33** G5
Westhoughton Golf Club
  WHTN BL5 .... **33** E4
Westhoughton High School &
  Community Leisure Centre
  WHTN BL5 .... **33** H4
Westhoughton
  Industrial Estate
  WHTN BL5 .... **33** G3
Westleigh Methodist School
  LEIGH WN7 .... **49** F3
Westleigh St Pauls CE
  Primary School
  LEIGH WN7 .... **49** G3
Wigan & Bolton
  Health Authority
  BOL BL1 .... **18** D5

Wigan Golf Club
  CHLY/EC PR7................
Wigan RUFC
  WGN WN1 ....
Wingates CE School
  WHTN BL5 ....
Wingates Industrial Estate
  WHTN BL5 ....
Withins Comprehensive
  School & Leisure Centre
  BOLE BL2 ....
Woodlands Hospital
  WALK M28 ....
Woodside Junior School
  BOL BL1 ....
Worsley Business Park
  TYLD M29 ....
Worsley Road
  Industrial Estate
  FWTH BL4 ....
Worsley Trading Estate
  LHULT M38 ....
Worsley Wharton School
  LHULT M38 ....
Worthington Lakes
  Business Park
  WGN WN1 ....

Notes

Notes

 **Street by Street** QUESTIONNAIRE

Dear Atlas User
Your comments, opinions and recommendations are very important to us.
So please help us to improve our street atlases by taking a few minutes
to complete this simple questionnaire.

You do NOT need a stamp (unless posted outside the UK). If you do not want to remove this page from your street atlas, then photocopy it or write your answers on a plain sheet of paper.

Send to: The Editor, AA Street by Street, FREEPOST SCE 4598,
Basingstoke RG21 4GY

ABOUT THE ATLAS...

Which city/town/county did you buy?
_____

Are there any features of the atlas or mapping that you find particularly useful?
_____
_____
_____

Is there anything we could have done better?
_____
_____
_____

Why did you choose an AA Street by Street atlas?
_____
_____
_____

Did it meet your expectations?

Exceeded ☐   **Met all** ☐   **Met most** ☐   **Fell below** ☐

Please give your reasons
_____
_____
_____
_____

ML

continued overleaf

Where did you buy it?

For what purpose? (please tick all applicable)

To use in your own local area ☐   To use on business or at work ☐

Visiting a strange place ☐   In the car ☐   On foot ☐

Other (please state)

LOCAL KNOWLEDGE...

Local knowledge is invaluable. Whilst every attempt has been made to make the information contained in this atlas as accurate as possible, should you notice any inaccuracies, please detail them below (if necessary, use a blank piece of paper) or e-mail us at *streetbystreet@theAA.com*

ABOUT YOU...

Name (Mr/Mrs/Ms)

Address

                                                                    Postcode

Daytime tel no

E-mail address

Which age group are you in?

Under 25 ☐   25-34 ☐   35-44 ☐   45-54 ☐   55-64 ☐   65+ ☐

Are you an AA member?   YES ☐   NO ☐

Do you have Internet access?   YES ☐   NO ☐

Thank you for taking the time to complete this questionnaire. Please send it to us as soon as possible, and remember, you do not need a stamp (unless posted outside the UK).